**Austria
under the Iron Ring
1879–1893**

Austria

Under the Iron Ring

1879=1893

William A. Jenks
Washington and Lee University

The University Press of Virginia
Charlottesville

FOR ELAINE AND TOM

Preface

Scholars have scrutinized the diplomatic history of the great European states between 1871 and 1914 intensively and productively, but the review of internal developments within these states has not attracted as much attention. This is particularly true of Austria-Hungary if one excepts the large number of volumes, some of them first-rate, on the general subject of the "nationalities question." The full story of ministerial and legislative activity after 1867 awaits its delineators. At the University of Vienna some superior dissertations have illuminated certain aspects of Eduard von Taaffe's personality and achievement as Austria's Minister-President between 1879 and 1893, but a full-scale appraisal has not appeared in any language.

Lack of source material inhibits the researcher, for the civil disturbances of 1927 in Vienna wiped out most of the Austrian cabinet minutes of the 1867–1914 period. Before the great fire writers such as Moses Mehring, Paul Molisch, and Ludwig Brügel luckily had scanned many of the protocols and incorporated them into their works. In the Austrian State Archives there are surprisingly few collections of private papers of the leading men of Taaffe's time. The Plener collection is rewarding, but Hohenwart's and Horst's are remarkably scanty. A peek at some papers still in private hands indicates that much has been destroyed or is still restricted. Arthur Skedl's collection of what Taaffe did not burn is disappointing until one reaches the Czech-German negotiations of 1890–91. An important running commentary upon affairs in Vienna is the diplomatic correspondence of the German Embassy there. No doubt Ambassador Prince Heinrich Reuss and his staff depended essentially upon German Liberal deputies and upon the German Liberal press for most of their comments, but there were times when they had direct access to the Austrian cabinet.

Nearly a decade of investigation and writing has multiplied my debts. The Fund for the Advancement of Education granted me a Faculty Fellowship to begin this study in 1954–55, and a concurrently held Fulbright Research Award to Austria was of much help. Washington and Lee University awarded Glenn Grants for the project in 1954, 1959, and 1962, and this university gave its encouragement, moral and financial, for a second year in Vienna, 1961–62. Duke University generously underwrote summer research in 1954, and a Faculty Fellowship from the Social Science Research Council in 1961–62 allowed me to finish the last details. I should also mention a very welcome Fulbright Travel Award for 1961–62.

In Vienna the personnel of the Austrian State Archives, of the Library of the University of Vienna, and of the Library of the Nationalrat have been uniformly helpful and pleasant. I owe special thanks to Hofrat Dr. Gebhard Rath, General Director of the Austrian State Archives, to Dr. Walter Goldinger of the Verwaltungsarchiv, and to Dr. Erika Weinzierl of the Haus-, Hof-, und Staatsarchiv. Hofrat Rath kindly has permitted me to repeat much of the material which first appeared as "Taaffe's Cabinet and the Nordbahn Controversy 1883–1885," in the *Mitteilungen des Österreichischen Staatsarchivs,* 1957. Valuable suggestions and encouragement have come from Professor Hugo Hantsch and Dr. Fritz Fellner of the University of Vienna and from Dr. Wilhelm Schlag and Dr. Anton Porhansl, the directors of Fulbright affairs in Austria during my two years there.

Translations from the German are my own, as are all errors which appear.

Without the interest and the generosity of Mr. William Bell Wisdom and the Fidelis Foundation, this study could not have appeared. I am also most grateful to Washington and Lee University and its Glenn Grant Publication Fund, which contributed decisively to the cost of publication.

WILLIAM A. JENKS

Lexington, Virginia
March 18, 1965

Contents

**Austria
under the Iron Ring
1879–1893**

1 The Irreducible Facts

If geography exerts a compelling influence over society and its forms, Eduard von Taaffe's Austria had little chance of viability from the day Franz Joseph agreed to Dualism. Stretched like a partially obscured crescent moon across the map of Central Europe, it linked the Bay of Cattaro (Kotor) with Czernowitz (Chernovtsy) in the Bukowina and Tarnopol (Ternopol) in Galicia. The skinny Montenegrins who brought cheese and ice and sumac wood to the bazaar in pleasant Cattaro had distant brethren in the Ruthene bumpkins who stared at the chattering students in the streets of the Bukowinan capital or at the decently uniformed soldiery of the great Galician *Kasernen*. The Austrian frontiers bulged toward more civilized folk in the west and north, touching upon the shores of the Bodensee and enveloping the "natural frontier" of the Erz Gebirge. Here the Austrian German recalled the mud-caked huts of his virile ancestors and the passes through which later and more cultured forebears brought precious lessons to the Slavs.

The casual student of geography rarely sensed the angularity, the absurdity, of the Austrian state's contours, for his gazetteer clamped the hull that was Austria upon the kernel which was Hungary. The result was a marvelously rotund commonwealth in the heart of Europe, through which coursed the romantic Danube. The two states enjoyed a common market and a

common policy, the formulation of which aged the chief ministers in both capitals. There was also a common burden in
maintaining great-power status and, after 1878, in administering
Bosnia and Herzegovina.

The union with Hungary guaranteed a degree of respect from
the other powers of Europe, and the marriage of convenience
between the developing Austrian industrial complex and the rich
yield of Hungarian fields and plains admittedly was preferable to
the economic nationalism in the Danubian basin after 1918. The
long frontier with Hungary was opportunity as well as irritant.
But physical geography has its complement in human geography,
and it was the encounter with the stubborn human factor which
made Taaffe's era memorable. Industrialism, nationalism, socialism, militarism—all demanded an accommodation from the
statesmen of Europe after 1870. Taaffe sometimes surrendered
without struggle, sometimes improvised upon patterns obtaining
elsewhere, sometimes dug in and refused to go beyond his
master's prejudices and his own estimate of the possible in a state
which had to face the moral and pecuniary costs of a string of
military and diplomatic misadventures.

It was a state in 1880 of something over 22,000,000 subjects.
About 17,700,000 were Roman Catholic, testimony to the long
years of faithful Habsburg service against Muslim and Protestant. If the upper levels of the bourgeoisie affected a taste for
anticlericalism, the country folk were as pious as ever. In the
poorer town districts indifferentism often reigned. Into such
humble surroundings both revivalism and materialistic socialism
would intrude, with results lasting down to the present. But
Franz Joseph never failed to appear on high and holy days, and
in his simple devotions he personified the state's fundamental
allegiance to the ideals and culture of the Roman communion.
Next in number were the Greek Catholics, accounting for almost
half of Galicia's population. Their deference as Uniates to the
pope was a very comforting sign, for it was assumed in Vienna
that the lure of the Muscovite third Rome otherwise might play
havoc with a wartime defense of the exposed crownland. In the
1880s they were multiplying more rapidly than any other Chris-

tian denomination. The appalling poverty in which most of them lived somehow did not offset their natural vigor and resilience.

Their neighbors in Galicia were either Roman Catholic Poles or Jews. Over two-thirds of all Austrian Jews lived in Galicia during Taaffe's era, though their intellectual, financial, and journalistic influence radiated from Vienna. Over a million strong in 1880, the Jews were increasing at a rate which outstripped every other religious community. Immigration played a part, but anti-Semites insisted that the true tempo was obscured by the tendency of the Jews outside of Galicia to go over to Christianity. The argument revealed the problems of classification, if nothing else. In Taaffe's fourteen years of service, the most discussed of all issues which had religious connections were those which dealt with the relations between the Austrian state and the Roman Catholic Church and "the Jewish question."

The Greek Orthodox had their strongholds in the far reaches of the empire, in the Bukowina and in Dalmatia. About half a million by count, their propinquity to the tsar and to Serbia was of great moment to later military commanders. Luther's disciples were dispersed throughout Silesia, Carinthia, the Bukowina, and Upper Austria. As the "true German faith," Lutheranism had surprisingly few adherents in Bohemia and Moravia. In these nationalistic battlefields the Calvinists had their concentrations, especially in the Sudeten districts. Both Protestant sects numbered only 400,000 in all of Austria.

Nationalism and industrialism posed greater challenges for Taaffe and his colleagues than did religion, however. Secular concerns were often indistinguishable from spiritual, for some anti-Semites took their cue from the scene of the Crucifixion while others ranted about Jewish "moneybags" and press lords. Again, a hope that "deserving" young Catholics from rural areas would get teaching posts was implicit in the debate over the Church's role in public education. But the waxing bitterness among national groups and between the beneficiaries and the depressed of the industrial areas overshadowed older quarrels of spirit and creed.

About 37 per cent of the Austrian population used German as their language of communication in 1880. The bare statistics did not convey the degree of continuing predominance which the Germans enjoyed when Taaffe took over, to be sure. Thanks to rationalization procedures in the eighteenth century and to the distrust aroused by the infidelities of 1848, the Habsburg monarchy had taken on a decidedly German cast. The earlier tendency to simple agglutination remained as an inspiring memory to the non-Germans, and the Magyars, so inspired, had made good their escape from the centralized German mold in 1867. But Franz Joseph did not possess the will or the mind to imagine an Austrian state that did not retain German as its cement, and the long affiliation of the armed forces, the bureaucracy, the aristocracy, the high clergy, and the merchant class with German culture and language reinforced his tenacious opinion. Taaffe had the enormous task of conciliating the natural German pride in German leadership with the surges of nationalistic enthusiasm which rolled in from seven other linguistic groups.

Czechs and Slovaks accounted for 24 per cent of the common population. The latter were a small part of the total, for most of them lived inside Hungary as an unhappy and suspect minority. The Czechs were bursting with a renewed sense of destiny, and the dream which at times possessed all of them was the re-creation of a great monarchy embracing Bohemia, Moravia, and Silesia. Infiltrations of Germans over the centuries militated against the dream, and sometimes factions arose which would accept a partition of the ancient lands of the Bohemian crown if the empire in turn would guarantee equality for their language in all state affairs. But a respectable press, a growing literature, and a flourishing dramatic and musical theater gave notice that the Czechs expected recognition as first-class citizens. Beyond the physical proofs of a mature nationalism, there were dynamic changes at work within the aristocracies of Bohemia and Moravia. Men whose ancestors had profited from the auctions and confiscations of the seventeenth century were learning the Czech language and spouting the constitutional arguments which bourgeois lawyers had fashioned. The peasants who trooped into mill towns noted that the nobleman of the district they were abandoning was trying to accustom his tongue to their rough sounds, while the foremen and owners of the factory were obstinately German. It would be a race between extreme nationalism and socialism in such towns, and in the end socialism did not survive the national enmity.

If Czechs and the more passive Slovaks were demanding treatment as equals, the Poles, who made up 15 per cent of the population, had achieved something more than formal equality. The Germans of Austria had never worked too hard at administering the broad expanses of Galicia, though they refused in 1868 to grant the crownland a special status comparable to Hungary's. By a series of ordinances and by imperial approval of Diet legislation, however, the central government, always glad to have the Polish Club's support in the Reichsrat, did in effect allow Galicia a great deal of autonomy. Polish was the language for the bureaucracy and for the schools. German survived only in the administration of railways and the postal service. Eternally poor and harassed by natural disasters, the crownland received steady grants of money from the central treasury and representation in the Austrian cabinet. The gentry (szlachta) did not compete in wealth and show with the haughty families of Bohemia and the Austrian duchies proper, but they rivaled their Magyar counterparts in the zeal with which they guarded their social and economic interests. A sizable number of truly feudal clans sparred for high place at court, with the result that the best administrative plums went to sons of the szlachta. Galicia was a paradise when compared to the Prussian and Russian shares of the extinguished Polish state. Rather, it was paradise for the Poles there.

The empire's real underdogs were the Ruthenes, who lived rather compactly in eastern Galicia and the Bukowina and who totaled 13 per cent of the Austrian citizenry. Not infrequently humanitarians in the Reichsrat called them the helots of the Poles, and there was enough truth in the assertion to make freedom-loving Czechs wince over their own alliance with the Poles. The representation allotted the Ruthenes in parliament was farcical, and the few deputies they could elect rivaled the extremists in the German Nationalist camp in the number of protest votes they cast. Poverty and illiteracy were the order of the day, and the settlement of Polish landlords throughout eastern Galicia added economic pressure to the political. If the Magyars were left to manage their "barbarians" by the *Ausgleich* of 1867, much the same was true of the Polish relation to the Ruthenes. In the 1880s a conscientious clergy, some dedicated lawyers, and a respectable press strove to modify the bargain which Vienna had struck with the Poles. No one failed to note, as the Ruthene voices increased in urgency, that the Ukrainians beyond the frontier were ethnically identical with the Ruthenes. Alexander III's Russification policies reduced Ruthene hopes sharply, however, and Taaffe would have been a most unusual Minister-President if he had not profited from the fact. Austria made no trouble for Ukrainians who preferred to leave Russia for Galicia. At the same time every political observer who counted noses in close ballotings in the Reichsrat would have wagered, without takers, that the Polish Club had no reason to anticipate a change in Ruthene political fortunes.

Solidly entrenched south of the pretty towns of Klagenfurt and Villach were the Slovenes. Once the nationality most likely to succumb to German colonization and civilization, they had sufficiently recovered their individuality by 1880 to organize themselves politically as Liberals and Clericals. In Laibach (Ljubljana) they pressed the Germans, who had long been the mercantile leaders, and every year more of them perched on the hills above Trieste. They were not splendid warriors like the Croats, and they lacked the nationalistic fire which threatened to consume some of their younger Czech cousins. Clearly they expected to endure and to increase until ancient Slovenia was theirs once again. It was a tribute to their tenaciousness that many Alpine Germans quarreled with their Bohemian German colleagues over the identity of the enemy at the gate, especially when the Slovenes exhibited much greater amenableness as Taaffe's allies than did the Czechs.

If not as unhappy as the Ruthenes, the Italians were undoubtedly the most irreconcilable of Franz Joseph's peoples. Clustered about Trieste and inhabiting the picture-book South Tirol, they were the last of the children waiting for redemption by Rome. Italy's alliance with Austria and Germany muffled their protests a bit, but recurring irredentist parades and speeches in the motherland defied old-school diplomacy. The prosperity of Trieste, the opportunities to serve in the monarchy's fleet, the chance to entertain archdukes and giants of the Bourse in Meran (Merano) and Bozen (Bolzano) never diminished their inner yearnings for another rule. Numbering only 3 per cent of the Emperor's subjects, they would be the most enthusiastic to see the last of his eagles.

Their neighbors to south and east, the Croats and Serbs, had eyes upon Budapest and upon Belgrade rather than upon Vienna. The vast majority of their brethren lived beyond Austria's limits, and Vienna for them was the place where the King of Hungary usually resided. They elected deputies to the Reichsrat, who learned to quarrel handsomely with Italians and with each other. But only one person in fifty in Austria was Serbo-Croat, and he tended to live in neglected and earthquake-ridden Dalmatia. The final disposition of Bosnia and Herzegovina would change the Serbo-Croat factor decisively. In the 1880s, however, Austria seemed to prefer to put off such a conclusion for a while.

Like the Serbo-Croats, the Rumanians of Austria, less than 1 per cent of the population, remonstrated against the Magyarization of their relatives in Transylvania and covertly watched the Hohenzollern dynasty at work in Bucharest. Concentrated in the Bukowina, a land that was a medley of nationalities, they produced a small middle class that aped the strong German colony there but did little else to arouse approbation or suspicion in distant Vienna.

The antagonisms bred of nationalism poisoned the air of the Reichsrat. No less ominous were the complaints of subjects who felt the pinch and the insecurity which rapid industrialization brought in its wake. Though persons in farming and forestry made up 63.55 per cent of all employed in 1880, a figure that

dropped quite imperceptibly to 62.41 per cent a decade later, the
government was remarkably disinterested in tackling the agrarian crisis of the 1880s. Count Falkenhayn in the cabinet and a
host of rural deputies in parliament made loud noises over the
farmer's plight, but Taaffe, like statesmen of other countries
where mechanization was proceeding at a quick pace, fixed his
attention upon the new industrial proletariat, the hand workers
whom they had displaced, and the social disturbances which
were likely to erupt in congested urban areas. Liberals who
represented the prosperous chambers of commerce of humming
mill towns raged at the rural aristocrats and lawyers who insisted
on social insurance and factory inspection for industrial workers,
for the same gentlemen usually asserted that agricultural conditions did not permit similar benefits for farm hands and lumberjacks. No doubt unconsciously, Taaffe agreed with Marx that
the angry city mob was more deadly than the dispersed rural
proletariat. Furthermore, the German Empire under Bismarck
had turned first to the complexities occasioned by industrialism,
leaving agrarian woes to the chancellors of the 1890s.

In 1869 almost 20 per cent of persons employed in Austria
were in industry. By 1890 such persons made up a little more
than 21 per cent of the gainfully occupied. The percentages
indicate a rather deliberate tempo, but in actual numbers industrial workers had increased by almost 700,000. These were the
years of the "long depression," when supply seemed to stay
ahead of demand, and both wages and profits were modest. If
the rural population suffered intensely from overseas competition, epidemics, and natural disasters, the laborers in factory and
workshop contended with a stagnation that encouraged the
growth of radical doctrines. The average daily wage in Austria
in 1879 was about 88 kreuzer. It dropped to 86 in 1880, then
rose gradually but unspectacularly to 93 in 1885 and 1886. It
dropped to 90 in 1887 and was back at 93 in 1890. At no time
did it equal the level of 97 kreuzer attained in the early 1870s.
During the same period the price of a hectoliter composed of
equal parts of wheat, rye, and potatoes generally dropped.

Worth about 6.75 gulden in 1880, it stood at about 4.6 gulden in 1888 and thereafter increased at a slow rate. Real wages followed a similar pattern, for a laborer had to work about eight days for this mythical hectoliter of basic nourishment in 1880, but only five days for the equivalent in 1889. Without reliable figures on unemployment and subsistence wages, the foregoing projections lose some value. Certainly Taaffe's regime was more alarmed by unrest among the urban laborers than among the agrarian classes.

In the history of strikes and political disturbances among the proletariat, textile and steel workers have been especially prominent in Western industrial society. Austria had a flourishing textile industry at the end of the century, though steel and iron production was far behind German and British. More than 450,000 persons were engaged in making textiles in 1890, some in the fabrication of woolens, silks, and linens, but most in the turning out of cotton goods. Bohemia had in 1884 almost 53 per cent of all Austrian spindles, most of which were concentrated in Reichenberg (Liberec) and neighboring towns. Lower Austria and Vorarlberg were next in line. Power looms were becoming relatively common, and here, too, Bohemia surpassed all other regions. Hand looms were double the number of power looms, and their operatives congregated in northern Bohemia, Moravia, and Silesia. Woolens were the specialty of Brünn in Moravia, though Reichenberg also was active in their manufacture. In Galicia, cities like Lemberg (Lvov) and Biała were developing important factories, though production in humble homes still was general in eastern Galicia, Bukowina, and the Alps. The finest worsteds came from Bohemia, Lower Austria, and Silesia. In later years the accounts of Social Democratic parades repeated continually the names of such factory centers as Falkenau (Falknov nad Ohři), Graslitz (Kraslice), Vöslau, and Bielitz (Bielsko). Vienna was especially noted for shawls and carpeting. Silk was the specialty in the South Tirol and Gorizia, though the firms which controlled the production usually were Viennese. Reichenberg again led in the processing of flax into linen, though most of the weaving in Austria was still "domestic." Even in cities like Trieste and Fiume (Rijeka) the threadmakers nearly always worked at home.

There were only 140 steel mills in all of Austria in 1880, employing 16,625 persons. Broadly scattered throughout the empire, they were absent only from Vorarlberg and the Adriatic coasts of Dalmatia. Prague, Olmütz (Olomouc), Leoben, and Reichenberg were but some of the sites. The finishing of iron goods—scythes, nails, guns, knives, and stoves—often was a small-scale endeavor, with certain towns and districts holding onto skills of considerable antiquity. Threatening such craftsmen were the growing machine-tool plants, concentrated in Vienna, Wiener-Neustadt, Prague, Brünn (Brno), Graz, and Trieste. Indeed, in 1880 these enterprises had 20,675 workers, more than those in steel mills.

Railway cars were constructed primarily in Vienna, Prague, and Marburg (Maribor), and de luxe carriages for the nobility and the wealthy came from Moravia or from workshops in the imperial capital. Glass was essentially a Bohemian product, with crystal from Haida (Nový Bor), plate glass and mirrors from Pilsen (Plzeň), and beads from Gablonz (Jablonec nad Nisou). Some 30,000 workers participated in these varied endeavors. Leather goods, like glass, were more and more factory products. Shoes poured forth from Vienna, Prague, and Brünn for foreign consumption. The gloves of Vienna and Prague rivaled France's, and all of Europe knew the purses and wallets that also came from Vienna.

Paper mills had their chief site in Bohemia, with the remainder in Lower and Upper Austria and Styria. Compared to other industries, paper production was growing rapidly, whether the final goods were newsprint, cartons, playing cards, or papier-mâché. The Bohemian crownland also led in such items as beet sugar, chocolate, and substitutes for coffee. Beer from Vienna and Bohemia rivaled the best in Europe, while spirits from a variety of mashes were a common rural commodity. As the decade continued, urban distilleries captured more of the market. Vienna was noted for pharmaceuticals and perfumes, matches and candles, terra cotta and bricks. Majolica and faïence originated in Znaim (Znojmo) in Moravia and Budweis (České Budějovice) in Bohemia.

Many of the goods mentioned came from small workshops or from individual craftsmen. Indeed, much of the energies of social reformers in the 1880s went for the salvation of such modest artisans, who were squeezed by the cheaper selling prices of machine-made offerings and by the techniques of marketing which the industrialists had devised. The makers of violins were as dear to reformers as were the sweated operatives in sugar refineries, and this concern had its echo in the social legislation of Taaffe's period. The transport workers did not seem to attract so much attention. Their champions were rather the still weak Social Democrats, but in time the stevedores of Trieste, the tram conductors of Vienna, and the railwaymen of private and state lines would demonstrate their dissatisfactions with hours and wages. In the 1880s Taaffe seemed most intent upon reducing the chances of social infections among textile workers, steel workers, and miners. Austria had progressed just far enough in the use of power machinery to make large concentrations of labor worth while. The Minister-President's fear of socialism among the increasing proletariat, coupled with the German Conservatives' resolve to save the skilled craftsman, precipitated some of the most vital legislation of the latter part of Franz Joseph's reign. Industrialism, whether drawing workers into a factory discipline or obscuring the virtues of craft production, challenged Taaffe and Austrian lawmakers as vigorously as nationalism did.

Politics during Taaffe's era reflected much of the tension created by industrial and national discord. The Germans of Austria had always disagreed among themselves in regard to Joseph II's policies and the ideas propagated during the French Revolution. A large number of professional men, officers, businessmen, and aristocrats subscribed to the Liberal doctrines of representative government, basic civil rights, gradual education of all citizens, and religious freedom. A number of the older aristocratic families, the well-to-do of the smaller towns, and farmers were still loyal to the Church and suspicious of those who questioned her mission to teach and to guide. Within both major tendencies there was room for important variation.

The Liberals first quarreled among themselves over the occupation of Bosnia and Herzegovina. Would the Balkan adventure add luster to the monarchy and to the Germans who had generally directed Austrian affairs since 1867? Or would it add more Slavs who would join with their brothers already under the Habsburg standards in demanding a kingdom or kingdoms of their very own? Tied to the answer to these questions was the question of Austrian militarism. An army and navy employed in Slavic complications in the Balkans had minimal attractions for Liberals who remembered Windischgrätz' repression in Vienna in 1848 and who never relished the prospect of higher taxes. The alliance signed with the German Empire in 1879 influenced their ultimate decisions, but it is well to remember that Austrian Liberals had less reason than the National Liberals in Germany to rejoice over Bismarck and his accomplishments. Austrian Liberals were far less self-conscious when they paid sincere respects to British parliamentary practices. They feared coercion by the executive, and they remembered the Iron Chancellor's sovereign disregard of the Prussian Diet. When Franz Joseph convinced some of his Liberals that the state could not do without extra funds for the military, he won their hearts, not their heads.

The discord over foreign policy and preparedness scarcely masked their basic preoccupation, which was defense of Germanism. The split of 1879 ended in 1881 with the formation of a "United Left," but the elections of 1885 resulted in a formal division between a "German Austrian Club" and a "German Club." The latter was more forthright in its demand for a restoration of German leadership in Austria, but it was still too "Austrian" to satisfy some of its members. They wished to have the right to say what they pleased about Jews, who long had been the allies of Austrian Liberalism. The majority in the club refused to allow such autonomy, and so a secessionist minority formed the "German National Association" of 1887.

Anti-Semitism was hardly a monopoly of dissident Liberals. Among the Clericals it was strong, and the lack of rapport between the great princes of the Church and young parish priests who sensed the resentments of urban artisans and petty business-men stemmed from episcopal distaste for hurly-burly politicking and Jew-baiting. At the end of the 1880s the Christian Social movement was already outflanking the reserved bishops and the aristocrats who disdained appealing to the streets. For some years it was a pariah in the eyes of many Austrian Catholics, but its enthusiasm and knack at organizing the Viennese voters were impressive in the 1890s.

In Taaffe's day the German Clericals who did not choose to gravitate to the Christian Social organization had their own difficulties in deciding what the proper attitude toward national-ity should be. Count Hohenwart, whose federalist tendencies sufficed to keep the Liberals alarmed throughout the 1880s, managed rather neatly a coalition of Slovene and German Cleri-cals, Croats, and Rumanians. Less cosmopolitan Clericals ral-lied around Prince Alfred and Prince Alois Liechtenstein, who emphasized social security measures, the confessional school, and moderate advancement of the non-Germans of Austria. To secure their program, these Clericals, not unwillingly, subscribed to the general concept of large-scale powers for the diets of the crownlands. Such autonomist tendencies were too drastic for a few of the members, chief of whom was Georg Lienbacher, one of the more colorful of the politicians of the decade. Eventually Alois Liechtenstein grew weary of his lack of tactical success as a leader of the Taaffe coalition, and by 1890 he was on close terms with the most promising of the Christian Social demagogues, Karl Lueger, the future mayor of Vienna. For most of the Clericals outside of Vienna, complete fusion would not seem desirable for another decade and a half. The one thread which tied the more conservative hierarchy and aristocrats to the popu-lar movement was *Das Vaterland,* a Viennese daily which profited immeasurably from the shrewd editorializing of Karl von Vogelsang until his death in 1890. In his columns Jew-baiting alternated with serious and challenging studies of social problems, for *Das Vaterland* aimed at a grand alliance against Liberal plutocracy and anti-Catholic relativism.

The most radical German Nationalists of Taaffe's time were Georg von Schönerer and his essentially tiny following. Beginning as a Liberal, Schönerer exhibited a tempestuous affection for peasants who were threatened by international grain and livestock consortiums and for artisans who were losing out to the competition offered by large-scale industry. During the 1880s he moved from a working partnership with Jews and others who shared his views to the adoption of unmistakable anti-Semitism. In his own mind he differentiated between the wealthy and powerful Jews and those who struggled in the back alleys of Vienna to attain some status in a gentile world. This did not, however, deter him from moves to restrict peddling or to close the frontiers to Jewish refugees from Russia and Rumania. His greatest notoriety came from his passionate love for the Hohenzollerns, their empire, and their paladin, Bismarck. This fantastic devotion ended with a jail sentence, the loss of his title of nobility, and with the eclipse of the following, never great, that he attracted despite his dictatorial ways and bad temper. Franz Joseph and Crown Prince Rudolf were for once politically agreed when they contemplated Schönerer and his works. They did not interpret him as a profound enemy of economic liberalism who used German nationalism as no more than the sharp point of his offensive. He was treasonable irredentism incarnate, an insult to the Emperor's concept of honor and to the Crown Prince's respect for the workings of a parliamentary system.

If the Germans were so split that no Austrian government could hope to include representatives of the major tendencies in one cabinet, the Poles offered a bloc of dependable votes in their tightly organized Polish Club. As representatives of an aristocracy that came late into Austrian hands, of a country that never had renounced hope of resurrection, the genial members of the szlachta kept on the better side of practically every Minister-President and profited accordingly. They allowed Poles who held high bureaucratic posts or who might even be professors to represent some of the larger towns and cities, but a perusal of the club's changing roster indicated variations in first names rather than in last. The very greatest landowners might not win the privilege of sitting in the Lower House, for the gentry was jealous of men whose grandfathers had owned thousands of serfs. There was the Upper House for such persons, though even here the gentry had its own brothers and fathers to sponsor. A few in the club were happy to proclaim that they were Liberals, and they raised their voices against "confessionalism." But the great bond for all was Galicia. The ravages of floods and winter, the misery of thousands of peasants, the ambitions of Lemberg and Kraków, the eternal hope that railroads, army bases, and canals would bring money into the crownland—such considerations largely explained the club's traditional role as a government party. Since Taaffe was most traditional in recognizing the Polish right to control the Ruthenes of Galicia, he generally could count on Polish backing.

Czech political opinion was a classic example of Right, Center, and Left during the Taaffe era. The conservative landowners, often called *Feudalen* or Feudalists, were very much like the Polish szlachta in regarding themselves as a "court party" which was sensitive to the empire's basic military and diplomatic needs. Often more at ease in German than in Czech, they wanted historic autonomy in terms of an "independent" kingdom of Bohemia, to which the old dependencies of Moravia and Silesia would adhere. "Bohemian" was a geographical term to them. They recognized a Bohemian nation composed of two nationalities of equal status, who should have equal rights in school and in public offices. Rejecting universal suffrage, they expected to dominate Bohemia with the aid of the upper middle class. To Vienna they would consign the direction of the army, foreign affairs, and finance. A Bohemian diet and a chancellor for Bohemia should regulate all Bohemian affairs, however. In short, the Habsburg monarchy should be a federation of its historic-political *Länder*. What was good for Hungary was good for the other realms. Bohemia should enjoy *Staatsrecht,* a constitutional recognition of her historic status as an independent kingdom under the Habsburgs.

The Old Czechs or, more properly, the National Party, served as the moderates of the 1880s. Tactically allied with the Feudalists, they had lost most of their radical members through secession in the 1870s, and those who were left were typically "liberal" in their talk of representative government, equality for all nationalities, and a "free church in a free state." Angered by failure to secure status for Bohemia equal to Hungary's, they had quit the central parliament and the Bohemian Diet in the 1870s, but returned when they sensed that the voters had lost confidence in such abstention. In the 1880s they gave lip service to the idea of *Staatsrecht,* but essentially they fought for a true equality for both peoples and for an autonomy that would not allow either nationality an unfair advantage over the other.

Far more active were the Young Czechs, most of whom had deserted the National Party in disgust late in 1874. By 1879 they wanted to make the Diet and the Reichsrat ring with their demands for unconditional independence of the lands of the Bohemian crown, and their vociferousness led Franz Joseph to suspect that his crown would mean little to them if they obtained their desires. Insistent upon universal suffrage and full guarantees of civil rights, they inclined for national and social reasons to the Third French Republic. It was an irony that Crown Prince Rudolf was the only person in the "Establishment" who shared such dangerous sympathies, and he was careful to keep his thoughts from his father. The Young Czechs were resolute in their campaign to topple the "enemies of the people," and they succeeded in Taaffe's time in annihilating the Old Czechs. By doing so, they wrecked Taaffe's system and pushed him either to a compromise with the German Liberals or to a radical reconstitution of the electoral system. The Minister-President's experiment in reconciling the nationalities really was concluded in the Bohemian constituencies, not in the angry parliamentary caucuses of late 1893. At the very end the Young Czechs were with Taaffe, but this strange alliance was but the final proof that the veteran politician had lost his touch. To the Emperor the Young Czechs were an odd crew, whom he had no intention of humoring, with or without Taaffe.

Slovenes, Ruthenes, Italians, and Rumanians did not possess parties quite comparable to the Young Czechs. The Slovenes and Italians divided rather conventionally into liberal and clerical tendencies, but these rivals were as eager to forward nationality's cause as they were to expound educational and economic doctrine. The Ruthenes were usually unified by the fact that they had a visible devil to fight in the Poles. More, they were overwhelmingly peasant in composition and outlook, and the lawyers and teachers who represented them relished their opportunities as advocates of the oppressed. When the Ruthenes were not protesting the evils of Polish rule, they were reasonably vocal in behalf of civil rights and justice for all in Austria. The Rumanians were so few that their advocates rarely stirred beyond the confines of the Hohenwart Club's premises. The Rumanians of Austria contrasted shockingly with their Magyarized brothers in Hungary, but basic German Liberal sympathies for the Liberals of Hungary and Czech absorption in the issue of *Staatsrecht* militated against much discussion of the "Rumanian problem" in the 1880s. The Austrian Rumanians, painfully aware of the nature of Budapest's "Liberalism," had to wait for a decade or so before Christian Social leaders and a new heir to the throne took up the cause of the Rumanians in Hungary.

Outside parliament and the distorted electoral system, Marxian socialism was struggling to obtain the allegiance of the masses and enough respectability to escape constant police pressure. Far from united, its self-appointed leaders alternately preached cooperation with the bourgeoisie or total war upon a hopelessly corrupt society. Direct action shaded into outright anarchism, and Taaffe and his colleagues were understandably confused by the labels which both moderates and extremists adopted. Late in the 1880s Victor Adler slowly triumphed over the radicals and created for Austrian Social Democracy an image of practicality and patience. The Second International, for all of its proscriptions of revisionists and talk of an overwhelming general strike, was also remarkably practical and patient. Before Taaffe retired, his laws which offered some social security to labor were amplified, while his laws to crush social radicalism expired. Indeed, the Social Democrats stood with the Young Czechs in support of Taaffe's last political gesture, the proposed electoral reform of 1893.

The further democratization of Austrian political life was an issue that gave Adler and his party more and more popular support in the decade that followed. In a sense Taaffe's outraged supporters had reason to accuse the Minister-President in 1893 of toadying to the people, for the people were increasingly restive over the limited franchise that existed. The Lower House of the Austrian parliament was a nineteenth-century reminder of the medieval tradition of representation of interests. The voting population was divided into four "classes" or curias, each of which had deputies sitting in the more active branch of the legislature. When Taaffe assumed office in 1879, the curia of the great landowners had 85 deputies, the urban voters (who paid at least ten gulden in direct taxes each year) 118, the rural voters (also ten-gulden men) 129, and the chambers of commerce in the major cities 21. No one denied that the system favored the Germans and the wealthy, though practicing politicians knew that one could diminish German power by manipulation of the mandates assigned to the great landowners. In 1879 a deputy represented 27 voters in the curia of the chambers of commerce, 63 voters in the great landowners' curia, 1,600 voters in the urban curia, and 7,900 voters in the rural curia.

A distinct improvement came in 1882, when the tax requirement for urban and rural voters was dropped to five gulden. At least 400,000 more votes were cast in 1885 than in 1879, but vast numbers of citizens still lacked the right to take part in representative government. Furthermore, the Emperor had wide latitude in picking the men of the cabinet, for ministerial responsibility as the French or the English of the 1880s knew it did not actually exist in Austria. Taaffe was Franz Joseph's personal choice, and he lasted as long as he secured the basic financial and military measures which the dynast insisted on having. It was necessary to construct a working coalition, though defeats on hotly contested issues did not call for resignation or revamping of the ministry unless the Minister-President

decided that he needed to heed the adverse vote. Ministers who
had lost the confidence of the coalition eventually had to go, but
the none too homogeneous majority which Taaffe depended
upon allowed a cabinet member a considerable margin of error
before it united to oust him. Parliament had the right to question ministers on specific policies and bills and to impeach those
who acted against the constitutional laws, but the latter possibility never came to pass. Taaffe preferred bureaucratic technicians for his associates, and so the ministers who represented
Germans, Czechs, or Poles were appreciably removed from active politics. They lasted as long as they did not outrage completely those deputies of their nationality who were in general
support of Taaffe's system. They retired when their fellow
nationals of the majority insisted on a change.

Taaffe's manipulation of the influential factors in Austrian
politics did not, unhappily for him, take place in a vacuum.
Austria-Hungary's great-power status and especially the occupation of Bosnia-Herzegovina required agility in diplomacy, while
the very nature of the bargain struck in 1867 compelled every
Austrian Minister-President to come to some kind of terms with
the Magyars on defense, tariffs, banking, and, after 1878, on the
jointly administered provinces in the south. There were para-
doxes and collisions as the complex monarchy tried to blend two
domestic policies with one foreign policy, and usually it was
Taaffe who seemed to be most out of step. As the man responsible for Franz Joseph's lands west of the Leitha River, he
assumed office just as Bismarck and Andrássy were perfecting a
defensive alliance against Russia, and he relinquished his onerous responsibilities a month or so before Crispi returned to
sublimate Italian irredentist yearnings through civilizing mis-
sions to the "lesser breeds" of Africa. The Austrian cabinet
between 1879 and 1893 depended largely upon elements, Slavic
and "clerical," which were suspect to Bismarck and the arbiters
of Italian policy. There were Czechs who combined an ethnic
reverence for Muscovy with a sincere admiration of the democratic premises of the Third French Republic. There were Poles
whose anger over Prussia's attempt to Germanize Posen shaded

their well-developed distrust of Russian performances. Austrian Clerical Conservatives, also Taaffe's allies, found it difficult
to apportion their contempt between a Bismarck who failed to
win a Kulturkampf and an Italian state that had stripped the
pope of the center of Catholic Christendom. The Slovenes, the
fourth and least important element of Taaffe's system, symbolized the growing failure of Germans to convert the people of the
old marchlands to Teutonic Kultur as well as the South Slav
determination to block an Italian regeneration in the Adriatic-
Alpine complex.

It should be quickly stated that Bismarck and the Italians had
done a great deal to shear the Habsburg monarchy of valued
possessions or prestige only a decade or so before Taaffe became
Austrian Minister-President. When Franz Joseph assented to
the alliance with the Hohenzollern empire in 1879 and to the
Triple Alliance in 1882, he recognized his expulsion from Germany and Italy and sanctified the concept of a "peaceful penetration" of the western Balkans. Obviously neither of his allies
intended to subordinate its own interests to Austro-Hungarian
advantage, and Taaffe's system was the Emperor's conscious
attempt to reinsure his family's future against Pan-Slavism and
the radical ferment which attended industrialism and urbanism.
He remembered 1848 as well as 1866.

Assuredly the alliance of 1879 was the fundament of all
Austro-Hungarian calculations. Its clauses were formally secret
for some years, but no wide-awake newspaperman or diplomat
failed to guess that Russia was the foreseen antagonist. Bismarck's eagerness to secure help in case of joint Franco-Russian
intrigues permitted Andrássy to insist upon his empire's freedom
from involvement in a German-French war over Alsace-
Lorraine. The violently anti-Russian Magyars and practically
all types of opinion among German Austrians applauded defensive arrangements against the massive enemy to the east. It is
doubtful, however, that any noteworthy political faction would
have liked an agreement to underwrite the decisions of 1871, for
even the German Nationalists in Austria resented the implication
that Bismarck would need reinforcements against a decadent

France. Bismarck repeatedly, through dispatch and speech, underlined his total disinclination to back Austro-Hungarian probes into the Balkans. Since a succession of foreign ministers in Vienna reiterated the monarchy's hope for purely economic and peaceful advances in that region, he had reason to remind them of his enthusiastic approval of their restricted objectives.

Irritated by Russia's patronage of the Bulgarians, Milan of Serbia had placed his country under a virtual Austro-Hungarian protectorate in 1881, and this seeming delimitation of spheres of influence gratified the German Chancellor, who was glad to leave the Balkans to others. The French move into Tunisia in the same year solidified Italian sentiment for an alliance that would end what had been an embarrassing decade of isolation following the seizure of Rome. Gladstone's victory in Great Britain in 1880 was a blow to Austro-Hungarian peace of mind, for his contempt was a matter of public record. The friendly cooperation of 1877–78 between Disraeli and Andrássy seemed to evaporate in other hands, but the joint enemy, Russia, squared matters by suggesting a revival of the Three Emperors' League in 1881. The new conservative alliance provided for prior agreement in a spoliation of the Ottoman Empire and guaranteed each partner the benevolent neutrality of the other two if it found itself at war with a fourth power other than Turkey.

With an outpost in Belgrade and reasonable assurance of Russian quiescence, the Foreign Office in Vienna could afford a degree of hauteur in its negotiations for the famous Triple Alliance. Bismarck had indicated to King Humbert's envoy that the key to an alliance lay in Franz Joseph's domain, and at first Kálnoky for the Dual Monarchy refused to agree to come to the aid of Italy if France attacked. Under some pressure from Berlin he finally yielded the point, for responsible circles in his empire were fearful that an isolated Italy might fall into radical or republican ways. The same influential circles stiffly rejected the Italian request for a formal mutual guarantee of frontiers. The ranking Roman Catholic great power still did not feel that a formal Italian recognition of Austria's right to the Irredenta was

worth an acknowledgment of the destruction of the Papacy's
temporal power. To be sure, the phrase in the alliance which
promised to maintain "social and political order" indirectly
ratified the Italian seizure of Rome, and the lack of a specific
statement on territorial integrity was more of an Austro-
Hungarian loss than a gain. There was a surety that Italy would
not join Russia against the Habsburgs, of course. In 1882
Kálnoky wanted no more, for an active participation by Italy in
an Austro-Russian war would allow Rome to sit in on the future
partitioning of Balkan regions.

Irredentism did not disappear, and genuine friendliness between Bismarck's junior partners never developed. The young
Oberdank, plotting the eradication of Franz Joseph at Trieste,
died at the hands of Austrian executioners, and the "correct"
and "loyal" attitude of the Italian government throughout the
messy affair did not wipe out the resentments of the public in
either country. Austria-Hungary signed a defensive alliance in
1883 with Rumania against an unnamed, but easily recogniz-
able, eastern foe, but Kálnoky did not deign to notify Italy of his
move. Bismarck, too, saw no reason to tell Rome of the renewal
of the Three Emperors' League in 1884, and, not surprisingly,
Mancini sent troops to Massawa on the Red Sea without telling
his rather distant allies beforehand.

A sudden development in the Balkans and the rise of an ersatz
Bonaparte on the French scene brought the temperamental Central powers into some degree of harmony between 1885 and
1887. The extremely sensitive Alexander III of Russia fumed
over the way Prince Alexander had united his Bulgaria with
Eastern Rumelia, and he vowed he would drive the shrewd
young man from that satellite land, which somehow did not
respond properly to Muscovite direction. With Austrian money,
though without Kálnoky's blessing, Milan of Serbia provoked a
war with the enlarged Bulgaria, lost decisively, and begged for
his patron's mediation. When Alexander failed to listen to
reasonable arguments, Kálnoky warned that Austria would
move into Serbia and that Bulgaria could then expect a Russian
occupation. In the end Bismarck prevented serious trouble

between Austria-Hungary and Russia, and the undeniably force-
ful Alexander retired in favor of a German princeling who had
an officer's commission in the Hungarian army. This Ferdinand
of Saxe-Coburg-Koháry weathered the Russian storm, but the
Three Emperors' League was dead. Bismarck retrieved a neutrality agreement of sorts from the debacle, for his empire and
Russia promised not to join another power in an attack on each
other, and he also promised German moral and diplomatic
support for a Russian descent upon the Bosporus.

Bismarck's risky undertaking had its inspiration in the French
Republic. The dashing General Boulanger in 1886 had elec-
trified the Paris boulevards with his glamour and his far from
sphinxlike advocacy of a return to *la gloire*. Since no French-
man could envisage a national revival without the redemption of
Alsace and Lorraine, Bismarck strove desperately to extinguish
the Balkan fires and to fabricate anew those alignments which
could nullify a Russo-French entente.

Susceptible to blackmail on all sides, he placated Alexander
III with the key to a lock which he devoutly hoped the British
would keep under active surveillance. When the rather tough
Robilant made it clear that Italy wanted some precise gains from
a renewal of the Triple Alliance, Bismarck was amenable. A bit
shaken from the near-encounter with Russia, Kálnoky dared not
withstand too long an obvious Italian decision to move into the
Ottoman preserves. Austria-Hungary did avoid a commitment
to help Germany against France and to back up Italy in North
African areas. On the other hand, the Habsburg state promised
to consult with Italy should the *status quo* in the Near East
demand revision, to inform Italy of her dispositions and intentions there, and to share with Italy the lands which the sultan
might lose. Italy made the same promises, of course, and the
special treaty of 1887, embodying these mutual obligations,
opened the Balkan world to Italian penetration. To underline
the Austro-Hungarian surrender (for Kálnoky obviously took no
pleasure in adding an Italian element to the explosive penin-
sula), Italy acceded to the Austro-Hungarian defensive treaty
with Rumania in 1888. Meanwhile England, Italy, Austria-

Hungary, and Spain exchanged notes and views concerning Egypt, Constantinople, "the Turk position in Bulgaria," and other sore spots. Sometimes called the Mediterranean Entente of 1887, the varying phrases employed did little to reassure Austria, even if they did create some sense of security in Italian minds hypnotized by the magnificence of the British navy.

The less than pleasant Bulgarian crisis and the higher than anticipated cost of renewing the Triple Alliance left Austro-Hungarian diplomacy in some disarray. War was averted, to be sure, and Kálnoky could argue that an encouragement of Italian colonial schemes, even if in the Balkans, tended to distract the irredentists. And, given the delicate balancing of forces which makes the period 1878 to 1914 uncommonly attractive to more harried generations, it was time for Franz Joseph's establishment to harvest a few small victories. Crispi returned to office in the autumn of 1887, and soon Italy and France were locked in a violent economic and propaganda war. Such a development forced the Italian premier to cater to opinion in his allies' lands, and he was soon dissolving irredentist clubs and dismissing colleagues who trafficked in anti-Habsburg sentiment. The co-operative Crispi fell from power before the Triple Alliance was renewed in 1891, but it was Germany rather than Austria-Hungary which paid the price which rumors of a Russo-French entente allowed Italy to demand. Should Italy and Germany formally recognize in the future that they could not maintain the *status quo* in Cyrenaica, Tripolitania, and Tunisia, the latter would back an Italian occupation or comparable action in these regions.

Obviously Russia was the chief anxiety for Austria-Hungary's Foreign Ministry during Taaffe's era, and the fact that Taaffe depended upon three major Slavic peoples for most of his legislative program inevitably perplexed and alarmed Bismarck. The unspoken question in all German Austrian minds was: What will our Slavs do in case of war with tsardom? Franz Joseph and Taaffe acted upon the premise that gradual "emancipation" and a move to equality with German Austrians would keep the Habsburg Slavs loyal. Prussians who disliked Poles and who

actively worked to dislodge them from Posen were not likely to
grant such a premise, and Taaffe rarely won praises from the
Hohenzollern government while Bismarck lasted. Rather, the
German Empire preferred the resolute Magyar government,
which in turn often sickened over Taaffe's patronage of Poles,
Czechs, and Slovenes. Furthermore, the dominant Magyar cli-
que in Taaffe's time called itself Liberal, and its affinities with the
Austrian German Liberals added to the ordinary trials of dualistic collaboration.

Koloman Tisza, Hungarian Minister-President from 1875 to
1890, epitomized the constant Magyar determination to make
Hungary fully equal to Austria without paying half of the costs of
defense and administration. Convinced that the dualistic structure and the Habsburg dynasty were good for Hungary in its
current stage of the historical process, he never allowed his
loyalism to interfere with the benefits which tariff policy could
guarantee a great agricultural state that was deliberately shrug-
ging off its dependence on Austrian industry. Magyar talk of
special arrangements with the German Empire's industrial complex was partly good business, partly resentful rejection of a
partner who dared to give breaks to Slavs.

Magyarization was a vivid contrast to Taaffe's "reconciliation
of the nationalities," and Budapest was as contemptuous of the
historic Croats as it was of the almost submerged and "unhistorical" Slovaks. It disdained the kind of alliance which German
Liberals and German Conservatives in Austria were willing to
consummate with the Poles and sometimes the Italians, for
Magyar "pro-Serb" policy in Croatia was nowise comparable to
Vienna's renunciation of authority in Galicia. Rumors of a
coronation in Prague or newspaper reports of Crown Prince
Rudolf's encouragements to the Croats aroused in Bismarck and
Tisza the same degree of concern, and necessity alone bred
courtesy between Taaffe and his longtime Hungarian counterpart. The lines of alliance were not always clear, for Tisza, the
German Liberals of Austria, and Bismarck could not always
view society and diplomacy through the same lenses. All were
willing to reduce the influence of the Roman Catholic Church,

but Bismarck belabored the Austrian Liberals for faithlessness
to their emperor and found Magyar intransigence against Russia
a real block to the allaying of Alexander III's suspiciousness.
They did possess a common nuisance, if not threat, in Taaffe.
With his dependence on Slavs and Austrian German Catholics,
he was a perfect target for their fulminations. As corollary, the
impetuous but effective German Austrian group which rallied
about *Das Vaterland* consistently lumped "Judaeo-Magyarism"
with "corrupt and Semitic Austrian Liberalism." If they could
not quite fit Bismarck with their archfoes, they certainly abstained from the usual adoration he aroused in German circles
and crowed over that misadventure of his which Liberals described as a Kulturkampf. Tisza was proper in his dealings with
Taaffe, for each was essentially "the Emperor's man." They
were reasonably frank in their estimates of what each could do
with a fractious opposition, and they realized that Franz Joseph's
obsession for a decently organized and well-functioning army
was the ultimate determinant of their tenures and actions.
Austria and Hungary were reasonably prosperous, attained
balanced budgets, and generally drew back from risky Balkan
adventures in Tisza's and Taaffe's time. In the more vital
problem of the nationalities, they pursued diametrically opposed
policies. If proof is needed of Franz Joseph's basic refusal to see
his dynasty's problem whole, it is this incredible disharmony
between the two realms.

And yet Taaffe and his era would be unimaginable if Franz
Joseph had not continued to try, sometimes bemusedly and
usually no more than doggedly, to cope with the "Austrian
problem." The partnership of the erstwhile playmates lasted
fourteen years, and in that time Taaffe had the task of reconciling his master to the realities of a Europe whose material civilization was at a zenith. Franz Joseph was sometimes an apt and
enthusiastic collaborator, aware of the social and economic
problems his government faced. On other occasions Taaffe
obviously had trouble persuading him to forget the memories of
1848 and the pleasantly autocratic calm of the 1850s. Had ruler
and first minister fully agreed at every juncture, they still would

have failed to eradicate many of the nationalistic and social bitternesses which afflicted Austria. Yet they tried to create the bases for a viable society, and if their common effort revealed their own personal pessimism and caution at many points, they were nonetheless making the effort. A re-examination of their major triumphs and defeats should at least raise the question of the propriety of speaking of Taaffe's era as a time of muddling through to well-tempered dissatisfaction.

2 The First Victory: The Defense Bill of 1879

Julius Andrássy's success in securing general European approval in 1878 of the Dual Monarchy's occupation of Bosnia and Herzegovina occasioned a major change in the internal administration of the Austrian half of the monarchy. For almost a decade German Liberals had acted as Franz Joseph's chief advisers in cabinet and in parliament, but the controversy over including, however provisionally, another large segment of Slavs within the empire destroyed the unity and so the effectiveness of the Liberal regime. The Liberals had already shown signs of fatigue and of a lack of imagination after years of governing, and many welcomed the chance to shed responsibility.

After thirty years of rule Franz Joseph's tastes had changed little. As Andrássy informed Prince Heinrich Reuss, the German Ambassador, on the eve of the decisive vote on the Treaty of Berlin, the Emperor wanted a man from the high aristocracy for his next Minister-President. Unfortunately, there was a dearth of intelligence in such circles, thought the Magyar aristocrat. The Bohemian nobility offered possibly the best selection, but its scions were too much involved with Czech nationalism. Count Ferdinand Trauttmansdorff was Andrássy's sole nominee, and he had begged off on the grounds that he did not command either the requisite nerves or oratorical skill.

Though Andrássy sensed an increase in conservative sympathies among the voters in Austria, he shied away from recommending a decisively conservative cabinet. Count Karl Hohenwart, whom he personally esteemed, was impossible, for the Emperor knew well that a turn toward clericalism would enhance Liberal chances for a landslide in the elections scheduled for the summer of 1879. Though sympathetic to Liberal ideas as long as the Liberals vouchsafed an efficient government to finance his diplomatic moves, Andrássy complacently regarded the bickering among his erstwhile partners as a sound crisis that would end in a new consolidation of political forces that would better understand his policy.[1]

Suddenly, on February 2, 1879, stories began to circulate in Vienna of an imperial summons relayed to Innsbruck to the Statthalter of Tirol resident there, Count Eduard Franz Josef von Taaffe. The Taaffe family had migrated from Ireland to Habsburg dominions after the final defeat of James II in 1690. In Ireland the family's roots went back to the rich and important Sir Richard Taaffe of the thirteenth century, and William Taaffe, a strong supporter of Queen Elizabeth in the turmoil of 1596–1603, was Count Eduard's direct ancestor.

In 1822 Count Ludwig Patrick von Taaffe married Princess Amalie von Bretzenheim de Regecz, and Eduard was the second son of this union. His father served forty-four years in various official capacities, notably as Minister of Justice and as president of the Oberste Gerichts- und Kassationshof. Born on February 24, 1833, Eduard, thanks to his father's court connections, became a playmate for Franz Joseph, the future emperor. By 1848 Eduard had completed his preparation for the University of Vienna, where he undertook the study of law. Finishing his examinations with distinction in 1852, he entered the imperial bureaucracy in an era still remembered for authoritarianism tempered by competence. He moved rapidly from his first post in Lower Austria to the direction of the district administration of

[1] See Reuss's dispatch No. 31, A 385, Jan. 22, 1879, *German Foreign Ministry Archives, 1867–1920,* microfilmed at Whaddon Hall for the General Library, University of California, Berkeley, ser. I (hereafter cited as UC-1), reel 214, frames 14–16.

Prague in 1861. In the interim he saw service in unhappy
Hungary, temporarily reduced to a pattern of geometrically
equalized circles ruled by youngish German-speaking civil serv-
ants similar to himself in training, if not always in social prestige.

In Prague, before he was thirty, the promising young official
publicized the concepts which would guide him in later years as
Minister-President. Addressing his subordinates in the capital
of a crownland already vibrant with revived Czech national
sentiment, he described state service as a very difficult career.
To meet its complexities, especially in areas rent by the claims of
rival ethnic groups, one had first to honor the Emperor's prescription of equal rights for all. Second, officials must be "above
the parties," willing to grant justified petitions and prompt to
avert unnecessary collisions. Less important for the future, but
a rather amusing foretaste of the genial and cavalier disregard
for details that irked his proper opponents of later years, was the
new director's frank admission that he was an enemy of verbal
redundancy and of time-consuming quill driving.[2]

In 1863 Taaffe moved to Salzburg as *Landeschef* of that
crownland, and, for a very brief period in 1867, he was the
Statthalter of Upper Austria. The disastrous Austro-Prussian
War of 1866 forced a complete change in Habsburg affairs, and,
named Minister of the Interior and, later, chief deputy for Austrian affairs to the Imperial Chancellor, Count Friedrich Ferdinand Beust, he participated fully in the negotiations with the
Magyars that eventuated in the Compromise of 1867. Beust later
admitted that Taaffe's aristocratic friends regretted this sudden
call to Vienna, with its overtones of appeasement, if not surrender. The "foreign" Chancellor, symbol of Franz Joseph's
impotent resentment of Bismarck's victory in 1866, nevertheless
found Taaffe indispensable in dealing with the not overfriendly
Austrian officialdom and courtiers.

At the end of 1867 a predominantly German Liberal cabinet

[2] *Der politische Nachlass des Grafen Eduard Taaffe,* ed. Arthur Skedl
(Vienna, Berlin, Leipzig, and Munich, 1923), pp. 15–17. Hereafter cited
as *Politischer Nachlass.*

under Prince Carlos Auersperg assumed direction of Austrian affairs. Taaffe surrendered the pivotal Interior portfolio in favor of the less important Defense post, but when Beust's interference in internal affairs caused Auersperg's resignation in 1868, the Emperor's childhood friend assumed the presidency of the ministry. Overshadowed by his more doctrinaire colleagues, Taaffe did his best work in securing from a mulish Lower House a ratification of the principle of compulsory military service. The Defense Bill of 1868 was to last for ten years, and the Hungarian parliament agreed to set the war strength at 800,000 men.

Within the cabinet, Taaffe, Johann Berger, and Count Alfred Potocki found themselves increasingly at odds with the centralist majority. The Emperor seemingly solved the impasse by accepting their resignations in January, 1870. This "bourgeois" Liberal coup was meaningless, for a steady desertion of the Reichsrat by Clericals, Poles, Rumanians, Slovenes, and Italians, coupled with the continuing refusal of the Czechs to take their seats there, compelled the survivors of the Liberal experiment to step down in April, 1870.

Count Potocki next attempted to form a ministry in which Taaffe served as Minister of the Interior from April, 1870, to the time of Potocki's admission of failure in February, 1871. During this period Taaffe became a life member of the Upper House, having served earlier as a deputy for the Bohemian landed curia in the Lower House. When the Emperor decided to replace Potocki with a thoroughly federalist ministry in 1871, Taaffe declined to join the venture. He recommended himself for the post of *Statthalter* of the Tirol, and Franz Joseph consented.[3]

His recall from Innsbruck in 1879 nevertheless surprised the "informed circles." Prince Adolf Auersperg and Baron Orczy briefed the German Ambassador on the new candidate, whose chances Andrássy indirectly had heavily discounted several weeks earlier. Franz Joseph had exhausted all possibilities, so

[3] Taaffe's early career is well sketched by Georg Beck, "Die Persoen-lichkeit des Grafen Eduard Taaffe" (unpubl. diss., Vienna, 1949), pp. 29–86. See also *Politischer Nachlass,* pp. 9–11, for Taaffe's own brief auto-biography, and Richard Charmatz, *Österreichs innere Geschichte von 1848 bis 1907* (Leipzig, 1909), I, 80–102.

he had to plead with his long-time friend to undertake the search
for an effective combination. Auersperg was convinced that the
Statthalter of the Tirol had a special talent for getting out of
prickly situations. If no orator, he met a variety of men well. In
view of the impossibility of securing a reliable majority, such an
ingratiating person was mandatory. But the German Empire
should not fear a move toward clericalism. The impending
elections might even be radical in result if the ministry were
anything but *verfassungstreu*, that is, loyal to Liberal constitutional principles. Taaffe had summarized his attitude toward the
Czechs in homely fashion. One must leave the drawing-room
doors wide open, but never go out to meet them in the vestibule.
Any attempt to strike a compromise before they returned to
parliamentary life would encourage them to make new demands. Their leaders were barely able to enforce the policy of
abstention during the Auersperg cabinet's lifetime. One could
now expect the ripe fruit to fall. In short, they would re-enter
the Lower House unconditionally.

Taaffe's ministry would have no pronounced coloring, for he
was looking for worthy experts in every party to carry on provisionally. Most of all, he and those who were negotiating for him
wanted a united cabinet. The last sessions of the Delegations
had proved the folly of disunity in the face of Hungarian resolution.[4]

Though Andrássy was sorely tried by Liberal intransigence
toward his Bosnian policy and had expressed to Prince Reuss a
positive lack of concern over the internecine squabbling among
the Liberals in the Lower House, he especially requested Ernst
Plener, an outstanding moderate Liberal, to heed Taaffe's request to consider the Commerce portfolio. For several days
Plener, who dreamed of transplanting English parliamentary
manners to Austria, and Count Franz Coronini, who was well
known for his conciliatory nature and who also had grown up
with the Emperor, bargained with Taaffe, stipulating a reduction
in army costs and the general retention of Liberal accomplish-

[4] Reuss's dispatch No. 55, A 700, Feb. 8, 1879, UC-1, reel 214, frames
32–33.

ments. Franz Joseph summoned both men, clearly to undermine their determination to obtain cuts in defense costs, while
General Julius Horst, the Liberal Defense Minister, upheld his
commander-in-chief with very pessimistic estimates of future
reductions. While Plener and Coronini played the old game of
recommending or disapproving of possible colleagues, Taaffe
made specific overtures to Karl von Stremayr, the experienced
Minister of Education in past Liberal cabinets, and undoubtedly
to Horst. On February 10 Taaffe unexpectedly notified Plener
and Coronini that his efforts had failed and that he would return
to his post in the Tirol.[5]

The tactics followed by Taaffe and the Emperor in February,
1879, are still difficult of analysis. Undoubtedly apprised by
Andrássy and leading Liberals of their estimates of the situation,
Reuss reported to Bismarck that Taaffe had made up his mind to
seek an honest parliamentary regime based on the fractions
which had voted for the Treaty of Berlin. Men who had finally
agreed to an adventurous foreign policy had little else to unite
them, however. Some had demanded a cut of 7,000,000 gulden
in the army's budget and a clear and constitutional position on
the question of occupying Bosnia. The Emperor and Taaffe
would not meet such terms, and so the former had asked the old
cabinet to continue as caretakers through the summer elections.
Adolf Auersperg and Dr. Josef Unger had positively declined,
but the rest, with Stremayr as chairman, agreed to carry on.

A few days later the Emperor drafted Taaffe for the ministry
most vital in an election year—Interior.[6] He and the people
wanted a parliament that could function, the ruler informed
Reuss, for no one could form a government with the incumbent
deputies. Taaffe would direct the new elections "in a conservative sense."[7]

In March the Emperor's "new man" conferred with Count

[5] Ernst Plener, *Erinnerungen* (Stuttgart and Leipzig, 1921), II, 144–
48; *Politischer Nachlass,* pp. 243–48.

[6] Reuss's dispatch No. 62, A 834, Feb. 14, 1879, UC-1, reel 214, frames
35–36.

[7] Reuss's dispatch No. 79, A 1026, Feb. 25, 1879, UC-1, reel 214,
frame 39.

Heinrich Clam Martinič, who represented the pro-Czech landed aristocracy in Bohemia, and with Franz Ladislaus Rieger, the Old Czech leader. Auersperg earlier had correctly reported that Taaffe wanted an unconditional Czech return to the Lower House, but Clam Martinič shrewdly exploited Taaffe's desire for a conservative parliament by demanding the surrender of a certain number of the German Liberal seats in the Bohemian landed curia to his Feudalists. He warned against a short-term agreement and predicted that Czech attendance in the Lower House would depend upon the proposals the government made to the diets, particularly to the Bohemian Diet.[8] Liberal sources never denied that Taaffe spoke bluntly in trying to contain the most extravagant Czech desires or that indiscretions within the badly splintered Liberal ranks speeded his negotiations.[9] In Styria and in Lower Austria party spokesmen of the anti-Bosnian fringe encouraged radical attacks upon an electoral system which favored the great landlords. Since many of these aristocrats, when elected to the Lower House, had favored Liberal experiments after 1867, their resentment was considerable. Such sniping especially angered Carlos Auersperg, and on June 24 he agreed to an electoral compromise with the Feudalists that would guarantee the latter 10 of the 23 seats at stake. He did so without consulting with his party associates, and a Prague dispatch quoted him as saying, "The compromise with the Feudalists is a patriotic sacrifice, which was demanded by authoritative quarters."[10] Three years later, when Taaffe's policies had thoroughly alienated him, he asserted that he had concurred in order to restore life to parliament.[11]

Taaffe actually hoped in 1879 for a coalition ministry in which German Liberals might collaborate with aristocratic and middle-class Czechs to settle the latter's claims within a proper parlia-

---

[8] *Politischer Nachlass,* pp. 377–82.

[9] Gustav Kolmer, *Parlament und Verfassung in Oesterreich* (Vienna and Leipzig, 1902–14), II, 546–47; Ernst von Plener, *Reden* (Stuttgart and Leipzig, 1911), p. 485.

[10] *Neue Freie Presse,* June 25, 1879, *Abendblatt.*

[11] For discussions of the compromise, see Kolmer, *Parlament,* III, 3–6; Charmatz, *Geschichte,* II, 7–9; Plener, *Erinnerungen,* II, 154–57.

mentary environment. Stremayr attempted to enlist Eduard
Herbst, the best known of the Liberal leaders, but this eternal
individualist haughtily declined. If Taaffe thought, said Herbst,
that he could find a majority outside the German Liberals, he
had slight knowledge indeed of the parliamentary situation.[12]

The elections proved Herbst's inaccuracy. Forming with the
equally obdurate Eduard Sturm a "Committee of the 112," he
helped continue the extremist vendetta with Andrássy and the
Emperor by provocatively recalling the number who voted
against the Treaty of Berlin. A Liberal Club, composed of
deputies who were willing to accept the new position in the
Balkans, issued an electoral manifesto which the official press
found very much to its liking.[13] The moderates avoided the
proscription which the irreconcilables had planned for them, but
the landed aristocrats in several crownlands, worried over left-
wing Liberal talk of reforming the privileged curial system,
rejected these very moderates, who were still open-minded about
Taaffe and a new approach to nationalistic compromise.
Altogether the Liberals lost 49 seats: 21 in the landed curia, 20
in the rural curia, and 8 in the urban curia.[14] The elections of
1879 were revolutionary in the sense that the Liberal representation thereafter could do little save annoy the Conservative-
Clerical-Slavic combination which Taaffe finally decided upon.
The Liberals' friends, the Ruthenes, dropped from 14 to 3, while
the unabashedly opportunistic Polish Club went from 49 to 57.
The Czech Club, when the Czechs finally decided upon active
participation, amounted to 54 members, while a loose aggrega-
tion of German Clericals, Slovenes, Croats, and Rumanians
made up a "Right" of 57. These three fractions accounted for
168 votes, but the electoral reform of 1873 had raised the
number of deputies to 353.[15] Taaffe faced 174 outright adversaries among those elected in 1879, and consequently he was always

[12] Beck, "Die Persoenlichkeit," pp. 109–10; letter of Hugo Salm to
Stremayr, May 22, 1879, in *Briefe zur deutschen Politik in Österreich von
1848 bis 1918,* ed. Paul Molisch (Vienna and Leipzig, 1934), pp. 212–15.

[13] Reuss's dispatch No. 202, A 2699, May 12, 1879, UC-1, reel 214,
frames 67–68.

[14] Plener, *Erinnerungen,* II, 156.   [15] Charmatz, *Geschichte,* I, 116.

searching for some support by independents.[16] The figures are
of basic importance in understanding Taaffe's problems and
overall strategy. He had to alternate concessions with hints that
he might turn to a more Liberal policy when he bargained with
Conservatives, Slavs, and Clericals. To underline his point, he
preferred to keep open a line to the Liberals as long as possible.
When convinced that he could not maintain such a delicate
equilibrium, he seized upon electoral reform as a means of
salvation.

The German Embassy relayed soothing reports of the elections to Bismarck, whose suspicion of the Poles in particular and
Slavs in general did not erase his uncomfortable memories of
encounters with doctrinaire Liberalism. Reuss first predicted a
decrease in the influence of the Polish Club, though he noted a
concern in Budapest over the Slav revival in Austria.[17] Later he
emphasized the relatively modest autonomist claims advanced in
Dalmatia, Bohemia, and Galicia. Everywhere there was an
attempt to be *gut kaiserlich*.[18] Franz Joseph expressed similar
views of the elections to Reuss, and he was quite satisfied that
Taaffe had procured the proper results without ordering "state
organs" to interfere. With his usual dispassion, he admitted that
such interference sometimes might be needed and that he would
not shrink from prescribing it.[19]

An undated memorandum in Taaffe's hand, presumably written in the early stages of the election campaign, reveals the
precepts which guided the future Minister-President as he
searched the scene for potential collaborators. The future cabinet was to consist of moderates who would neither excite the
Liberals' concern nor impede the return of the Czechs. He
wanted men who would be conservative and yet respectful of
constitutional norms. They had to support the irrevocable Bos-

[16] *Ibid.*, II, 10; Kolmer, *Parlament,* III, 12.

[17] Reuss's dispatch No. 268, A 3690, June 30, 1879, UC-1, reel 214,
frames 106–112.

[18] Reuss's dispatch No. 277, A 3907, July 10, 1879, UC-1, reel 214,
frame 117.

[19] Reuss's dispatch No. 298, A 4149, July 18, 1879, UC-1, reel 214,
frames 131–32.

nian decision without relinquishing a voice in future Balkan moves. Finally, they had to realize that a cabinet composed of outspokenly partisan elements would negate the election results and unduly harass the Emperor.[20]

To realize his aims, Taaffe took refuge in vagueness, which his Liberal colleagues tended to interpret as confusion or weakness. Four of them definitely were seeking the relief of retirement, and on July 28, Johann Chlumecky, the Minister of Commerce, finally contrived a conference with "the man of the future." The latter admitted to *pourparlers* with Czechs and Conservatives, who wanted a totally non-Liberal ministry. Only the Emperor, admitted Taaffe, could decide between a Feudalist-Clerical-Nationalist ministry and one composed entirely of Liberal elements. Chlumecky and most of his colleagues who were present ruled out the chance of the latter eventuality. Thanks to the election results, such a cabinet would not have a chance. Attempts to secure a coalition had to continue, even if certain posts remained unfilled up to the opening of parliament. At that time, recommended Chlumecky, the attitude of the Czechs and their Feudalist allies would determine the choice of the new ministers.

In Ischl the Emperor refused to countenance the complete exclusion of the German Liberals. Should the Czechs decide to re-enter the Reichsrat, they would receive one or two seats in the ministry.[21]

The tenseness of the moment encouraged the choice of relatively inconspicuous men. Count Julius Falkenhayn received the Agriculture assignment because of his first-hand experience as a gentleman farmer and his identification with the Clerical Conservatives. Reuss reported to Berlin that Baron Karl Korb-Weidenheim, the new Minister of Commerce, was a young man of talent, if indeed a stranger to this field of activity. Alois Pražak, Minister without Portfolio, was acceptable to many

[20] *Politischer Nachlass,* pp. 249–50. Skedl's note, dating the memorandum as of early August, 1879, is not warranted by the internal evidence.

[21] Letters of Chlumecky to Pretis, July 28 and Aug. 1, 1879, in *Briefe,* ed. Molisch, pp. 221–23; Plener, *Erinnerungen,* II, 167.

Germans because he had led the Czechs of Moravia in their
return to the central parliament in 1874.[22] The *Neue Freie Presse,*
Vienna's most influential Liberal paper, accused Falkenhayn of
writing a most superficial brochure on Austrian finances, hooted
at Korb-Weidenheim's reputation as an efficient manager of his
own estate, and deplored the "anti-dynastic and scandalous"
speeches which Pražak had once uttered.[23] Such harsh judg-
ments ended in the confiscation of the offending issue.

   Julius Glaser, one of the retiring Liberal ministers, besought
his fellow Liberals not to go into the opposition preached by the
Neue Freie Presse. If the Liberal deputies failed to support the
Liberals in the new cabinet, the Right inevitably would profit. It
would be far more clever to let the Czechs hound Taaffe, for in
the end such maneuvers would again bring a purely Liberal
government into power. Horst, the astute yet honorable Minister of Defense, was willing to make an honest bargain over the
government's obligation to ask for a new military bill, and
Taaffe's appointment of Korb indicated a desire to have as many
Liberals as possible in the ministry.[24]

   At the end of August, 1879, the two discordant wings of the
Liberal Party assembled in Linz to formulate a program for the
coming session of the Reichsrat. A subcommittee of five, of
whom four had opposed the Berlin settlement, worked out a
manifesto against concessions to non-Germans which would
"violate" the fundamental laws of the empire and against defense
expenditures which would threaten imperial financial stability.
Ernst Plener, the one member of the subcommittee who had
assented to the Treaty of Berlin, later asserted that this declaration was by no means a challenge to the new Taaffe regime and
vigorously denied the rumors that the party had secretly decided
to forbid any Liberal to become a part of the coalition.[25] Alois
von Czedik, the many-sided director of the Westbahn, kept

   [22] Reuss's dispatch, not numbered, A 4555, Aug. 14, 1879, UC-1, reel
214, frames 140–41.
   [23] Aug. 14, 1879, *Abendblatt.*
   [24] Letter from Rudolf Auspitz to Eduard Suess, Aug. 16, 1879, in
Briefe, ed. Molisch, pp. 225–26.
   [25] *Erinnerungen,* II, 169.

Stremayr well informed of the sentiment of some of the diehard Liberals toward his presence or the presence of other Liberals in Taaffe's cabinet, and Herbst's private declaration to Czedik that anyone who entered the cabinet was lost indicated clearly that the opponents of the Bosnian adventure had little hankering for the Taaffe experiment. On August 31 the Viennese newspapers openly reported that the party had voted to forbid any Liberal to take part in the ministry, and Czedik wrote Stremayr that only the unforgiving Herbst could have originated such a story. Czedik assured Stremayr, however, that at least forty deputies would secretly form a "conservative" club within the general Liberal framework to support Stremayr's retention of his post and the entry of more Liberals into the cabinet.[26]

Czedik's prediction of a club favorable to Taaffe's coalition did not come to pass, and inspired sources actually alleged that Taaffe was pleased by its nonappearance. He preferred to have this ostensibly cooperative core of Liberals operate within the regular Liberal Party, where they could nullify the animosity of the "Bosnian fraction."[27] Just as his press chiefs were making the best of the turbulent organizational moves that preceded the opening of the Reichsrat, a sizable number of those who had voted against Andrássy's diplomacy announced the creation of the Progressive Club (*Klub der vereinigten Fortschrittspartei*). They stressed careful scrutiny of all foreign policy in the interest of peace and demanded drastic paring of the expenses of the occupation.[28] Paradoxically, they did not enroll Herbst, who was normally regarded as the apostle of opposition to the new Balkan policies. He and at least twenty-six others who had voted against the Berlin arrangements joined with such moderates as Plener, Czedik, and August Weeber, a lawyer from Olmütz, in forming the larger Liberal Club (*Klub der Liberalen*), whose program was more general in its insistence on economy in finances and upon deliberation in meeting nationalistic demands. Plener was so outraged by the independent moves of the

[26] Letters of Aug. 30 and 31, 1879, in *Briefe,* ed. Molisch, pp. 226–27.
[27] *Das Vaterland,* Oct. 16, 1879.
[28] Richard Charmatz, *Deutsch-österreichische Politik* (Leipzig, 1907), p. 171.

Progressives that he confidentially proposed to Eduard Suess, the renowned geologist, that all moderate Liberals join with the Clerical Center Club to form the government's party in the new Reichsrat. Such a move, he argued, would drive Herbst into the arms of his true friends in the Progressive Club and provide a nucleus for the ministry which would succeed Taaffe's.[29]

Liberals like Plener underestimated Taaffe's staying power. The Liberal displeasure over Auersperg's compromise of June redoubled when the Emperor praised the Czechs in his customary speech from the throne for having returned to parliamentary life "without detriment to their own legal convictions and notwithstanding the difference in their point of view."[30] To sensitive German politicians, such phrases were more than a courteous bow to Czech sensibilities. They might well lead to a recognition of full autonomy for Bohemia, Moravia, and Silesia. Two days later the Czech deputies and their aristocratic allies proclaimed in both houses of the Reichsrat that their re-entry signified no surrender of their federalist principles.[31]

The Liberals in the Lower House could only send a minority reply to the address from the throne, but the Liberal majority in the Upper House contrived a distinct rebuke for Taaffe and the Emperor. A respectful but stern paragraph called upon the government to be mindful of the constitution. It should meet Czech desires by due process of law and not by administrative decree. The peers ignored Taaffe's pleas for a milder statement, which would unite rather than separate, and the almost unheard-of appearance of three archdukes and all four cardinals at voting time did not prevent the Minister-President's defeat, 78 to 59.[32] Prince Reuss heard from high court circles that Taaffe's employment of Archdukes Albrecht, Karl Ludwig, and Ludwig Victor had not particularly edified the Emperor, since these gentlemen were loath to engage in a battle already lost.[33]

[29] Undated letter, possibly of Oct. 20, 1879, in *Briefe*, ed. Molisch, pp. 231–32.
[30] Kolmer, *Parlament*, III, 3–6, 15.   [31] *Ibid.*, pp. 17–18.
[32] *Ibid.*, pp. 19–25.
[33] Reuss's dispatch No. 446, A 6218, Nov. 3, 1879, UC-1, reel 214, frame 202.

Franz Joseph imperturbably ignored the Upper House's attempt to demonstrate its lack of confidence. It was time to renew the empire's military program, and as supreme war lord he was determined to allow no side issues to interfere with the chief matter at hand. As he listened carefully to his advisers, he inevitably remembered that armed might, far more than marriage in recent centuries, had saved Habsburg dynastic interest. Against Turk and Louis XIV there had been the marvelous Eugene of Savoy. Archduke Charles had been one of the few to halt Napoleon, if never conclusively. In the disheartening years of 1848–49, Radetzky and Windischgrätz again proved that superior generalship and discipline could hold the line against subversion. Obversely, what ruler knew better than he the cost of military unpreparedness?

Apart from an enthusiasm for regimental histories, uniforms, and traditions that middle age did not dim, the Emperor-King was mindful of the scenes of disorder in Paris in 1871 which a stern army alone ended. The army seemed still to be the instrument of order, whether it had to fire on mobs, fulfill international mandates, or inculcate a simple loyalty to ruler and state when their subjects were on its rolls. In 1869–70 a rising in Dalmatia required military measures, and the dispensation from the European powers to occupy Bosnia and Herzegovina by no means neutralized the native resistance to Austro-Hungarian units. Before the provinces were militarily secured, a third of the monarchy's army had been pulled into the campaign.

Equally important in stiffening Franz Joseph's resolve was the conclusion of a defensive alliance with Germany against Russia in October, 1879. Bismarck's countrymen had proved their brilliance in battle in 1866 and 1870–71, and it was flattering to secure their offer of aid in case of a Russian attack. Andrássy steadfastly declined to give guarantees in case France attacked Germany over Alsace-Lorraine, but neither he nor his sovereign could afford to rule out the possibility someday of a Franco-Russian coalition. The statistics were distinctly unsettling. In terms of total mobilization (not the same thing as war footing), Austria-Hungary could place 1,100,000 against Russia's

2,600,000 and Italy's 900,000. France could match the German Empire's 1,542,000 with a surprising 1,555,000.[34] Such figures explained Franz Joseph's absolute repugnance to talk of reductions. The alliance with the Hohenzollerns was undreamed of security, but Bismarck expected more than press acclaim and dignified court dinners. The new responsibilities in the Balkans were proof that England, too, still regarded the Habsburg monarchy as a great power worthy of a civilizing mission. Not since the turn of the tide in 1848 had Franz Joseph enjoyed greater prestige.

Would his parliaments dare spoil the empire's refurbished glory? Would the German Liberals of Austria torpedo the military system their cabinet had sponsored in 1868? There were indeed signs in late 1879 that an unknown number of Liberals would compound their disagreeable reception of the Treaty of Berlin with unimaginative demands for cuts in defense costs.

Franz Joseph personally conferred with his Austrian and Hungarian advisers on September 26 in regard to extending the Defense Law of 1868. Though Horst informed him that both governments were agreed on maintaining the war strength at 800,000 men and in trying to obtain a ten-year approval of this figure, Tisza expressed doubt that his parliament would bind itself for such a lengthy term. Andrássy and Taaffe energetically supported the ten-year proviso. Knowing that he would have to secure a two-thirds majority in his Reichsrat for any period beyond one year's approval, Taaffe saw no sense in an uphill campaign that would end only in a three-year dispensation.

The Emperor then intervened. Tisza's suggestion of a three-year approval would appear strange and would jeopardize future demands for a decennial authorization. It would be better to ask for one year's sanction, for this obviously had the mark of the provisional and would require a simple majority in the Reichsrat. Under imperial and Austrian pressure, Tisza retorted that his task would be eased if Taaffe first won the Austrian parlia-

---

[34] *Stenographische Protokolle über die Sitzungen des Hauses der Abgeordneten des Reichsrates,* IX Session, pp. 583–84, Dec. 3, 1879. Hereafter cited as *SPA,* with pages and date.

ment's acquiescence. Andrássy dared to question the Emperor's preference for a one-year term (if the parliament proved to be obdurate), for he strongly discountenanced any measure that would give oppositional forces a chance to create trouble in the following year. In the end Franz Joseph ordered a strong fight for the decennial provision. Should parliamentary opposition be insuperable, then the two cabinets might confer further on a three-year or a one-year extension.[35]

Das Vaterland succinctly portrayed the Austrian government's basic dilemma as it turned to the Lower House for approval. To ready the existing army and the Landwehr for combat, the state had to remedy an insufficiency of officers, of ammunition for target practice, and of properly modernized fortresses. The oppressive imperial deficit nonetheless interposed a veto upon an increase in defense spending.[36] It would be triumph enough to sustain a war strength of 800,000 for another decade, and this consideration spurred Taaffe to a stubborn rejection of Hungarian proposals to increase the imperial budget. If he demanded more appropriations, the opposition would argue against a war footing of 800,000.[37]

To sweeten the tempers of both parliaments, the Imperial Defense Minister in October proposed furloughs for 18,000 men then under arms. The German Ambassador was quick to relay to Heinrich von Haymerle, Andrássy's successor as Austro-Hungarian foreign minister, his government's concern over such a reduction, but Haymerle replied that it was very important to soothe the deputies of each realm as they began their study of the renewal of the Defense Law. The authorities could recall the furloughed soldiers to their units in a very short time in case of emergency, so the army's effectiveness was not imperiled.

From his retreat at Varzin, Bismarck directed Reuss to point out to Haymerle that the arguments used to justify leaves for 18,000 could apply just as well for 100,000. Indeed, it would be

---

[35] Haus-, Hof-, und Staatsarchiv, Vienna, Ministerrath für gemeinsame Angelegenheiten, Protokoll vom 26 Sept., 1879, RMRZ 241. Hereafter, citations will give only RMRZ number and date of these protocols.
[36] Oct. 10, 1879.   [37] RMRZ 242, Oct. 13, 1879.

most economical of all to furlough the entire army. Did the
Russian troop concentrations along the Galician frontier mean
nothing? Of course, instructed the Chancellor, Reuss was to
deliver these comments in as forbearing and as circumspect a
way as possible.[38]

Already, on October 15, the government had sent the Defense
Bill to parliament. As before, the Reichsrat was to surrender for
another decade its right to modify the peace strength of 253,000,
the war strength of 800,000. Such renunciation required the
acquiescence of two-thirds who cast ballots. A month later
Taaffe, most of his colleagues, and leaders of the chief parliamentary clubs met to discuss the government's case. The
Minister-President had warned Heinrich Clam Martinič, Hohenwart, and Kazimierz Grocholski, the "boss" of the Polish Club,
that he would yield to a "party ministry" if the Defense Bill
failed to pass.[39] It was clear from the statements advanced by
Hohenwart and Grocholski in the meeting that they believed
him.

August Weeber, who was to be the decisive figure in the
government's final victory, carefully avoided committing the
Liberal Club to a direct refusal. His colleagues would support
an extension "for a longer period of years" only if the regime
promised to effect savings in defense outlays. Eduard Sturm,
who had voted against the Treaty of Berlin and now represented
the "irreconcilables," accented the constant rise in costs of material and sourly predicted that the cabinet would use the strength
it derived from a passage of the military proposal to execute the
constitutional amendments which the Right already had
planned. In a final effort to persuade the moderate Liberals to
rally to the Emperor, Horst and Stremayr, honorable if not
outspokenly partisan Liberals, spoke of the absolute necessity of
maintaining the established military force and stressed the right
of future Delegations to make cuts in the war budget.[40]

To a degree the pleas were telling. After Weeber reported the

---

[38] Reuss's dispatch No. 441, A 6145, Nov. 1, 1879, UC-1, reel 214,
frames 194–200.

[39] *Politischer Nachlass*, pp. 254–57.   [40] *Das Vaterland*, Nov. 17, 1879.

tenor of the conference to the Liberal Club, his associates accepted Czedik's resolution to grant a ten-year renewal if the military authorities would reduce the peacetime strength to 230,000 men. Franz Joseph lost no time vetoing compromise proposals, telling the presidium of the Lower House that speedy passage of the unchanged governmental proposal was imperative. Horst also wrote Weeber that the cabinet was unanimous on the Defense Bill. Though he was most distressed over this breach with his closest political friends, he could not conceal his conviction that the Liberals were using the military issue for partisan purposes. They should realize that the general public did not understand or laud their attitude.[41]

The great debate began on December 1, and the Progressives provided the chief opposition. Those who had supported the reform of 1868 maintained that a reorganization at that time was inescapable. Thanks to the army's ability to overspend its budget, however, they would fight a second ten-year dispensation. Did not the recent defeat of the Turks show that bravery and a sufficient supply of bayonets could not withstand the deadly germ of financial disorder? Furthermore, Austrian authorities had committed frequent blunders, and it was foolish to garb such gentlemen with a cloak of infallibility. People had forgotten that Austria lost in 1866 not because of lack of valor or of troops and equipment but because of factors best left unexplored.[42]

Czech reaction was mixed, though all spokesmen admitted they would vote for the proposal. Julius Grégr, the powerful Young Czech, grumbled that hundreds of millions went for militarism, while the question of subsidizing the cultural interests of entire nationalities ended in haggling over a few gulden. Rieger, while disclaiming all connection with Taaffe's collaborators, was unmistakably Austro-Slavic in asserting that the Czechs, with an Austrian past and future, had to do what was necessary to secure Austria's safety. Heinrich Clam Martinič

[41] Letter of Nov. 25, 1879, in *Briefe,* ed. Molisch, pp. 232–33.
[42] Speech of Eduard Sturm, in *SPA,* IX Session, pp. 514–16, Dec. 1, 1879; of Adolf Wiesenburg, *ibid.,* pp. 547–49, Dec. 2, 1879; of Johann Fux, *ibid.,* pp. 552–54, Dec. 2, 1879.

quite casually noted that he and his friends would keep the Czech banners flying no matter who was minister and no matter what form the military laws might take.[43]

Grocholski harped on the theme of maintaining the empire's great-power status, for his people had every reason to keep Austria-Hungary as independent as possible of diplomatic domination by the German Empire and as reserved as possible in its relations with the other oppressor of the Poles, Russia.[44] Prince Alfred Liechtenstein, the German Clerical Conservative, argued that the clumsy dualistic system would never work if political passions were annually stirred up, or at least it would work only to the advantage of the more united Magyars.[45]

Taaffe judiciously left the government's exposé of the bill to General von Horst, who presented a multitude of statistics showing that Austria-Hungary spent less on every soldier than did the other four continental powers and that it called up a smaller percentage of men for service in peace or in war than did the others. The reorganization of the imperial forces, begun in 1870–71, would be completed only in 1892–94, and he vigorously opposed the "dangerous" recommendations coming from the opposition.[46]

By a tally of 178 to 152, the Lower House adopted the provision keeping the army's war strength at 800,000 on December 4, after the defeat of Czedik's motion to reduce the peacetime strength to 230,000. This was small comfort for Taaffe, who still needed a two-thirds majority for the decennial grant. Next day this vital part of the plan received 174 affirmative votes, whereas 220 were needed. The cabinet nevertheless sent the original bill to the Upper House, whose members were proverbially more dependable. After a very brief debate, replete with patriotic sentiments, the peers unanimously accepted the proposal on December 13.

Conferring with his Hungarian colleagues a few days earlier,

---

[43] *SPA,* IX Session, pp. 560–61, Dec. 2, 1879; pp. 637–42, Dec. 4, 1879; p. 608, Dec. 3, 1879.
[44] *Ibid.,* pp. 527–28, Dec. 1, 1879.   [45] *Ibid.,* p. 551, Dec. 2, 1879.
[46] *Ibid.,* pp. 584–86, 590, Dec. 3, 1879.

Taaffe was sure that the war strength would remain as before, but he feared that the size of the contingent for peacetime purposes might still be undecided by the time the Delegations met. When the Hungarian ministers informed him that their Upper House was likely to press for energetic and expensive measures in the occupied provinces, he urged the Hungarians to rein in their parliamentarians. Otherwise his carefully arranged majority in the Austrian Lower House might well collapse.[47]

To force a sufficient number of perplexed moderate Liberals to join the government's allies, Franz Joseph summoned Weeber to a private audience on the same day that the Upper House returned a favorable verdict. According to Weeber's full account of the conference, he told the Emperor that his moderate friends expected a dissolution of the Lower House in the not distant future. Taaffe's majority and its opponents were too evenly matched. If the moderates yielded and voted for the Defense Bill, they would face sure defeat at the hands of an aroused German electorate. Now that the Czechs openly proclaimed their national ambitions, it was incumbent upon patriotic German Austrians to fight for moderation.

Franz Joseph refused to concur with Weeber's assumption that the Lower House would prove to be short-lived. No great constitutional questions were coming up after defense needs had been met. When Weeber cautiously expressed his fraction's distrust of Taaffe's ability to guarantee stable conditions, the Emperor irritably reminded him that every effort to form a new ministry from the Liberal Party had ended in frustration. Continuing pressure on the present ministry would only drive it further to the Right. He asked if the Liberals really expected to force the Hungarian parliament and the Austrian Upper House to give in to them in rejecting the government's plan. Recalling the arguments that accompanied each renewal of the *Ausgleich,* he said he would not endure any scheme that would permit annual recriminations between his two parliaments.

Weeber entreated the Emperor to promise economies, quite nominal, in the existing defense budget, but his firm interlocutor

[47] RMRZ 245, Dec. 8, 1879.

referred him to the Upper House's example of requesting savings
when it accepted the government's bill. Though Weeber promised only to relay the imperial comments to his colleagues, the
Emperor was in good humor at the close of the audience.[48]

Meanwhile, Taaffe and Horst were sparring with Tisza to
avert Hungarian actions that would exacerbate opinion in the
Austrian Lower House. Both Austrians swore that the Defense
Bill would pass as desired, but they heartily disapproved of
Tisza's decision to submit the bill, approved by both Hungarian
houses, to the Emperor before the Austrian Lower House
reached a final decision.[49] While these Austrian cabinet members held off an obvious Magyar demonstration of loyal coopera-
tiveness, Haymerle and Andrássy (present for the Delegations
meeting) worked assiduously to break down Liberal resistance.[50] Czedik, no doubt himself under heavy pressure, implored
Horst to secure an imperial promise of future economies,
roughly what Weeber had hinted would be sufficient to save
face.[51]

On December 17, as if to underline Czedik's sincere pleas for
a statement on retrenchment, the Lower House again failed to
approve the decennial arrangement. The affirmative votes had
increased only by six. When both houses elected delegates to a
commission to settle the marked differences in opinion, Taaffe
and Horst appeared to give unconditional promise that they
would do everything possible to reduce costs of the defense
program. They also assured the conferees that the Reichsrat
could repeal the entire Defense Law anytime it so desired. With
such an explicit recognition of parliamentary primacy, a majority
of the committee of the Lower House entrusted with defense
affairs decided once again to ask for the desired two-thirds
approval.[52] Weeber and Czedik went along with this majority and
asked the Liberal Club to ratify their actions. The ensuing poll

[48] *Briefe,* ed. Molisch, pp. 235–43.   [49] RMRZ 249, Dec. 16, 1879.
[50] Reuss's dispatch No. 529, A 7043, Dec. 17, 1879, UC-1, reel 214,
frame 221.
[51] Letter of Dec. 15, 1879, in *Briefe,* ed. Molisch, p. 243.
[52] *SPA,* pp. 865–66, Dec. 20, 1879.

indicated that 35 favored their representatives' action, 30 were opposed, and 7 cast blank ballots.[53]

The weary Lower House voted yet a third time on December 20, and the government won four votes in excess of the two-thirds required. Thirty-seven Liberals accounted for Taaffe's victory. Of these, twenty had previously voted in opposition, while seventeen had not voted.[54] Hisses and booing from the "irreconcilables" greeted those who changed their minds. Even Eduard Suess, the university professor and party stalwart, brought storms of derision upon himself by avowing that he voted only for the sake of the empire.[55]

Both cabinet and opposition had employed intimidation, and a letter composed by Horst just after the votes were counted expressed great concern over the willful obstruction of some of the Liberals. Did they not realize that every party which fought military subventions in every European state was committing suicide? States had to be prepared for tough political and social crises, but only the German Liberals, of all the political groups in both Austria and Hungary, took pleasure in trying to negate such preparedness.[56]

An anonymous pamphlet of 1880, admittedly written by a member of the Austrian Lower House, reflected the anger which gripped many diehard Liberals during the last stages of the passage of the Defense Bill. Printed in Leipzig under the title, *Der Weg Bergab,* it rehashed most of the economic arguments used by the bill's foes and also offered such astonishingly frank interpretations of the government's motivation that a cabinet meeting of March 15, 1880, busied itself with the possible repercussions.

The loss of Lombardy and Venetia was the loss of an integral

---

[53] *Neue Freie Presse,* Dec. 20, 1879. Weeber's and Czedik's reasoning is explained by Alois von Czedik, *Zur Geschichte der k.k. österreichischen Ministerien, 1861–1916* (Teschen, Vienna, and Leipzig, 1917), I, 322–23.

[54] *Das Vaterland,* Dec. 21, 1879.

[55] *SPA,* pp. 876–77, Dec. 20, 1879.

[56] Haus-, Hof-, und Staatsarchiv, Vienna, Nachlass des Ministers Julius von Horst, Karton 2 (Korrespondenzen 1850–1904), item 14. Hereafter cited as Nachlass Horst.

part of the imperial body as far as the ruling circles were concerned, asserted the author. They wanted compensation, and it was easy to discern the weakening Turkish hold over the lands between Croatia and Dalmatia. Austria had not a shadow of right there, the people were poor and turbulent, but 850 square miles were an honorable replacement for the 826 square miles lost in Italy. More, with the abolition of absolutism and the coming of Dualism, the army alone remained as a focus of interest, concern, and affection. Save for a nominal right of the people's representatives to approve its expenses, the army remained free of popular interference. Its very unity allowed the fiction of a united state to live on.[57]

But Austria-Hungary was no great power. It was but a secondary state, thanks to thirty years of unsound administration by its ruler. Two alternatives faced Austria's ruling caste: withdrawal for decades from any participation in great-power maneuvers and concentration on financial recovery and economic prosperity or further insistence on upholding the glory, reputation, and great-power status of the empire at the cost of every policy that would enhance the health and security of the citizens.[58] *Der Weg Bergab* made no effort to hide its disrespect for the Emperor, for an aristocracy consumed with a passion for soldiering, for all who could not rationally endure the thought of trailing any other power in number of bayonets and cannons.

Its often penetrating comments presaged an intensification of Liberal resentment against Taaffe and the hopeful Czechs. Liberal-oriented cabinet members withstood the denunciations of their more excitable party colleagues for a while longer, but the unwelcome compulsions of December, 1879, left all Liberal circles uneasy. Some expected Taaffe to make a fatal error that would force Franz Joseph to recall experienced Liberals to power. Meanwhile, no responsible leader in either club permitted talk of the slightest collaboration with "the ministry above the parties." Containment of the Czechs, restraints upon the Poles, absolute check upon the Clericals—with such negative policies Liberalism moved into the even more rancorous decade of the 1880s.

[57] *Der Weg Bergab* (Leipzig, 1880), pp. 5–7.   [58] *Ibid.*, pp. 53–54.

3 Full Breach with the Liberals

The "irreconcilables" who contested the Defense Bill to the end honestly did worry over the state's deficit and were correct in supposing that the Emperor looked upon the army as his personal possession. The Bosnian adventure had earned their disapproval because it confronted parliament with an accomplished fact and also because it might add more Slavs to the empire in the proximate future. German Liberals were uniformly proud of Germandom's role as a civilizing agency among the Slavs, but the Czech renaissance of the nineteenth century had indicated that protégés did not remain tractable. In Bohemia, the richest land in Austria, the contest between Germans and Czechs was moving toward a climax, and Taaffe's transparent wooing of the long-time underdogs was bound to antagonize all shades of Liberal opinion.

Thoughtful Liberals had yielded to the crown's will when resistance to the Defense Bill no longer seemed sensible, but Taaffe's delicate yet definite moves to persuade the Czechs to resume common deliberation with the rest of Austria in the central Reichsrat seriously alarmed them. *Raison d'état* could excuse ultimate approval of an expensive military establishment, but the compromise in the Bohemian landed curia and the appointment of Pražak to the cabinet were significant threats to the German position in Bohemia and consequently in Austria. The Czechs had dutifully voted for the Defense Bill, and it was

assumed that they expected concessions in return. Indeed, the
simple return of the Czechs to the Reichsrat implied recognition
of some of their claims.

In the six months which preceded the final decision on the
Defense Bill, Taaffe shrewdly managed the Czech assumption of
full political responsibility. It is clear from Heinrich Clam
Martinič's complaints that the Emperor's chief minister refused
to allow the Czech fractions to proclaim their basic constitutional convictions prior to taking their oaths of office in the
Reichsrat and likewise declined to summon the Bohemian Diet
before the opening of the Reichsrat in the autumn of 1879.[1] But
Pražak's appointment to the cabinet in August was a favorable
augury, followed by some hard bargaining between Taaffe and
the leading Czech politicians in September. At the right moment, he agreed, the latter could issue a statement deploring the
existing constitutional framework. In addition, the cabinet
would work toward equality of opportunity in positions in the
bureaucracy and toward an electoral reform favorable to the
Czechs.[2]

The cost to the Czechs? Ostensibly, they were to act respon-
sibly as parliamentarians. Responsible parliamentarians in an
institution as fraction-ridden as the Austrian Reichsrat had a
duty to search for sympathetic partners, and on September 18
the Czechs caucused with the Poles and the German Clerical
Conservatives. Taaffe had indubitably impressed upon all of
these groups his master's desire to keep some Liberals in the
cabinet as part of a scheme to maintain a "ministry above the
parties." It was likely that the German Liberals in the Reichsrat
would protest loudly over new policies, however, and only the
most naïve believed that Taaffe could be unhappy over the
Czech-Polish-German Clerical Conservative bloc that was forming.

When joined by the Slovenes, these elements made up the

---

[1] Letter and Memorandum of July 27, 1879, in *Politischer Nachlass*,
pp. 382–88.

[2] Gustav Kolmer, *Parlament und Verfassung in Oesterreich* (Vienna
and Leipzig, 1902–14), III, 7.

"Iron Ring" that was the fundament of Taaffe's system between 1881 and 1890. In his first two years of office Liberals sat with him in the cabinet. After 1890 some of them seemed ready to end their hostility and to collaborate in a Bohemian settlement. During the most vital years of his regime, however, it was the Iron Ring that delivered the votes, spelled out the concessions and policies desired, and learned, sometimes fitfully, that coalitions do not reward all their component elements equally. Taaffe never was completely subservient to the Poles, Czechs, and German Right, for a quick resort to the Liberals was always possible. Bismarck, another *Kaiserminister,* had long perfected the art of juggling governmental majorities, and Taaffe almost as expertly exploited those divisions within the Ring that imperiled its vaunted solidity. From the beginning Old and Young Czechs had uneasy relations with Polish, Czech, and German aristocrats. Policy concerning education and religion would be a major source of embarrassment, obviously. German Clerical Conservatives in turn could not go too far in applauding concessions to the Czechs or big monetary grants to eternally poor Galicia. An intensely interesting dialogue developed between Taaffe and these partners once the last Liberal quit his cabinet. Though tired of agonizing with Liberal collaborators, he could not give in supinely to all that the partners wanted. The interplay eventuated in some of the most fruitful legislative activity of his reign. But it also threw into vivid relief the future of the Germans as the empire's ranking culture bearers.

The Czechs were their chief challengers, since the "historic" Poles were in secure control of Galicia and the "historic" Italians waited for final redemption by the government in Rome. On the day the Lower House resumed its session in the autumn of 1879, Heinrich Clam Martinič and Rieger submitted to the Emperor what was to become a famous Memorandum. In accord with the bargain struck in September, its contents remained unpublished. Though rumors hinted at the existence of "demands," the German Ambassador with some relief wrote to Berlin that Taaffe had secured a victory that could not be underestimated. He had prevailed upon the Czechs to admit they would be content with a decentralization of administration.[3] Had Bismarck's envoy known of Franz Joseph's thought at the time, he would have hesitated before writing of a victory. In the cabinet meeting of November 27 the Austrian monarch declared that the time would come when his ministers would have to work a change in Article 19 of the Fundamental Laws, for, as long as it stood, there could be no progress.[4] It was not enough, in short, to declare that all nationalities were equal in rights, with an unquestioned guarantee of their language and ethnic individuality.

He was very much aware of what the Czechs had spelled out as their "rights" in the Memorandum, which was published with his and Taaffe's consent as soon as the Defense Bill passed. What were the Czech expectations, as they awaited some reward for their loyal support of the armed forces?

The first part of their Memorandum laid down regulations which would ensure parity in the bureaucracy and in the courts. In all offices and courts of first instance, the valid medium of communication should be the language used by a majority of the population subject to such offices and courts or used by the autonomous officials who were "correlated" with such offices and courts. In all other offices and courts, whose jurisdiction included several districts, or the entire crownland, or which were located in the crownland's capital, German and Czech were to be the official languages. Courts and offices of first instance were to use their own language in corresponding with superior or equal courts and offices. Superior courts and offices were to answer in the language employed by the inferior organs. Every inhabitant had the right to use his own language in his petitions and other legal documents, and all of the subsequent proceedings had to be carried out in his chosen language. To enforce these projected regulations, the Czech Memorandum declared that oral and

[3] See Reuss's dispatches Nos. 446 and 447, A 6218 and A 6219, Nov. 3, 1879, *German Foreign Ministry Archives 1867–1920*, UC-1, reel 214, frames 204–6.

[4] Moses Mehring, "Die deutsch-böhmische Sprachenfrage während des Ministeriums Taaffe (1879–1893)" (unpubl. diss., Vienna, 1924), p. 140.

written proficiency in both tongues was an absolute necessity. The government was to transfer bureaucrats and legal officials who lacked dual proficiency to assignments requiring only one language. In every provincial office, however, there was to be at least one official well versed in both. In Silesian court proceedings, Czech and Polish were to have equal footing with German.

The second part of the Memorandum stipulated equality for the Czech language at the University of Prague, in the Mittelschulen, and in industrial schools. In the future the Mittelschulen would share subventions in a manner proportionate to the population statistics and tax contributions of the two nationalities in Bohemia and Moravia.[5]

Two days after the publication of the Memorandum, Taaffe acquainted the entire cabinet with the limits to which they might go in meeting Czech desires. There were but two absolute prohibitions. Any concession would apply to the individual crownland, never to the empire as a whole. The claims of seven tongues made an empire-wide linguistic decree or law impossible. In the second place, new language regulations would under no circumstance affect or modify official correspondence with the military establishment.[6] With such restrictions in mind, a ministerial committee under Pražak settled down to serious work and in four months elaborated new Language Ordinances for Bohemia and Moravia. Before this task was completed, however, two separate crises had persuaded the Liberal members of the cabinet that they could not continue to collaborate with Czechs and German Clerical Conservatives.

These same Liberal ministers, Horst, Stremayr, and Korb, had cajoled enough members of their party to accept the Defense Bill the third time it was offered to obtain its passage. In return, they officially declared that they had Taaffe's promise that he would not shift further to the Right. To their consternation the Minister-President informed them after Christmas that he had to relieve Stremayr of the Education portfolio and give it to Baron

[5] Kolmer, *Parlament,* III, 58–59.
[6] Mehring, "Die deutsch-böhmische Sprachenfrage," pp. 36–37.

Kriegsau, the candidate of the German Clerical Conservatives.[7] Stremayr was to remain as Minister of Justice, but he did not hide from the German Ambassador his resolve to quit the cabinet should the new Minister of Education develop policies contrary to his own principles. Reuss then relayed home his prediction that such a resignation would be the first dangerous crack in Taaffe's system of government by coalition.[8] When Stremayr, at Taaffe's behest, sounded out a picked group of moderate Liberals on Kriegsau's acceptability, he found only one who refrained from opposition. In fact, this caucus demanded that all Liberals step down from the cabinet should Taaffe persist in awarding the highly controversial Education post to a man beloved of the Clerical Conservatives.[9] Their concern was intensified when the four bishops of Bohemia abruptly announced that they would forbid their communicants to send children to the public schools if the cabinet did not initiate a reform of the imperial educational system.

Bismarck heard from Reuss that Franz Joseph, to all appearances, intervened to keep Stremayr and his like-minded colleagues in the cabinet. The "temporary" Minister of Finance, Emil Chertek, gave his place to Kriegsau, while Education went to Siegmund Conrad von Eybesfeld, the *Statthalter* of Lower Austria, who was reputed to be *verfassungstreu*. Reuss surmised that the Czech Memorandum and the bishops' declaration had reminded the crown "that it would be risky to rely on these elements." The Liberals had permitted the Bohemian electoral compromise only because the Emperor had wished it. They were essentially loyal to him, and he had to treat them accordingly, particularly in view of the majority they still controlled in the Upper House.[10] Haymerle later confirmed Reuss's suspi-

[7] Letter from Horst, Stremayr, and Korb to Emperor, June 12, 1880, in Haus-, Hof-, und Staatsarchiv, Vienna, Kabinettsarchiv, Geheimakten, I. Ministerwechsel in Österreich 1870 bis 1918, Karton 41, ad 2544.880. Hereafter cited as Kabinettsarchiv.

[8] See Reuss's dispatch No. 38, A 453, Jan. 24, 1880, UC-1, reel 214, frame 249.

[9] *Neue Freie Presse*, Feb. 8, 1880.

[10] See Reuss's dispatch No. 71, A 769, Feb. 8, 1880, UC-1, reel 214, frame 265.

cions concerning the Emperor's reactions to the Bohemian bishops. He had denounced them emphatically to the nuncio, who
disclaimed all personal responsibility and denied that Rome had
supplied inspiration of any kind.[11]

The second crisis which persuaded the Liberal ministers that
they could not get along with their Rightist colleagues developed
as Taaffe sought approval for his Discretionary Fund
(*Dispositions-Fonds*). This fund subsidized the "official press"
and the men who prepared the "handouts." If parliament refused the necessary subsidies, it would deliver an annoying
rather than a critical blow against the government. Early in
April the Liberal Club and the Progressive Club decided to
demonstrate their lack of confidence in the cabinet by voting
against this Austrian version of a "reptile fund."[12]

To forestall such mischief, Taaffe granted the Vienna corre-
spondent of *The Standard* of London an interview. Vowing that
he would never head a purely partisan ministry, he repeated his
hopes for a truly conservative Center that might balance Right
and Left. In an obvious bid for a change of heart among
moderate Liberals, he plainly stressed the impossibility of fulfill-
ing what the ultramontanes wanted in educational affairs.[13]
Facing the clubs in the Lower House a few days later, he
reiterated what was already a formula. His cabinet would not
encourage those national aspirations which were unhealthy for
the empire. At the same time it would try to keep every nationality from feeling that it was deprived of its inborn and histori-
cally acquired rights.[14]

Neither his generalities nor his specific comment on ultramon-
tane educational objectives prevented disaster on April 13, the
day of the intensely awaited vote. The ministers who had seats
in the Lower House voted confidence in themselves, grimly
reported the *Neue Freie Presse,* and Taaffe, when the recorder
reached the letter *S* in the roll-call vote, left the scene, flushed

[11] See Reuss's dispatch No. 77, A 816, Feb. 11, 1880, UC-1, reel 214,
frames 269–70.
[12] *Neue Freie Presse*, April 6, 1880.
[13] *Ibid.,* April 9, 1880, *Abendblatt.*
[14] *Ibid.,* April 12, 1880, *Abendblatt.*

and with a forced smile on his face. The opposition was twelve
votes ahead. The Ruthenes, automatically anti-Polish and so
anti-Taaffe, joined the Liberals. Actually, the absence of a few
disaffected Clericals, of a few Liberal Poles, and the abstention
of some landowners from Moravia who usually observed the
signals given by the Right made possible the defeat, by two votes,
of the Discretionary Fund. When it was clear that the opposition had whipped the ministry, Herbst led the Left benches in a
wild demonstration, while Rieger angrily shouted that the
nonpresence of two pious Tirolese had at last permitted the
extremes to meet.[15]

Herbst's savage exultation and Rieger's cry of frustration
illustrated perfectly the growing dilemma within the cabinet. Its
ministerial committee was polishing the last phrases of the forthcoming Language Ordinances for Bohemia and Moravia, which
Rieger desperately needed for the political future of the Old
Czechs. Concurrently, Horst, who was absent from Vienna at
the bedside of his desperately sick daughter, wrote Korb that
there was no use trying to keep a coalition going. A homogeneous ministry of the Right was the only solution, for a continuation of the existing chaos was a disservice to the Emperor.[16]

The sovereign's presence at the cabinet meeting of April 18
confirmed the gravity of the situation. Taaffe admitted that the
government appeared to be impotent because of the decided lack
of confidence on the Left and because of a lack of resolution on
the Right. But, before retiring, he felt obliged to push for the
budget, taxes to support military expenses, and a few other
fundamental measures. Falkenhayn and Pražak vigorously opposed all talk of resigning, and Florian Ziemialkowski, who had
been Minister for Galicia in the cabinet since 1873, accepted the
idea of stepping down only after parliament had gone home. In
the absence of Horst and Stremayr, who was ill, Korb energetically advocated immediate resignation. The coalition had
failed, and promises of full support from the Right were un-

[15] *Ibid.*, April 14, 1880.
[16] *Briefe zur deutschen Politik in Österreich von 1848 bis 1918,* ed.
Paul Molisch (Vienna and Leipzig, 1934), pp. 248–49.

acceptable to the Liberals in the cabinet. The Emperor, obviously displeased by Korb's suggestion, refused to consider a "partisan" solution. If the ministers of Korb's point of view relinquished their posts, he would replace them with men of the same general orientation. Thanks to this peremptory comment, the entire ministry decided to carry on with the important legislation still to be enacted.[17] Stremayr, probably well briefed on the course of the discussion, wrote Horst that he was saddened by the thought of four more weeks of enduring an impossible situation.[18]

The publication of the Language Ordinances on April 19, 1880, completed the discomfiture of the Liberal ministers. Angered by the Kriegsau intrigue and embarrassed by their lack of influence with the Liberal parliamentary groups in the matter of the Discretionary Fund, they were only partially prepared for the indignation which their political friends manifested when they read the provisions of the new linguistic regulations. Worst of all, these executive ordinances bore Stremayr's signature as Minister of Justice. For the rest of his days he was never allowed to forget the "Stremayr Ordinances."

What were these new dispensations for the two crownlands where Germans and Czechs were the contenders for supremacy? In the future all provincial officials—political, legal, and administrative—would execute documents, settlements, and the like in the language employed or requested by the citizen who was making use of their services. Should the said citizen make a statement, they were to take it down in the tongue he utilized. Documents brought in as subsidiary appendixes or as aids, if already drawn up in one of the two chief languages, required no translation. Administrative and legal directives or proceedings not initiated by the person to whom they applied were to be drawn up in his language. Should the person so involved speak neither of the two chief languages, the officials would draw up the relevant papers in one of the chief languages anyhow. The

[17] Letters from Korb to Horst, in Nachlass Horst, Karton 2. The letters are not dated but obviously were written on April 17 and 18, 1880.
[18] Heinrich Friedjung, *Julius Freiherr von Horst* (Vienna, 1906), p. 22.

nature of the case and the actual abode of the person concerned
would decide which language was apposite. In case administrative and legal processes involved communes rather than persons,
the bureaucracy would act as they did with individual citizens.

All official notices for universal dissemination had to appear
in Czech and German. Communal officials had to publish notices for their particular commune in the language used in its
confines. Court stenographers had to record testimony in the
language used by witnesses. Judicial personnel had to inform a
person accused of criminal acts of the charges made against him
in his own language. The same rule applied to the principal
proceedings, the statement of the state's attorney, and the defense's statement. Where several persons of different linguistic
backgrounds faced a joint trial, the court had the right to decide
what languages to use in the principal proceedings. In civil
cases the language of the court's decision had to coincide with
the language employed by the parties. Should the principal
parties use different languages and refuse to agree on one, the
court would promulgate its judgment in only one tongue. It
issued its orders for the execution of the verdict, naturally
enough, in both languages. Public offices had to maintain regis-
ters of landed property and of business firms in both languages.
The language employed by autonomous organs would prevail in
any correspondence such organs had with political, legal, and
administrative officials. This rule, however, did not disturb
procedures already followed by communal offices which exercised the functions of district political offices.[19]

What precisely did Stremayr's Ordinances mean, aside from
the complicated procedures which they sanctified? First of all,
they clearly defined Czech as a *Landessprache* in both Bohemia
and Moravia, and so they outraged many Germans who continued to describe Czech as merely *landesüblich*. The first term
created an official status for the Czech language. Previously the
Germans had insisted that Czech was merely a language used in
certain crownlands. In the second place, the Ordinances guar-

[19] Kolmer, *Parlament,* III, 87–89.

anteed every Czech an honest break in his dealings with bureaucrats and judges. From 1880 on there would be increasing
demand for officials in the outer services who were bilingual.
Since the Germans readily and frequently admitted their troubles
in learning Czech (if not always their inherent distaste for an
"inferior" vehicle of expression), it was clear that the Czechs
would gradually replace many Germans in state jobs. As long as
the inner services did not require Czech, the Germans could
count on some positions for their ambitious sons. Here was the
situation which angered the Czechs and yet did not calm the
Germans.

In retrospect Stremayr insisted that he had consented to new
linguistic regulations only after considerable watering down of
Czech demands, and Heinrich Pollak, his journalist confidant,
alleged that Stremayr alone kept Taaffe from even greater sur-
renders to the Czechs.[20] A scholar who had an opportunity to
read the minutes of the cabinet meeting of April 14, 1880, before
they were destroyed confirmed Stremayr's assertions.[21]

Liberal newspapers, however, decided that Stremayr was the
man to belabor. The *Neue Freie Presse* depicted him as the
unblushing signer of ordinances which deprived two million
Germans of rights they had possessed in Bohemia for centuries.[22] The *Brünner Zeitung,* the voice of the Progressive Club,
announced that the thin band which heretofore had linked Stremayr with the Liberals was broken. Whether he stayed with the
ministry or left it was immaterial to the German Left.[23]

On May 1 the German Left in the Reichsrat relentlessly closed
in on Stremayr through the classic expedient of an interpellation. Why did the cabinet feel that the Ordinances were called
for? How could the executive power reconcile them with the
provisions of the Fundamental Law?[24]

[20] Carl von Stremayr, *Erinnerungen aus dem Leben* (Vienna, 1899),
p. 60; Heinrich Pollak, *Dreissig Jahre aus dem Leben eines Journalisten*
(Vienna, 1898), III, 273.
[21] Mehring, "Die deutsch-böhmische Sprachenfrage," p. 40 n. 1.
[22] *Neue Freie Presse,* April 27, 1880.
[23] Quoted in *Das Vaterland,* April 30, 1880.
[24] *SPA,* IX Session, pp. 2870–71.

It was Stremayr's unhappy task to answer these questions. He insisted that his colleagues were putting into these Ordinances what had long been practiced. The cabinet promised absolutely not to subjugate imperial administration and justice to "nationalistic aspirations or to struggles for linguistic evolution." In other words, the Czechs had best be satisfied for the moment. The Germans should be glad that the inner services remained untouched.[25]

The Germans, save for the Clerical Conservatives, saw no reason to rejoice over what was left to them. In the Lower House, Count Gundacker Wurmbrand of the Graz Chamber of Commerce requested the cabinet to prepare a bill which would give the German language the status of an official tongue, to be used in the bureaucracy, in the schools, and in all phases of the state's public life.[26] Then Herbst moved that a special committee of twenty-four deputies review Stremayr's reply to the Liberals' interpellation. His proposal naturally implied that the cabinet had exceeded its power by pre-empting parliament's right to implement the Fundamental Laws.[27] A further indication of increasing German ire was the leading editorial of May 14's *Neue Freie Presse*. It defied Taaffe to stand against the resistance of the Germans in Austria, which, based as it was on strong legalities, would prove to be tougher than the turbulent activities of a Czech Tabor or the stupid passivity of peasants led by fanatic priests. "Austria will be German or nothing."

On May 24 the Liberals of the Upper House, who had accepted the Defense Bill without a murmur and who had been partially responsible for breaking the resistance it had stimulated among the Liberals in the Lower House, subjected Taaffe to a most unpleasant session. Cardinals and archdukes had not sufficed to persuade them to forgo a statement rigidly critical of Czech autonomist desires at the beginning of their sessions, and actually there was a logical correlation between their vote for the armed services and their determination to uphold centralism.

[25] *Ibid.*, pp. 2978–81, May 5, 1880.
[26] *Ibid.*, Beilagen 202, May 10, 1880.
[27] *Ibid.*, Beilagen 207, May 10, 1880.

Typical of the resentment shown by these Liberal peers were the tactless comments delivered by Anton von Schmerling. He graciously acknowledged that it was suitable for a person to use his own language for the first years of school, to hear it in his church, and to cultivate his own knowledge of its grammar and literature. Such freedoms had their limits, however. They should not be enjoyed at the cost of the common Kultur. His colleagues had no desire or need to proclaim German the state speech in Austria, for the world had already given it that rank. Where in England, Germany, France, or Italy did men learn Czech, Polish, or Magyar? The introduction of Magyar and even Croatian as service speeches had already injured the imperial army. Would future generals be able to put across their ideas to their troops, short of translations?[28]

Taaffe, rather surprisingly, counterattacked with vim and frankness. He and his fellow ministers were not depriving the Germans of their rights, and he would never permit any invasion of the executive's prerogatives by a parliament or by a commission that might number fifty members.[29] Stremayr, who had ceased attending cabinet meetings because of illness, did not show up to give the Ministry of Justice's case.

Two days later Stremayr, Horst, and Korb begged the Emperor to allow them to give up their portfolios, sending a letter to Taaffe as well to request his acquiescence.[30] Rather briefly they reminded Franz Joseph that a *Mittelpartei,* which they deemed imperative for the functioning of a coalition, had not evolved. Actually, some of their colleagues in the cabinet, afraid that the Right's effectiveness would dwindle, had hindered its development. In view of the increasing tension between Right and Left, which led to greater Rightist influence over the cabinet, they preferred to step down.[31] On May 29 the Emperor requested them to reconsider their action, and the disaffected three yielded to his wishes. In an attempt to restore to these

[28] *Stenographische Protokolle über die Sitzungen des Herrenhauses des Reichsrates,* IX Session, pp. 257–58. Hereafter cited as *SPH.*
[29] *Ibid.,* pp. 258–59, May 24, 1880.
[30] Letter to Taaffe, in *Politischer Nachlass,* p. 257.
[31] Kabinettsarchiv, Karton 41, ad 2544.880.

reluctant advisers some of the prestige they once had enjoyed in Liberal circles, he refused to receive a deputation of Czechs from predominantly German areas of Bohemia when he learned that they wanted to complain of German excesses and oppressions. As Haymerle delicately put it to Reuss, the Emperor was not pleased with the turn of recent events.[32]

But nothing had really changed, as the correspondence of the early summer, necessitated by Stremayr's absence from Vienna for recuperative purposes, amply proves. Horst wrote that he and Korb could see no point in carrying on and that Taaffe himself, rather confused, spoke vaguely of things having to be settled one way or another soon.[33] Conrad wrote Stremayr that the Emperor definitely wanted no changes in the cabinet and that Herbst did not expect or desire the departure of the Liberal ministers. The tone of this letter reveals a degree of pressure, possibly from the Emperor, for Stremayr doubtless noted the insertion of a statement that another would administer "his" Ordinances should he retire.[34]

On June 12 Horst finished a long letter to the Emperor in which he again detailed the grievances which he shared with Stremayr and Korb. In this renewal of the request to be relieved of their duties the ministers were as frank as one could be with a ruler noted for a long memory, and it is clear that Horst wished to leave to posterity an apologia for their joining and retiring from the cabinet.

The arguments were familiar. The coalition had never worked because no *Mittelpartei* had arisen and because Taaffe would or could not keep his promise not to favor the Right. The vote on the Discretionary Fund was proof of the lack of influence the Liberals in the cabinet had with the Liberals in parliament; it was useless and dishonorable to serve any longer in a cabinet which should mirror the point of view of the fractions which made up the Right.

The three ministers nevertheless expressed themselves

[32] See Reuss's dispatch No. 286, A 3408, June 5, 1880, UC-1, reel 214, frames 328–31.
[33] Letter of June 9, 1880, in *Briefe,* ed. Molisch, p. 249.
[34] Letter of June 12, 1880, *ibid.,* p. 249.

strongly against any increase in autonomy for the crownlands, which would be a pernicious drain upon the state's power. They could not work with a majority which demanded extremely dangerous concessions and which repeatedly and insultingly piled abuse upon those ministers who had served in the previous cabinet. Since there no longer was any chance of the entire cabinet's resigning, the three chief Liberals suggested that their own replacements be nominees more sympathetic to the majority.[35]

On June 26 the Emperor finally allowed Horst, Stremayr, and Korb to give up their responsibilities. Kriegsau joined them in leaving the cabinet, for he had been a great disappointment to his backers. Julian von Dunajewski, a power in the Polish Club, took over Finance, but Taaffe tried to balance this obvious bow to the Right by picking two men, Moriz von Streit and Alfred von Kremer, from the German bureaucracy to fill the Justice and Commerce positions. Since both men passed as being *verfassungstreu,* their presence enabled Taaffe still to boast of a coalition.

Kremer wrote Taaffe the day he assumed his new office that he was entering the cabinet only because of a direct request from Franz Joseph and despite his conviction that he would collide with Rightist colleagues. Taaffe's reply seemingly deprecated the possibility of such clashes, and so Kremer entered upon his duties.[36] The German Embassy had kind reports to make to Berlin of Streit's and Kremer's expertise and assumed that Taaffe would maintain a coalition. At least party matters might now allow of easier handling, for two of the retiring Liberals had been members of Auersperg's cabinet. As such, they had seen their old political friends daily and had suffered the inevitable consequences of growing isolation.[37]

Once the pleasant summer was past, party deliberations began anew. The German Liberals of Bohemia clashed with police

[35] Kabinettsarchiv, Karton 41, ad 2544.880.
[36] Kremer's letter to Emperor, Dec. 21, 1880, Kabinettsarchiv, Karton 41, ad 239.881.
[37] See Reuss's dispatch No. 312, A 3891, June 27, 1880, UC-1, reel 214, frames 344–45.

authorities in Karlsbad (Karlovy Vary) over a torchlight parade
and with imperial censors over a resolution that declared war on
the Language Ordinances.[38] Vienna's Municipal Council expressed strong solidarity with its Liberal brothers in Bohemia,
and the cabinet wondered if it should punish such insolence.[39]
Taaffe was so much disturbed by the increasing hostility that he
went out of his way in November to insist to Berchem of the
German Embassy that he was not persecuting German-speaking
Austrians. The two met by chance in Budapest and had discussed the recent closing of the German Theater there. Taaffe's
conversations with members of the German Empire's diplomatic
representation were extremely rare, judging from the dispatches
filed from Vienna. Convinced that the Hungarians had closed
the theater in Budapest as reprisal for his system of government
in Austria, he quite firmly asserted that the Germans of Austria
were too numerous and powerful to require his aid or to suffer
anyone's persecution. In view of such facts, he had simply set
for himself the duty of representing those groups which had been
totally neglected during the many years of Liberal hegemony.[40]

Berchem was seemingly impressed, for he wrote home that the
Austrian Minister-President had indeed tried hard to maintain a
balance between the embattled nationalities. He had matched
his ministerial appointments, Language Ordinances, and manipulation of elections with the naming of Korb as *Statthalter* of
Moravia and of Felder, the Liberal mayor of Vienna, as *Landes-
marschall* of Lower Austria. Furthermore, he had strenuously
disciplined agitating Czech teachers and was directing a
property-tax reform in a Liberal sense. In short, Berchem was
not yet definitely anti-Taaffe, as he would be later. He had no
doubt of Taaffe's resolve to give the non-Germans a greater
share in the direction of affairs, but he had concluded that the
Austrian honestly preferred a coalition which embraced German
Liberals as well as German Clerical Conservatives.[41]

[38] *Das Vaterland,* Oct. 1 and 6, 1880.   [39] *Ibid.,* Oct. 6 and 7, 1880.
[40] See Berchem's dispatch No. 527, A 7118, Nov. 9, 1880, UC-1, reel
214, frames 401–2.
[41] See Berchem's dispatch No. 540, A 7227, Nov. 18, 1880, UC-1, reel
214, frames 417–19.

Kremer and Streit represented Taaffe's tenuous link with the Liberals. The Liberal press and politicians ignored these men, as well as Conrad, or else depicted them as tools of the Right. The Right, however, was not happy with these relics of the concept of a government by coalition, and the Viennese press often hinted that the majority wanted their heads. *Das Vaterland* disingenuously reported that Conrad and Kremer had sent congratulations to Herbst on his sixtieth birthday and on the following day admitted the possibility that one or two ministers might depart in order to save "the harmony of the whole."[42] A Tirolese Clerical journal, on the other hand, admitted that it would not regret Conrad's replacement by a more decisive person, who would not parry the wishes of Catholic Austria with pretty words.[43]

Conrad was to last until 1885, but Kremer begged orally to be relieved in October, 1880, and wrote formally to Taaffe on November 27 to secure this release. Taaffe temporarily dissuaded him, but Kremer finally informed the Emperor on December 21 that he could no longer work with men with whom he had such basic disagreements. Their reckless determination to get the three seats in the Upper Austrian landed curia for Clerical candidates had completely destroyed his willingness to stay on, to say nothing of Taaffe's disclaimer that he had instructed the *Statthalter* of Upper Austria to work for a Clerical victory.[44]

Again, the list of new peers decided upon in the cabinet meeting of January 5, 1881, was almost exclusively composed of representatives of the Right. Kremer and Streit were openly chagrined, for they submitted their resignations to the Emperor on January 13, protesting they could not continue to take responsibility for a dangerous course. Nationalistic passions were finally infecting the Upper House, which had been immune. The cabinet was unashamedly partisan, and so their continuance in office was useless.[45]

[42] Dec. 9 and 10, 1880.
[43] *Neue Tiroler Stimmen,* quoted in *Neue Freie Presse,* Dec. 11, 1880, *Abendblatt.*
[44] Letter of Dec. 21, 1880. in Kabinettsarchiv, Karton 41, ad 239.881.
[45] *Ibid.*

On the same day the cabinet met to consider a joint resignation. On January 14 it was decided not to quit as a body, but
rather to fill the vacant Justice and Commerce posts. Pražak
took over the former next day, while Baron Felix von Pino, the
Statthalter of Upper Austria during the elections which the
Liberals had protested, accepted the Commerce portfolio. Streit
and Kremer had been able to reduce the list of new peers,
overwhelmingly of the "federalist" persuasion, from 26 to 12,
but the leaders of the Lower House's majority retaliated by
forcing Taaffe to advise the Emperor to accept the Liberal
bureaucrats' resignations.[46] The breach with Liberalism was
complete.

Yet Taaffe gave up his attempt to have some working liaison
with the Liberals slowly and reluctantly. As a *Kaiserminister* he
hated surrendering totally to either side in the Lower House, and
a few months after Streit and Kremer deserted him, the *Pester
Lloyd* published a transparently inspired article "which truly
depicted the opinions and intentions of the Austrian Minister-
President." This Budapest report described Taaffe as being
discouraged by party excesses and by endless demands for concessions. No cabinet had ever been in a more dire predicament
than his, particularly over the Lienbacher bill to reduce the term
of compulsory schooling. The cabinet did not like the bill, the
Czechs were definitely opposed to it, but he had to reward the
Clericals to keep the majority alive.

Partly to blame for this sad situation were the Liberals, whose
cooperation Taaffe had sought from the beginning. He had
insisted, of course, upon cooperation with the Czechs, but he had
refused as a corollary to wage war on Hungary, as the late
Michael Etienne of the *Neue Freie Presse* had demanded.
Thanks to Liberal hostility, he had to make deals with the
Clericals.

The article concluded with the statement that there still was
time for a Liberal rapprochement with Taaffe. To save the
schools, the Liberals would have to accept his program of concil-

[46] See Reuss's dispatch No. 22, A 360, Jan. 18, 1880, UC-1, reel 214,
frames 441–42.

iating the nationalities. If they really wanted freedom, unity of the empire, and defense of their Kultur, they had only to reach out their hands for a lasting understanding.[47]

The *Neue Freie Presse* scorned this overture as a move to split the Left further. Taaffe's actions simply had not merited confidence.[48] *Das Vaterland,* which would have been much distressed by the conclusion of an alliance between Taaffe and the Liberals at the cost of the Clericals, refused absolutely to believe that the Minister-President had anything to do with the article.[49]

Why did the Liberals and the *Kaiserminister* fail to cooperate in the years following the Congress of Berlin? It is not enough to recount the last-ditch fight of the diehards against the Defense Bill or to refer to Herbst's megalomania and contempt for Taaffe as a person. Nor were the Liberal complaints about unbalanced budgets truly convincing in an age which worshiped but did not always practice financial conservatism.

The Liberals' failure to understand or to contain Taaffe stemmed from their inability to recognize the legitimate claims of the non-Germans in Austria. When the Czechs accepted Taaffe's terms in 1879, the Liberals thought only of their lack of success in the conversations of 1878 and decided to harass Taaffe and the Czechs until an agreement more to their liking was reached. The continuing backing which the Poles, the Czechs, and the Clerical Conservatives provided Taaffe down to the last years of his regime did not connote his complete subjugation to all of their demands. The Poles no doubt secured the maximum, but it should be remembered that Taaffe never met some of the fundamental requests made by the Czechs and the Clerical Conservatives. The Liberals underestimated the Emperor's determination to try in a limited way to gratify the desires of the non-Germans in Austria and overestimated the value of their support of any cabinet. The remembrance of their period of productivity acted as a subtle deterrent to their renewal of fruitful accomplishments, for they were hypnotized by a sense

[47] Reprinted in *Neue Freie Presse,* May 28, 1881, *Abendblatt.*
[48] May 29, 1881. [49] *Das Vaterland,* May 31, 1881.

of self-importance and by a feeling that no regime could last
without their aid. They realized dimly that the underprivileged,
whether in the economic or the ethnic sense, were turning to new
leaders, but they righteously spurned all advice to modify their
basic doctrines. That they never really believed in full freedom
for all under the Habsburg scepter was the core of the Liberal
tragedy in Austria, and the attempts of their apologists among
the historians of the Dual Monarchy to blacken Taaffe as a
superficial mediator among disastrously selfish factions cannot
hide their arrogant pride in their own Kultur. Horst, Stremayr,
and Korb quit in 1880 because they distrusted the direction
Taaffe might be forced to take. Their letters to the Emperor
nevertheless stated without equivocation that the Left was resolved not to support Taaffe. Here was the critical reason for
their retirement from the ministry, and behind their obdurate
attitude was Liberalism's undying conviction that Austria's sole
salvation lay in the recognition of the primacy of German culture
within Austria's frontiers. The Poles, the Czechs, and the other
Slavs were as suspect in 1882 as they had been in 1848. The
best-educated and most-experienced of the German Austrians
could not see otherwise during Taaffe's early, groping years, and
so their chance to work for a lasting solution with moderate
Czechs and Slovenes was fatally postponed. The logical result
of the Liberal failure to accept Taaffe's policy of national reconciliation was their eclipse by the rising Christian Socialists and
Social Democrats. For the latter two stressed conciliation and
compromise in nationalistic quarrels, and even if it is argued that
their social and economic programs won more votes than their
attitude toward the issue of nationalism, Schönerer's failure to
make Pan-Germanism a powerful movement prior to 1914 un-
derlines the extent of the Liberal miscalculation. The Liberals
dared not trust the fundamental liberties they loved to men who
did not understand the blessings of German Kultur.

4 The Czech University in Prague

The appointment of Pražak to Taaffe's cabinet and the publication of the Language Ordinances for Bohemia and Moravia only partially satisfied the Czechs who had returned to the Reichsrat. They had asked the Emperor to grant their language equality at the University of Prague, and Baron Conrad, the relatively new Minister of Education, announced in February, 1881, that an administrative ordinance would fulfill their request. Only the most rabid Germans opposed the idea of a Czech university in Bohemia, though many were determined to limit its operations as much as possible.

In the spring of 1880 the *Neue Freie Presse* presented an honest, if distinctly prejudiced, appraisal of the future of the University of Prague. Thanks to the increase of Czech Mittelschulen and Gymnasien, fewer Czechs each year had a command of German. The inevitable logic of things consequently required more Czech instructors and chairs at the University. When the Czechs in 1880 demanded complete linguistic parity there, they were appealing from practical necessity, whatever might be thought of the justification for their plea. The journal frankly admitted that, save for the brief Hohenwart ministry, the cabinets had administered the institution in Prague "in a way to protect its German character." Even so, the number of professors and *Privatdozenten* who lectured part time or exclusively in Czech increased from 10 to 41 in ten years. In addition, many German professors voted with their Czech colleagues on vital faculty affairs to demonstrate their "objectivity," their yearning for "sweet peace."

To the *Neue Freie Presse,* such matters were clear signs of decline. Not fewer than forty taught in a language unknown to cultured persons outside Austria, a language whose literature had a past sullied by numerous forgeries and a dubious future. Worst of all, it had no "present" as far as most academic fields were concerned, for intellectuals almost never used Czech as a medium of communication. Indeed, a great number of the scholars active at this very university could not understand it. In a certain sense there was reason to inquire if this institution deserved the title of "university."[1]

Conrad, who was responsible for preparing the Emperor for changes at the University of Prague, readily admitted to his sovereign that an exclusive utilization of the German language in all University activities would best serve state interests. But professors had increasingly employed Czech since 1848, and the Czechs had long demanded equality for both tongues in all the subjects offered. In view of the large numbers of Czechs who were enrolled, the promise of educational equality contained in Article 19 of the Fundamental Laws, and the fact that the Poles had two universities where lecturers used the Polish language, Conrad recommended a solution that would satisfy Czech wishes.

There were three possible procedures. The state might constantly increase the number of professors who would lecture solely in Czech and thus maintain a formal unity within the University while actually creating a dualism. Secondly, the state might divide the faculty into German and Czech sections under a common rector and academic senate. Third, there could be outright partition into what amounted to separate universities. On the basis of conferences and reflection Conrad opted for the final and most drastic solution. The Germans and the Academic Senate of the University felt that the other plans would do

[1] *Neue Freie Presse,* April 14, 1880, *Abendblatt.*

nothing to end tension and bickering. Cooperation between Czechs and Germans simply was not possible in University affairs. After partition the state could anticipate fruitful work by students of both nationalities, Conrad predicted, and he advised the Emperor, who had no desire to burden the budget, that total separation would cost little more than partial separation.

The Minister's negotiations with German and Czech professors had not settled disputes over endowment and scholarship funds, but Conrad noted that the state's ownership of the buildings and control of some of the estates whose incomes went for endowment gave him a powerful lever to enforce a compromise. As for German resistance to the Czech suggestion to allow relatively free movement of students from one university to the other for desired courses, he made no recommendation for either point of view. In answer to the expressed concern of the Bohemian *Statthalter* over the probability that candidates for future public service might not have sufficient command of German if they attended the Czech university, Conrad could only promise greater emphasis on the teaching of German in Czech Gymnasien. Would it not also be wise to separate examinations which tested qualifications for bureaucratic service from the usual university examinations? Clearly Conrad saw no way to hobble the Czech insistence upon having their own language as the medium for their university students in Prague.[2]

When the specific imperial decree appeared on April 11, it transformed the venerable Karl-Ferdinand University into the Carolo-Ferdinandea. Under the new dispensation separate German and Czech institutions would enjoy the common new name. The minority of the Lower House strongly protested this decision by fiat, and Taaffe, though never relinquishing the theory that the entire matter was one of executive prerogative, decided to submit a regular bill for parliamentary approval.[3]

---

[2] Haus-, Hof-, und Staatsarchiv, Vienna, Kabinetts-Kanzlei, Vortrag 1403, April 2, 1881. Hereafter cited as Kabinetts-Kanzlei.

[3] Richard Charmatz, *Oesterreichs innere Geschichte von 1848 bis 1907* (Leipzig, 1909), II, 39–40.

The *Neue Freie Presse* inferred from Czech editorial comments that the Czechs also were eager for full parliamentary treatment of the university question. After all, what one ordinance created another ordinance could destroy.[4]

The explanation appended to the government's bill continued to insist that the ministry had already partitioned the University and that parliament merely would approve a few special questions. Henceforth, German and Czech would be the languages prescribed for lectures in the separate faculties. Each faculty would receive half of future gifts made to the Carolo-Ferdinandea, unless the donors otherwise specified. No student could matriculate at both institutions, but he could attend lectures at the institution in which he was not matriculated. The cabinet promised, apart from the above provisions, to warn all Czech students that a complete knowledge of German was mandatory for state jobs.[5]

A second *mémoire* from Conrad to the Emperor indicates that the latter was not pleased that parliament would legislate the details of the partition. To persuade his master that a bill to expedite a settlement was necessary, Conrad implied that the state could not otherwise dismiss German claims to all of the endowment. Moreover, the Czechs needed guarantees that their sons could attend courses in the German university without spending half of their class time in such classes, as the Germans had insisted. In short, Taaffe required Czech help, and it would not be forthcoming unless the rest of the majority cut the German pretensions to reasonable dimensions. In meeting another criticism which Franz Joseph undoubtedly advanced, Conrad secured a statement from Pino that every Czech who wanted a career in state service would have to demonstrate an adequate knowledge of German. The cabinet, not the Reichsrat, would define the degree of competence expected.[6]

Rieger's *Pokrok* greeted the Emperor's formal approval of a purely Czech institution as a victory which provided strength for new battles. *Národní Listy* truculently reminded its readers that

---

[4] April 19, 1881.   [5] *SPA*, IX Session, Beilagen 344.
[6] Kabinetts-Kanzlei, Vortrag 1823, April 28, 1881.

the university was but a small payment on account, not a concession and not a loving service. The cabinet's proposal merely set aside a small part of the record of centuries of injustice.[7] Several days later *Pokrok* anxiously took up the Young Czech refrain. The fight would go on until everything that suggested German rule in the Czech homeland had been wiped out.[8]

The Education Committee of the Lower House meanwhile made some changes to hasten action and to reduce diehard German opposition. By juggling a few phrases the committee left in abeyance the issue of parliamentary versus executive competence in the creation of a "new" university. As a concession to academic custom, Latin continued to enjoy "its usual extent." The professors and lecturers were to serve in only one of the two new universities. Students might audit courses at the "other" university as long as they were spending at least half of their class time in lectures offered by the university in which they were registered. The parliamentary conferees explicitly declared the property of the old university to be the common wealth of the new universities.[9] They unanimously recommended these changes, a sign that for once the Germans and Czechs could manifest a spirit of mutual accommodation.

The chief criticism came from the *Neue Freie Presse.* The Liberal daily, noted for its suspicion of the military, gladly quoted the *Wehrzeitung* to the effect that the erection of the Czech "rump university," correlated with the Clerical insistence upon fewer years of compulsory schooling, would increase "that half-educated proletariat, of which we have a surplus, which fights shy of any physical exertion and is not capable of an intellectual exertion."[10]

The Czech spokesman for the committee, Professor Jan Kvíčala of Prague, defensively asserted that his people probably would denounce the compromise, in view of the "concessions" made to German sensibilities. For instance, the Czechs had renounced a unitary institution in which both nationalities would

[7] Cited in *Neue Freie Presse,* April 19, 1881, *Abendblatt.*
[8] *Ibid.,* April 24, 1881.   [9] *SPA,* Beilagen 371.
[10] *Neue Freie Presse,* May 25, 1881, *Abendblatt.*

receive a full guarantee of their rights. They had acquiesced in a terminology which obscured the question of parliamentary versus executive competence. The restriction of one professor to one institution worked hardship only upon the Czech academician, alleged Kvíčala, who also insisted that it would be Czech undergraduates who exercised the right to audit courses outside their own institution. Since the Czech intelligentsia was generally fluent in German, his points, for the moment, were just. Moreover, the actual presence of 93 German teachers, compared to 41 Czech teachers, made it most likely that many course offerings would only be in German.[11]

A few Germans arose to contest the committee's unanimity. Max von Scharschmid of the Bohemian landed curia wanted an entirely new university for the Czechs in Prague, not a plan that would permit continuing Czech infiltration of German academic positions.[12] Johann Fux, a Liberal from Moravia, was equally fearful of any program that stopped short of total separation. Joint use of properties would only cause future conflicts.[13] A Young Czech journalist, Jaromír Čelakovský, ingenuously informed the Lower House that the cabinet had promised the new Czech medical faculty equipment and collections equal to those left with the Germans, but his undiplomatic admission did not prevent a speedy acceptance of the bill.[14]

This orderly disposition of the proposal was a refreshing contrast to other legislative controversies between Czechs and Germans during the Taaffe era. Clam Martinič, sensing the German willingness to accept the inevitable if the German university received certain desired facilities and collections, successfully persuaded the Czech Club on May 30 to agree to a partition which the text of the actual law would spell out.[15] As a final step on May 31, 1881, the deputies also voted to request the cabinet's cooperation in instituting the Czech medical faculty no later than

[11] *SPA*, pp. 5916–19, May 30, 1881.
[12] *Ibid.*, pp. 5921–22, 5924, May 30, 1881.
[13] *Ibid.*, p. 5963, May 31, 1881.
[14] *Ibid.*, pp. 5969–70, May 31, 1881.
[15] *Neue Freie Presse*, May 31, 1881, *Abendblatt*.

the opening of the winter semester of 1882–83, a year after the activation of the other Czech faculties.[16]

Amity among deputies did not connote tranquillity among their constituents. The noisiest agitators of the era were university students, whose tendency to riot had colored many pages of European history. In retrospect their antics seem more chaotic than effective, and it is prudent to evaluate the effectiveness of their performances with marked caution. In the summer of 1881, however, the rival student bodies at Prague touched off disturbances which revived many of the antagonisms latent in the university issue and created serious doubts in Bismarck's mind as to the wisdom of Taaffe's "system."

The excesses began on a small scale on June 24, when German and Czech students created a brawl in the Canal'schen Garten. A crowd gathered, and the police dispersed onlookers and antagonists with no trouble.[17] No doubt the simultaneous elections in the Prague Chamber of Commerce, in which the Czechs openly were trying to wean the influential Jewish vote from Liberal candidates, had some effect upon student sensibilities.[18] The *Neue Freie Presse,* thoroughly exercised by the reports from the Bohemian capital, provocatively announced that no German was safe any longer in that city. The Czechs were pursuing Germans as they would a wild animal, knowing that their leaders were in high favor with the regime. To put an end to the German university, the Czechs were singling out German students for special attack.[19] Why did not Taaffe protect Germans from the brutal fists of a Czech "Bubocratie"? Rieger should realize that founding a university did not automatically ensure a nation of culture.[20]

On June 28 the German student organization "Austria" left Prague, 40 strong, for an outing to Kuchelbad on the Moldau. At first accompanied merely by invited female guests, they had far less welcome guests in late afternoon when a deputation of

[16] *SPA,* p. 5984, May 31, 1881.
[17] *Neue Freie Presse,* June 24, 1881, *Abendblatt.*
[18] *Ibid.,* June 22 and 23, 1881.   [19] June 25, 1881.
[20] *Ibid.,* June 25, 1881, *Abendblatt.*

young Czechs, never absolutely identified as University students, accosted them and invited them to sing the "People's Hymn." Because of German noncompliance or simply because of over-heated comments from both sides, bottles, glasses, and stools began to fly through the air. A boat stood nearby, ready to transport the Germans back to Prague at the end of what should have been a pleasant frolic, and in crisis it served as a refuge for the seemingly outnumbered Germans. Two dozen gendarmes arrived in time to avert a really bloody encounter, and they covered most of the students who escaped to the boat. Some fourteen had taken to the woods, arriving home by train. A crowd standing upon the Podskal Bridge showered the returning boat with stones, but the police intervened effectively to get these students, as well as those who had taken the train, safely home.[21]

Newspaper comment was violent. On June 30 the govern-ment confiscated *Pokrok, Národní Listy,* and *Czeske Noviny* for "hate articles" against German students.[22] The *Neue Freie Presse* wrote on July 1:

The Germans in Austria . . . must be disavowed as bas-tards if they ever forget the day on which peaceful citizens in the Bohemian capital were exposed to the attack of the rabble and the cudgel beat time to the tune, "conciliation of the nation-ities. . . ." This was not a question of driving the Germans away, no, the Czechs openly wanted to prepare a massacre, and it is no thanks to the officials that they succeeded only in part.

Taaffe revealed his discomfiture over the ugly scenes in Prague by issuing an unusual communiqué which stated that he had requested Baron Weber, the *Statthalter* of Bohemia, to leave the cure at Karlsbad to complete the pacification of the capital. Weber, pleading ill health, had declined.[23] The Minister-President had told his colleagues that the incendiary actions of the German students were but a part of the general Liberal offensive to return to power, and it was clear that he wanted a

[21] *Ibid.,* June 29 and 30, 1881.   [22] *Ibid.,* June 30, 1881, *Abendblatt.*
[23] *Ibid.,* July 5, 1881.

stronger hand in Prague.[24] Weber's lack of a sense of responsibility completely upset the Emperor, who was receiving first-hand reports of the disorders from Crown Prince Rudolf. From Ischl, Taaffe received the order to suspend press and association rights in Prague if necessary. Naturally the sovereign also recommended the appointment of a reliable official to carry out the duties of the *Statthalter*.[25]

Bismarck meanwhile dispatched a worried message to Count Berchem. German opinion in the Hohenzollern realm was out of humor with the Austrian cabinet's feeble handling of the excesses, reported the Chancellor. Such weakness encouraged baiting from the other nationalities, apart from the satisfaction it brought the Czechs. Berchem should employ German influence discreetly in the press to make known Germany's justified indignation, while the Chancellor implied that he would discourage demonstrations of German solidarity within Germany, which could only benefit Czech designs. Warming to a theme which he publicly developed a year later, Bismarck launched into a savage tirade against Herbst and his associates, whose political incompetence and constitutional obstinacy went far to explain the insults inflicted upon Germans in Prague. Franz Joseph realized the Germans were the only lasting foundations for the unity of his empire and army, but their parliamentary leaders wanted him to surrender monarchical rights which alone guaranteed the continued existence of Austria. Consequently he could no longer depend upon the German Austrians.[26]

At the end of July, Rieger had an audience with the Emperor and an hour-long conference with Taaffe. *Politik* revealed, no doubt through Rieger, the government's serious displeasure and concern over the incidents. At the same time it assured the Czechs that no one in high places accepted the interpretation placed upon events by the opposition, whose puny combat-

---

[24] Paul Molisch, *Geschichte der deutschnationalen Bewegung in Oesterreich* (Jena, 1926), p. 115.

[25] Oskar von Mitis, *Das Leben des Kronprinzen Rudolf* (Leipzig, 1928), pp. 56–57.

[26] See Bismarck's dispatch, A 4271, July 7, 1881, UC-1, reel 214, frames 493–94.

iveness had now become laughable.[27] In the cabinet Franz
Joseph said it would be necessary to keep a tight rein over the
professors of both nationalities, for they seemed to be behind the
turmoil.[28]

Bismarck vied with the Czechs in his scorn for Liberal maneuvers. He wrote from Kissingen in late July that he was not
surprised to hear of German Austrian disgust with the political
impotence of their chief party. Such discontent would be a sign
for the better if Herbst and men like him, blockheads all, were
eliminated as party leaders. Instead of being loyally dynastic,
they had forced a parliamentary regime upon a state of mixed
nationalities, just to control it. Always pushing the empire's
center of gravity further to the Left, they forced the sovereign to
seek aid elsewhere. Austrian Liberals were more impossible
than the German Empire's variety. To apply Herbst's brand of
parliamentarianism to Austria was an act worthy of a lunatic
asylum. Bismarck pompously dogmatized that the German
Empire itself could not absorb such a system, because of the
leaders' imbecility and because of the lack of integrity which
every parliamentary regime developed.[29]

The School Commission of the Austrian Upper House, picked
in the days of Liberal ascendancy, justified Bismarck's comments
on Liberal ineptness in the months which followed the Lower
House's acceptance of a Czech university in Prague. It stalled
action for eight months, probably because its members realized
that a majority of the peers now were Taaffe's appointees or
reasonably sensitive to Taaffe's desires. Rieger emphasized
Czech displeasure with the delay by accusing Conrad of playing
favorites in the university issue. The latter plaintively told
Count Berchem that he had "noted" the appointment of fourteen
Czech and only four German professors to the Carolo-
Ferdinandea since assuming office. Moreover, he had hinted

[27] Quoted in *Neue Freie Presse,* July 28, 1881.
[28] Paul Molisch, *Politische Geschichte der deutschen Hochschulen in
Österreich von 1848 bis 1918* (2d ed.; Vienna and Leipzig, 1939), pp.
178–79.
[29] See Bismarck's dispatch, A 4647, July 29, 1881, UC-1, reel 214,
frames 508–10.

delicately to the German diplomat that Franz Joseph wanted no
German students from Jena or Leipzig to come to Prague to join
their German fellow students there in a parade.[30]

On the day the School Commission's majority brought in a bill
directly opposed to the regime's desires, the *Neue Freie Presse*
printed an incredibly condescending *précis* of the whole question
of a Czech university. Apart from the threat to existing order in
the state, the new university would harm Czech national interests. By destroying the ancient bond which linked them to the
most intellectually developed nationality, a bond which had
placed them high above the cultural *niveau* of other Slavic
peoples, the Czechs were retrogressing.[31]

The School Commission's majority was quite prepared to
expedite the divorce of Czech culture from German civilization.
Instead of a separation of the University into two branches,
public funds would build an entirely new, well-equipped institution for the Czechs. This solution would have left intact all of
the then existing properties and rights of the University—to the
Germans.[32]

The most interesting speeches delivered by members of the
commission's majority, who of course realized the futility of their
cause, centered upon the future of the controversial university.
Leopold von Hasner, the distinguished jurist and ex-Minister of
Education, predicted that attendance would drop by at least half
under the Lower House's program. By halving the enrollment,
the best-paid chairs would soon be but moderately well remuner-
ated. The best minds would depart, only mediocre students
would be satisfied with the talent left, the institution would
simply become second-rate.[33] Dr. Josef Unger, equally desir-
ous of leaving the contested seat of higher learning to the
Germans, manifested a painfully unconvincing solicitude for the
Czech intelligentsia. When all of the chairs at the proposed
Czech university were filled, death alone would make room for

[30] See Berchem's dispatch No. 319, A 6242, Oct. 30, 1881, UC-1, reel
214, frames 565–66.
[31] Feb. 9, 1882.   [32] *SPH*, IX Session, pp. 737–38, Feb. 9, 1882.
[33] *Ibid.*, pp. 756–57, Feb. 9, 1882.

the bright young Czech scholars. After all, no German university could profit from their gifts, for they would not be able to
lecture in German. His final scene was dreary indeed—"a university isolated, at a standstill, desolate."[34] Such predictions
were made in vain, for on February 10, 1882, by a vote of 82 to
55, the Upper House accepted the bill as written by the Lower
House.

Das Vaterland described the rather exciting vote witheringly.
An attendance of 90 members was average in the Upper House,
but more than 130 appeared to decide on the Czech university.
Cardinals, prince-bishops, and a mere archbishop looked up at
Clam Martinič and Rieger in the gallery. Why was such a minor
matter the subject of wearisome and passionate quarrels?
Because the "German National" party did not want the peoples
of the monarchy to live together in peace. They wanted segregation until, with the right conditions, they could Germanize or
subjugate the non-Germans.[35] The *Neue Freie Presse* merely
announced the death of the old, Austrian, famous Upper
House. From now on it would be a partisan battlefield, where
numbers, not arguments, would win the day.[36] *Politik* hailed the
victory as one which marked for the first time a parliamentary
recognition of the right of the Czechs to a national existence in
Austria. Eulogizing Taaffe and Conrad, it also paid special
attention to the gratifying appearance of the cardinals and
princes of the Church. *Pokrok* emphasized the Emperor's constant influence, while *Národní Listy* was content to rejoice over
the defeat of the resolution which would have specifically required a command of German for state examinations.[37]

Within the context of the rapidly growing antagonism between
Czechs and Germans, the decision to approve a Czech university
in Prague actually was attended by a minimum of rhetoric and
demagoguery. No German denied the right of the Czechs to
have a university, while the Czechs put up little fight to secure a
full half of the facilities involved. They were sure of future

[34] *Ibid.*, pp. 798–99, Feb. 10, 1882.   [35] Feb. 10, 1882.
[36] Feb. 11, 1882.
[37] Czech opinions quoted, *ibid.*, Feb. 11, 1882, *Abendblatt.*

grants, of course, and it is doubtful that they honestly believed that the regime would especially favor the Germans in the distribution of these appropriations. For a while their students might have to audit courses given by German professors in fields not covered by their own faculty. But the break had come. The Czech renaissance finally had an intellectual home of its own.

The retention of German as the basic language of communication in Austria was an issue that conditioned much of the debate over the final acceptance of the Czech university in Prague. Though the Reichsrat had not specifically required a proof of proficiency in German in state examinations when it formulated the mode of dividing the Prague institution, its members fully expected the cabinet to make some rules that would guarantee the enlistment of bureaucrats adept in German.

In a cabinet meeting of March 12, 1882, which canvassed means of ensuring a command of the German language among future bureaucrats, the Emperor remarked that he put special weight upon learning German in secondary school—not just in Bohemia, but in all of the Austrian lands. Conrad admitted the possibility of a law prescribing compulsory training in the German language at such a level, if such a law simultaneously compelled Germans to learn the language of the nationality which shared a *Land* with them. Dunajewski heartily approved the idea, for no one had to go to a Gymnasium against his will. Pražak contested this interpretation, for Gymnasien were institutions of public instruction, and existing laws forbade pressure or compulsion against a nationality in such institutions. Pražak nonetheless was willing to chance such a law.[38] Such a bill never emanated from the cabinet, possibly because of the Emperor's hesitation over coercion of the Sudetenlanders or because the ministers did not feel entirely sure of their legal position.

The professors of the University in Prague, when polled by the government on a proposed regulation of state examinations, unanimously approved the maintenance of a single examination

---

[38] Moses Mehring, "Die deutsch-böhmische Sprachenfrage während des Ministeriums Taaffe (1879–1893)" (unpubl. diss., Vienna, 1924), p. 141.

commission for all candidates. A majority of them also desired proof of the candidate's oral and written mastery of German, though a minority settled for a test of oral ability. In the cabinet Dunajewski opposed the majority opinion among the professors that *Reprobazion* should be the lot of any candidate who failed to demonstrate facility in German, and Taaffe directed Conrad to reword the regulation to allow a candidate to choose the academic subject in which he desired to prove his knowledge of German.[39]

Conrad returned on June 9 with a rephrased regulation, which permitted the commission, when re-examining a candidate deficient in German, to ask a few questions from subjects other than the one which he had chosen for his German test. Dunajewski, Pražak, and Ziemialkowski emphatically disapproved. The Finance Minister argued, rather illogically, that professors would wink at the man who was skilled in his subject and shaky in German. The German ministers, Pino and Zeno Welsersheimb, Horst's successor as Minister of Defense, contented themselves with sententious comments on the absolute need of officials to know German, and Taaffe compromised the issue by suggesting that the examiners allow an unsuccessful candidate to take his German test in the same academic subject he had chosen previously. Having yielded to his Slavic colleagues on this matter, he placated the German ministers by recommending stern instructions to the examiners not to be indulgent on re-examinations.[40]

When the Emperor met with the cabinet for a last perusal of the regulations, he raised some of the points which had already been compromised. Obviously convinced that the German language was indeed the cement of his empire, he approvingly called special attention to the original comments made by the majority of professors at Prague. In law examinations they had recommended passing two subjects in German and also a special

[39] Verwaltungsarchiv (Staatsarchiv des Innern und der Justiz), Vienna, Österreichische Ministerratsprotokolle, No. 46, May 20, 1882. Hereafter cited as MRP, with number and date of protocol.
[40] MRP 52, June 9, 1882.

written test in German to accompany regular state examinations. Conrad tactfully cited "expert" advice against such proposals. First, the adoption of such procedures would create hurdles for Prague students that did not exist at other Austrian universities. Second, the composition of a paragraph in a particular language did not necessarily prove verbal command of that language. Third, the custom of linking subjects in the general field of law (*Handels- und Wechselsrecht, Strafrecht und Strafprozess*) meant in effect that law examinations would comprise two "subjects."

Conrad also was able to reassure the Emperor on the question of re-examinations. Franz Joseph had wondered if it was sufficient to allow a candidate to offer the same field in the retesting of his proficiency in German. Conrad admitted to similar doubts in the beginning, but he had come to the conclusion that questions from other fields might not really be practical. When the ruler lectured the entire cabinet on the unqualified duty of Czech Gymnasien to teach their pupils expertness in German, his auditors countered with some politely worded objections. The Minister of Education was sure that making German an obligatory subject was not the answer for the moment. And, to force instruction in other subjects in German would inspire parents to enter lawsuits on the basis of Article 19 of the Fundamental Laws. Taaffe soothed the Emperor by declaring that Czech nationalists eventually would "see the light" and insist upon adequate preparation in German in secondary schools, but the Emperor's tone during the rest of the conference did not indicate that he was convinced.

He was quite worried, for instance, that the rule permitting the Rigorosen for the doctorate to substitute for certain state examinations might allow persons who were poor in German to enter the bureaucracy. Conrad assured him that candidates had to pass at least one subject in German in the Rigorosen, and the Emperor made it clear that he expected total fulfillment of this guarantee. He also gave orders that the professors in Prague desist from creating difficulties, whereupon Dunajewski remarked that their pecuniary interest would probably be the most effective restraint. In conclusion Franz Joseph pronounced the regulation to be absolutely minimal. As such, the cabinet had to enforce it rigidly. If the secondary schools did not offer completely effective courses in German, all other governmental decrees would be illusory.[41]

The decree of June 29, 1882, retained the examination commission for both institutions. A candidate could take his state examination in either German or Czech. In the latter case, however, he had to use German for at least one subject. If he failed to demonstrate an adequate degree of proficiency, he faced a re-examination in the same subject. Those who offered the doctorate in lieu of state examinations for certain positions also had to utilize the German language in one of the subjects offered for the Rigorosen.[42]

The Young Czechs immediately raised howls of protest, which Rieger and Clam Martinič insisted were serious and dangerous. Alfred von Kraus, the new *Statthalter* of Bohemia, was inclined to agree, but Pražak scoffed at the "noise." It would cease, he predicted, because the Czech professors were willing to recommend compliance with the decree.[43] When Kraus came to Vienna, filled with forebodings over the possibilities of conflicts in the common use of archives and similar facilities, Conrad and Taaffe remained untouched by his fretting. If bureaucrats were disobedient, he should stop their salaries, said Conrad.[44] The *Statthalter* actually was most interested in the speedy establishment of a Czech medical faculty, for this was essential to the Czech program. Aided by pressure from Czech party leaders, he did secure the cabinet's appointment of a special commission which would pass on the possibility of activating the Czech medical faculty in the autumn of 1883.[45]

During the budget debate of February, 1883, the Czech Club unabashedly stipulated the creation of the medical faculty as the

[41] MRP 57, June 26, 1882.

[42] Gustav Kolmer, *Parlament und Verfassung in Oesterreich* (Vienna and Leipzig, 1902–14), III, 283.

[43] Letter of Aug. 11, 1882, Kraus to Taaffe, *Politischer Nachlass,* pp. 393–95; MRP 67, Aug. 19, 1882.

[44] MRP 83, Oct. 29, 1882.   [45] MRP 99, Dec. 19, 1882.

price of its support of the government, Taaffe reported to the cabinet. Conrad quoted the special commission's opinion that the step was feasible, even if some equipment might be lacking in the beginning. The cabinet, after brief discussion, voted to tell the Czech Club that it would indeed propose a supplementary credit to finance their desired faculty.[46] Finally, in March, 1883, Conrad yielded once again to Kraus and the determined Czech leaders. Although he had preferred to delay the appointment of faculty members, he had no desire to create special difficulties for himself. He also preferred leasing land for the use of the new faculty, but his opinion collided with the strong view of the *Statthalter* and the Czechs, who wanted to buy the land outright. He therefore recommended meeting these special Czech requests by the supplementary credit already promised, and the cabinet agreed.[47] Nonetheless, Crown Prince Rudolf wrote his Liberal friend Moriz Szeps that the Czechs were not happy over affairs in Vienna. Taaffe was as tenacious as a tapeworm, he added with some irritation, and there was no hope of dislodging this ministry of "Deliriums nehmens."[48]

As if to substantiate the strictures of the heir to the throne, Czech students of theology sent a deputation to Cardinal-Prince Friedrich Schwarzenberg complaining that they had to take their preliminary training vow in German when they registered for their first course.[49] Schwarzenberg did not want a separate Czech faculty of theology, which the petitioning students certainly were hoping for, because such an arrangement would decrease the chances of a student's learning both tongues. Consequently, he asked the cabinet for a totally independent theological university. At first the cabinet was disinclined to remove the seminary from the German section to which it had been assigned.[50]

---

[46] MRP 17, Feb. 21, 1883.   [47] MRP 20, March 3, 1883.

[48] Letters of Feb. 1, 19, and 23, 1883, in *Kronprinz Rudolf: Politische Briefe an einen Freund, 1882–1889,* ed. Julius Szeps (Vienna, Munich, and Leipzig, 1922), pp. 36–38.

[49] Kolmer, *Parlament,* III, 284.

[50] MRP 67, Aug. 19, 1882. See Molisch, *Politische Geschichte,* pp. 53–54.

For three years the issue recurred spasmodically. Dunajewski and Falkenhayn began to think more favorably of a completely separate faculty of theology, and the Emperor was quite happy with the idea of one Carolo-Ferdinandea University, with German, Czech, and theological sections.[51] Yet Schwarzenberg died in 1885 before anything concrete was done. His successor, Count Franz Schönborn, was less amenable to Czech arguments, to "national eccentricities."[52] For five more years nothing happened.

Then, on the eve of the seeming rapprochement with the Germans, Rieger easily persuaded the Czechs still sitting in the Bohemian Diet to petition the government to erect a special Czech theological faculty, and in July, 1890, when the chances of keeping the Czechs interested in a deal with the Germans looked quite forlorn, the ministry consented to the establishment of a separate institution in 1891.[53]

The episcopacy rather than the Germans had opposed such a move, and few Germans looked upon the new separate faculty as a threat to their position. The Germans were vexed rather by a modification of rules which applied to state examinations in law. The Czechs had never ceased to protest the rule which compelled a candidate to prove his command of German in one of the subjects offered for the doctorate and in the state qualifying examination. The examiners had "conditioned" some of the Czech aspirants because of faulty German, and in the budget debate of 1889 the Czechs again besought the regime to make a change. Taaffe granted a small concession. Candidates could take the *rechtshistorische* examination in either language, but a student still had to prove competence in German when he took the examination in jurisprudence and political science. If he failed to demonstrate this in one of the subjects offered, he had to wait six months for a re-examination.[54]

No single quarrel that engaged Germans and Czechs in Bohemia aroused as little permanent distrust as the changes in the

[51] MRP 24, March 29, 1883.
[52] See Reuss's dispatch No. 144, A 4520, June 4, 1884, UC-1, reel 215, frames 373–75.
[53] Kolmer, *Parlament,* IV, 195.   [54] *Ibid.*

ancient Karl-Ferdinand University. William H. Dawson summarized the history of the institution in Franz Joseph's last years quite fairly when he wrote:

For over thirty years the concordat of 1882 worked so well that no serious proposals to interfere with it were made. From the first the two universities enjoyed a prosperous career, each going its own way, while loyally respecting the traditions which were a common intellectual possession. To say that does not mean that during those years the Czech national movement had lost in strength and that the relations between the two nations had changed greatly for the better, for the contrary was the case.[55]

Taaffe's last regulations on the taking of examinations in law assumed that somehow young Czechs who were ambitious would master the language of their rivals. The Emperor never deviated from his belief that the imperial bureaucracy could not function without German as the great bond of communication, but he and the ministers and the two peoples of Bohemia never formally agreed upon a system which would deliver young Czechs properly fluent in German.

Czech students calmly attended their classes most of the time, often registered for courses given in German at the German university, and picked up a sufficient acquaintance with German to meet the revised requirements of 1889. They learned German as an optional subject in their own secondary schools, and the more radical of their mentors, the Young Czechs, would tolerate no closer accommodation with "the second language of the kingdom."

As tempers grew worse toward the end of Taaffe's era, it became apparent that enforced teaching of the rival idioms in Bohemian schools would have embroiled the youngest generation in the vital but unfortunate contest. Both sides seemed to agree that it was enough to call out the university students when either felt sufficiently menaced. It was a tribute to the settlement of 1882 that the University in Prague survived these ephemeral clashes with more than a modicum of academic respectability.

[55] Gray C. Boyce and William H. Dawson, *The University of Prague* (London, 1937), p. 59.

5 The German Counterattack: *Staatssprache*

The Language Ordinances of April 19, 1880, and the establishment of a Czech faculty under the general rubric of the Carolo-Ferdinandea University added new impetus to the German desire to legalize the German language as the official tongue of Austria. Though the Upper House's School Commission held up the final decision on the University in Prague until early 1882, Crown Prince Rudolf was complaining to German Liberal politicians of Taaffe's Slavicizing policies. In time, he predicted, the German provinces would secede from the empire along the Danube, making the whole imperial idea a chimera. Plener wrote his revered father that such views should hearten the Liberals, especially since Rudolf was amiable and well disposed to the party.[1]

It will be remembered that such Liberal stalwarts as Herbst and Wurmbrand had introduced motions critical of the Language Ordinances and calling for German as the *Staatssprache* in May, 1880. These motions did not undergo committee scrutiny until December, 1880, for the committee had Polish deputies as its president and secretary and its meetings were not frequent.[2]

---

[1] Haus-, Hof-, und Staatsarchiv, Vienna, Nachlass Plener, Karton 17, Nos. 63–64, letter of Oct. 11, 1881. Hereafter cited as Nachlass Plener.
[2] Richard Charmatz, *Oesterreichs innere Geschichte von 1848 bis 1907* (Leipzig, 1909), II, 37.

Czech members of the committee upheld the cabinet's right to issue the Ordinances, and Rieger accused Herbst of taking part in an anti-Austrian German Nationalist movement. When Pražak, speaking for the cabinet, promised the Germans that the government would not prescribe Czech for the inner services of the courts in Bohemia and Moravia, he merely angered his Czech countrymen into insisting upon such a step in the future. As expected, a majority of the committee refused to hear of an investigation of the ministers for exceeding their powers. Indeed, a Rumanian and a Slovene asked for a similar ordinance for Bukowina and the South Slav areas.

Taaffe met with the committee on April 2, 1881, and told its members it would be dangerous to approve German as the *Staatssprache* by a simple parliamentary majority as long as there was no real conciliation among the nationalities. He insisted that the executive alone had the right to decide what language the state's officials would use. Such decisions would vary from crownland to crownland, depending upon the needs for simplification and economy as well as upon the peculiarities of individual crownlands and their inhabitants. Finally, a demand for one language as *the* state language was not in full accord with the provisions of Article 19 of the Fundamental Laws. Wurmbrand continued to insist upon an official medium for the army and bureaucracy, but the conferences came to a temporary end on April 5. Czechs and Germans turned their attention to the debate on Taaffe's new proposal for a Czech university in Prague, and for almost two years Wurmbrand's proposal lay dormant.[3]

The publication of further linguistic concessions to Slovenes, Czechs, and Poles in 1882 intensified the German Liberal determination to press for the recognition of German as the state language, for in areas the German had long dominated the Slavs were winning equality in the battle of the idioms. In April, 1882, Pražak ordered the Graz Oberlandesgericht to notify inferior courts of Carniola, of the Styrian court district of Cilli

---

[3] Gustav Kolmer, *Parlament und Verfassung in Oesterreich* (Vienna and Leipzig, 1902–14), III, 244–48.

(Celje), and of Slovene and linguistically mixed court districts of Carinthia that they should thereafter give Slovene parity with German and employ judges competent in both languages.[4]

The Czechs and Poles of Silesia petitioned the Minister of Justice in July, 1882, to grant their languages equality with German in that crownland. The cabinet's discussion of an applicable ordinance in the autumn of 1882 reveals much of the pressure and maneuvering to which Taaffe inevitably was subject. He summoned the *Landespräsident* of Silesia, Marquis Olivier Bacquehem, to confer with a rather small representation of cabinet officers on September 9. Pražak sketched a possible scheme, in which he promised no change in purely German districts save for the obligation of officials in such districts to accept letters in Polish or Czech from their autonomous counterparts in Polish and Czech districts. In mixed districts the language of the petition would determine the language of judgment *nach Thunlichkeit* (where feasible). If different languages were used, German would be the language of judgment. The Czech minister was sure no one would be satisfied by his proposal, but "something had to happen." When asked to comment, Bacquehem first blamed party leaders, not the masses of Poles and Czechs, for the agitation. These same circles would dislike the phrase *nach Thunlichkeit,* for everyone knew that judges in Silesia were hardly inclined to give verdicts *nach Thunlichkeit.* Germans would be the most ill-humored of all. They saw no solution to the language quarrel, so they felt there was no need to change the German monopoly. Even in Polish and Czech towns in Silesia official correspondence and records were in German, and the Slavic communities used German to communicate with each other. In his recent journeys throughout the Polish areas, undertaken at the Minister-President's request, he received no petitions on linguistic matters.

Bacquehem's forthright opposition incurred Ziemialkowski's quick displeasure. However important the Silesian chief executive's objections might be, said Galicia's representative, the state had to proceed with the fulfillment of Article 19 of the Funda-

[4] *Ibid.,* pp. 240.

mental Laws. Why not do for Polish and Czech what had been done for Slovene? A long postponement was out of the question.

To place the issue in a realistic light, Taaffe told Bacquehem and the ministers that Grocholski, chairman of the Polish Club, had directly asked for implementation of Article 19 in Silesia at the end of the last session of the Reichsrat. Despite Bacquehem's subsequent failure to discover mass discontent over the primacy of German in official life, he, as Minister-President, still felt that persons should be permitted to use Czech or Polish if they so desired. Pražak strongly urged his own formula for Silesian court procedure, but, persuaded by the others present, he dropped *nach Thunlichkeit* as a phrase which could make all ordinances confusing, if not illusory.[5]

A month later the cabinet considered two interpellations from members of the Silesian Diet. Three Slavic deputies petitioned for equality of languages in courts, while twenty-three Germans pleaded for the *status quo*. Taaffe was by now sure that he had to honor the Slavic request. As head of the political administration in Austria, he considered it his duty to synchronize the linguistic needs of the citizens with the officials who served them. Such was to be his reply to the interpellants.[6] On October 12 a directive regulating the languages used in Silesian courts appeared, and Bacquehem answered German protests in the Diet by comparing the Silesian ordinance with those applying to Bohemia and Moravia. The latter were more drastic, for the Silesian arrangements concerned only courts, judges, and public prosecutors, not "political" officials. In Silesia, too, the use of Czech or Polish exclusively in court was mandatory only if the principal involved knew only Czech or Polish. In an empire that rioted over shades of distinction, Bacquehem found it wise to note that the ordinance did not describe Czech and Polish as *landesüblich,* but as "languages which are in use in several judicial districts."[7]

The cabinet's extremely careful procedure no doubt reflected

[5] MRP 71, Sept. 9, 1882.   [6] MRP 75, Oct. 9, 1882.
[7] Kolmer, *Parlament,* III, 241–42.

Bacquehem's reservations, and Conrad, during the Silesian discussions, denied a Czech petition to found a private Gymnasium
in Troppau (Opava), a city which he deemed *urdeutsch* (fundamentally German). An appeal to the Reichsgericht reversed his
decision, thanks to the illness and absence of two of the Liberal
judges of the court. Conrad disclosed to Berchem of the German Embassy his resentment of such irresponsible Czech frivol-
ity "in expecting the cabinet to approve such a school in so
ancient a German center."[8]

If Conrad had sincere distaste for a Czech Gymnasium in
Troppau, his colleagues and superior were of quite another mind
when the Landesschulrat of Lower Austria, defying a ministerial
decision, refused to permit the building of a private Czech school
in Vienna. Interpellations for such schools dated from 1880,
and the cabinet's final approval of a project submitted by the
Komensky Association met with excoriation from the Municipal
Council of Vienna and with noncompliance from the provincial
school authorities.[9] Taaffe indignantly directed Conrad to
proceed sternly against the recalcitrant officials and to require a
justification from the *Statthalter* himself. The Minister of Education somewhat undiplomatically mentioned the "inveterate
dislike" the Viennese had for the Czechs and hinted that the
regime would regret wounding these extremely loyal citizens
where they were most sensitive. Pražak stiffly recited population figures to prove the Komensky Association's case, and
Taaffe's grave displeasure over the disobedience of bureaucratic
underlings carried the cabinet against Conrad's halfhearted defense of the Landesschulrat. Even Welsersheimb, voluble on the
subject of nationalism's threat to the army, recommended the
strongest possible punishment for these German officials.[10]
When the *Statthalter* reported in full to Conrad, the latter found
his explanation unsatisfactory. To prevent further incidents, he
dispatched to the Lower Austrian dignitary a very explicit statement of the compliance the cabinet expected in the future.[11] The

---

[8] See Berchem's dispatch No. 425, A 6559, Oct. 24, 1882, UC-1, reel
215, frame 12.

[9] Kolmer, *Parlament,* III, 107, 161.   [10] MRP 96, Dec. 4, 1882.

[11] MRP 99, Dec. 19, 1882.

intemperate language of the Landesschulrat in refusing to obey explained Taaffe's ire, for they had declared the school's establishment to be a political coup, not the satisfaction of a necessity.

Existing cabinet minutes do not pinpoint exactly the Emperor's reaction to talk of making German the state language. On May 21, 1883, he distinctly called for a regulation of the "language question" through administrative ordinances so that the use of German would not deteriorate further. Taaffe took pains to show the Emperor his reasons for an emphatic rejection of Wurmbrand's bill. First, the latter proposal called for a *Reichssprache,* whereas it could only be a matter of regulating the *Dienstsprache.* Second, if the cabinet acquiesced in a legislative solution, its right to issue ordinances in the sphere of linguistic regulation would vanish. Quite abruptly, Franz Joseph described the ideal ordinance as one which would prescribe German for all inner services and for communication between officials. This would make every official learn German, and if such a prescription were not enforced, the number of bureaucrats who did not know German would increase beyond what was already unfortunately the case. Pražak avoided a direct comment on what must have been a painful verdict from his ruler by mentioning the cooperation of the superior courts in enforcing existing language ordinances. Resistance in the Oberste Gerichtshof also would cease if its president relented, and he begged the Emperor to urge this matter upon that particular jurist.[12] Though no ordinance had yet tampered with German as the medium of the inner services, Pražak nonetheless was the symbol of the erosion of German as a great centripetal agency, and, by protesting Schmerling's obduracy on the high court, he was asking his master to weaken one of Germandom's heartiest defenders.

The sullen German resentment in Bohemia against the Ordinances of 1880 appeared in Franz Schmeykal's rejection in August, 1883, of Rieger's proposal for an extraparliamentary conference between the leaders of the two nationalities in Bohe-

[12] MRP 38, May 31, 1883.

mia. The arguments each political figure advanced were painfully familiar. Quite significantly, Schmeykal alleged that the
Czechs looked upon German as a *Landessprache* and not as the
only factually existing *Staatssprache* of the empire.[13] Inevitably
the German members of the parliamentary committee which
originally dabbled with Wurmbrand's proposal forced a brief
reconsideration of the motion that no one honestly expected to
pass.

In January, 1884, the Austrian public heard one of the most
important debates of the dying empire's last century. The osten-
sible topic was the Wurmbrand proposal, but the overpowering
issue was the question of the future compatibility of Germans
and Czechs under the Habsburg scepter. Franz Joseph admitted
to the cabinet early in the new year that, even if another policy
had guaranteed greater calm, the government, for the sake of the
empire's future, could not renounce the principle of equality for
both languages throughout Bohemia. He comforted himself
with the thought that this principle would exclude all who could
not master German from posts in Bohemia. He overlooked the
obverse of the principle, possibly because of his stubborn determination to insist on German in the bureaucracy. Expecting the
supporters of the Wurmbrand bill to push for a settlement that
would give German in Austria the status which Magyar enjoyed
in Hungary, he understood Taaffe's desire not to force these
same supporters to make a clear definition of the term *Staatssprache*. As long as there was no set definition, the cabinet had a
chance to maneuver. Indeed, Wurmbrand confided to Taaffe
that his bill was no more than a demonstration, and the cabinet
simply hoped to avoid unnecessary embarrassment.[14]

Radical nationalism among both peoples was growing, but it
had by no means triumphed. Taaffe still had powerful support
among the German Clerical Conservatives, while the leading
Czechs continued to be profuse in their sentiments of loyalty to
the empire. It was generally expected that the electoral reform

[13] Reprinted in *Das Vaterland,* Aug. 10, 1883.
[14] Paul Molisch, *Geschichte der deutschnationalen Bewegung in Oesterreich* (Jena, 1926), pp. 114, 129.

of 1882 would strengthen moderatism in the next elections, or at least that it would secure the victory of deputies more responsive to economic and social problems than to questions of extreme national honor. When the debate was over, however, a degree of marked concern gripped Vienna, for both sides had said too much to allow for worth-while compromises later on.

Professor Constantin Tomaszczuk from Czernowitz delivered one of the more venomous Liberal perorations, for he openly accused the Slavs of plots to turn Austria into a Slavic state as soon as possible. The constant Slavic reminders that they had numerical preponderance revealed their ambition. They would fight a legal sanction for German until it was time to consummate their own project, which was a Slavic official language.[15] It was Liberal strategy, of course, to embarrass the German Clerical Conservatives on *Staatssprache,* for in the coming elections it might be difficult to explain to German voters in the western rural districts why there was no need to recognize German as the empire's official language. Count Hohenwart's remarks were curiously unconvincing, for he could only argue that his Slavic friends accepted German as a necessary means of communication and comprehension.[16] Georg Lienbacher, the influential Clerical representative of rural communes in Salzburg, echoed Hohenwart's opinion that there was no need for an explicit declaration of German as the *Staatssprache,* but he also repudiated the committee majority's assertion that such a step would be unconstitutional. Though he hoped for a compromise between the guarantee demanded by Wurmbrand and the committee's refusal to entertain such a guarantee, he was ready to vote for the former in case of an impasse.[17]

The possibility of Lienbacher's endorsement of Wurmbrand's proposal momentarily elated the German Liberals and seemed to add to a sense of desperation on both sides of the Lower House. For four more full days some of the ablest figures in the House limned without ambiguity the unlucky fate which had overtaken

[15] *SPA,* IX Session, p. 11109, Jan. 24, 1884.
[16] *Ibid.,* p. 11117, Jan. 24, 1884.
[17] *Ibid.,* pp. 11119, 11123, Jan. 24, 1884.

a dynastic state whose peoples were manifesting an irrepressible impatience with the *status quo*.

The Czechs had the major task of refuting the German Liberal demand, and their spokesmen moved methodically from conciliatory arguments to thinly concealed threats. Rieger began rather goodnaturedly with the surmise that the German Liberals were stirring up controversy in order to have propaganda for electioneering in the approaching imperial balloting. When he expressed doubt that moral conquests could be made among the South Slavs after the adoption of German as the official tongue, the Left roared that it wanted none.[18] Heinrich Clam Martinič, almost at the end of his public career as a federalist and exponent of Czech aspirations, retailed the practical difficulties which Wurmbrand's bill would create. Would persons fluent in German alone be eligible as parliamentary deputies? How could any general law bring uniformity to all of the educational and bureaucratic problems found in the various provinces?[19] Dr. Eduard Grégr was not content to emulate these placid disquisitions. With a frankness born of anger, he bluntly raised the question of eventual independence for the "lands of the Bohemian crown." Should fate ever decree such a "mighty process," no petty expedient such as Wurmbrand's motion could hold it back. Why not admit that all of the talk for a *Staatssprache* simply meant Germanization? The villains behind the maneuver were the German Liberals, who were desperately trying to discredit the German deputies from Salzburg and the Tirol in the hope of coming to power again. But their hope was vain. They had lost out, not because they lacked national fervor, but because of their infidelity to the ideals of liberty. Their electoral "reform" had left the worker without a vote and had bestowed upon the peasant a ballot a hundred times less valuable than the one granted the burgher. What Liberal textbook had they consulted in writing their press law, which sacrificed every expression of opinion to the arbitrary action of bureaucrats and police? Their version of the right of assembly was a caricature, for the

---

[18] *Ibid.*, pp. 11143, 11148, Jan. 25, 1884.
[19] *Ibid.*, pp. 11163, 11169, Jan. 25, 1884.

approval of the tiniest gathering depended on the pleasure of the police authorities. Some day a true Liberal party would again arise, but directed by men who would teach love of one's own nationality without hatred for another's.[20]

The Polish Club joined with the Czechs in contesting the idea of German as the *Staatssprache*. Grocholski, chairman of the committee which considered Wurmbrand's motion, repeated the argument that the Lower House had no right to pass such a law and declared that the Emperor was the best possible guardian of the treasured "right of language."[21] Otto Hausner, despite the Teutonic ring of his name, derided a liberalism which forwarded all of the classical freedoms while denying the "freedom of language and nationality." To leave no doubt as to the targets of his strictures, he pointed to Posen and Metz as tragic examples of such limited liberalism.[22]

It was Ernst Plener, the paladin of Liberalism, who brought the sad debate to a near-riotous climax the same day that Hausner implied liberal responsibility for Posen and Metz. He explained that the German Liberals had not legalized German as the state speech when they were in power because they were confident that no more federalistic experiments would take place. They had failed to see that federalism would reappear, more dangerous than ever, through the pressure of an increasingly Slavicized bureaucracy. The Czech Memorandum of 1879 had been most alarming to the Germans, since it demanded parity for both languages in the inner services right up to the highest posts of the central bureaucracy. The Emperor himself, in opening parliament in 1879, had recognized, if indirectly, the concept of a Bohemian *Staatsrecht*. The Language Ordinances of 1880 were proof of the dangers facing the Austrian state.

Wurmbrand's bill was an honest answer to such dangers, for it would construct a dam against the ever-rising Slavic flood in the very heart of the empire. Galicia, South Tirol, and the Serbo-Croat lands were on the periphery, but Germans had to maintain

[20] *Ibid.*, pp. 11189–90, 11192–93, Jan. 26, 1884.
[21] *Ibid.*, pp. 11123, 11124, Jan. 24, 1884.
[22] *Ibid.*, p. 11203, Jan. 28, 1884.

their language in the heartland as a wedge against Slavicization.

Though Austria and Russia continued to be on less than the
best of terms, there was no need to appease the Slavs of Austria.
It was true that Polish mistreatment of the Ruthenes made the
latter look to Russia for relief. The Poles, however, were by
nature anti-Russian, and Plener was of the opinion that the
Czechs would be loyal to Franz Joseph in case of war with
Russia. If individual Czechs were disloyal, the Germans would
simply crush them. There was no point in trying to talk such
persons out of their opinions or in bribing them. The influential
Polish and Czech leaders were not Pan-Slavs in the sense of
being oriented toward Russia and certainly not in the sense of
hoping for expansion toward Salonika. Bluntly, they wished to
found a West Slav empire upon the wreckage of German Austria.

With heavy sarcasm Plener then denounced the Czech claims
that the election of Ferdinand to the Bohemian and Hungarian
thrones after Mohács had actually created Austria, claims which
stripped the Germans of any actual importance in the founding
of modern Habsburg power. Let the Czechs remember 1620,
when Austria would have been destroyed if the Czechs had had
their way! Plener was speaking to packed galleries, which liter-
ally exploded with applause, when, as do all politicians, he
appealed to past historical bitternesses. The president of the
Lower House rang for order and warned the galleries to cease
their demonstrations. When the galleries and the Left ignored
him, he ordered the former cleared. Plener's friends angrily
protested, and the president rescinded his order with the warning
that further "disorder" would compel him to enforce the rules
rigidly. Georg von Schönerer arrogantly demanded the removal of detectives from the gallery, but the harassed Czech
president merely asked Plener to continue.

The excitement was over. After a few stereotyped phrases
declaring that German honor demanded the legalization of German as the state speech, Plener ended by addressing the vulnerable German Clericals. Was it not typical that not a single one

of them dared to table Wurmbrand's motion? That their sole spokesman in the debate was "for us"? The day would come when the voters would demonstrate against them.[23]

The Lower House first voted on January 29 on the Polish motion to table Wurmbrand's motion. By the close vote of 174 to 167, it was lost. The galleries and the Left broke into fervent applause. They already had cheered Lienbacher, the dissident German Clerical, who temporarily deserted the Iron Ring by voting against the Polish move. Obviously the interest aroused among the citizens of Vienna had forced the rejection of face-saving strategies. Very few German deputies dared avoid committing themselves.

Laughter, hissing, and applause often interrupted the vital balloting. The Left ridiculed those deputies in Taaffe's cabinet who came to vote against the German Liberal proposal. Lienbacher's associates hissed him, and his enemies acclaimed him as he stuck to his promise to vote his convictions. The final tally, 186 to 155, was a decisive repudiation of Wurmbrand's bill, and the president had to order the clearing of the gallery because of its deafening disapproval.[24]

But the public actually had become exhausted, and there was little interest in Herbst's outdated demand for a parliamentary repudiation of the cabinet's Language Ordinances.[25] Though everyone knew the outcome of the debate, Germans and Czechs representing the contested lands of Bohemia and Moravia traded insults and statistics that were of interest only as indications of the steadily widening gulf between German pride and fear and Czech determination to obtain parity.

The final Czech orator, Vinzenz Hevera from Kolín in Bohemia, injected something of a novelty into the wearisome proceedings by contrasting the treatment given tiny Czech minorities in American states with the obstruction they had to fight in Austria. How did a country of 36,000,000 treat 85,000 Czechs scattered throughout the land? In Texas 2,669 Czechs received

[23] *Ibid.*, pp. 11217, 11221, 11223, 11228–30, 11233, Jan. 28, 1884.
[24] *Ibid.*, pp. 11282–85, Jan. 29, 1884.
[25] Charmatz, *Geschichte.* II, 39.

an official Czech version of the state's constitution. In Nebraska there was a translation of the governor's message for about 8,000 Czech readers. In Minnesota official bulletins were available in Czech for the 700 Czechs living there. In other American cities men who lived liberty and democracy were supplying Czechs with libraries and schools.[26]

Next day, just before the vote, Max von Scharschmid of the Bohemian landed curia observed that Hevera did not say whether or not these Czechs in the United States were opposed to the constitution or to the use of English as the national language. Had they been, he was sure that Americans would not have offered them the courtesy of Czech translation.[27]

On February 1 the Lower House rejected Herbst's motion, 176 to 161. The German Liberals, through Wurmbrand and Herbst, had expended much energy in trying to arouse all the Germans against "destructive federalism" and against cooperation with Taaffe's policy of gradual satisfaction of Czech objectives. The German Clericals had not yielded to the pressure, and so the Iron Ring remained intact. The shouts of the Viennese in the galleries were proof, however, that the dominant Germans were alarmed by the increase in Czech power. Nationalistic radicalism was bound to increase, and the barbs and thrusts of the debates were but small harbingers of unparalleled outbursts yet to come. If men of high cultural rank, basically free of the need to placate the vast masses of Austria, were unable to put aside petty taunts and near-blind obstinacy in 1884, their universally elected successors after 1907 were even less free to work toward fair solutions. Taaffe's Language Ordinances, in retrospect, were timely and just. Paradoxically, men who looked to the theoretical ideals of the French Revolution for guidance endangered his attempt to achieve harmony. Mesmerized by the dream of a smoothly running centralized administration, "modern and scientific," and all too conscious of the glories of their own Kultur, they paved the way for uncompromising demagoguery.

[26] *SPA*, p. 11362, Jan. 31, 1884 (*Abendsitzung*).
[27] *Ibid.*, p. 11389, Feb. 1, 1884.

As the German Ambassador put it in his report to Bismarck, all moderate politicians would have preferred avoiding this acrimony. Everyone expected the extremists on both sides to exploit this welcome opportunity, and the extremists had not disappointed expectations. The passage or rejection of Wurmbrand's bill could not have altered the *de facto* use of German as the *Staatssprache*. The debate, rather, prefigured the coming election campaign. In Reuss's opinion Grégr's harsh tone spelled his party's intensified drive to separate from the Old Czechs and Feudalists. Lienbacher's rally to Germanism was equally significant. Everywhere the national rivalry had waxed in strength.[28]

[28] See Reuss's dispatch No. 44, A 754, Jan. 29, 1884, UC-1, reel 215, frames 186–89.

6 The Electoral Reform of 1882

The reversal of power in the Bohemian landed curia in the elections of 1879 and the construction of a generally reliable coalition of Lower House parties were political events of primary importance for Taaffe's survival as the *Kaiserminister*. Rare upsets in the Upper House did not ruffle his debonair good humor, so one gathers from the occasional personal digs the Liberal press indulged in, nor did the famous reverse in the matter of the Discretionary Fund send him into retirement. But it was not easy to keep in one fairly compatible political alignment such elements as doggedly agrarian German *and* Czech-oriented aristocrats, purposeful Clericals from Salzburg and the Tirol, and the determinedly anticlerical bourgeois deputies who dominated Old and Young Czech councils. The Polish Club, to add to the complexity of the situation, also had its fringe of liberals who did not take kindly to the informal alliance that existed between the dominant szlachta members and the Roman Catholic Church. Taaffe performed his acts of political management with dexterity most of the time, though it strained his nerves and the Emperor's fortitude when the Czechs wanted more educational facilities, when the Clericals wanted to decentralize, if not de-emphasize, the existing educational system, and when the Poles wanted new railroads, more flood control, and a continuing dictatorship over all Galician schools as the price of falling in with Czech and Clerical desires. Club discipline was not always reliable, and the roll-call majorities, particularly when aggrieved deputies absented themselves, were dangerously slim.

At times Taaffe had to crawl to keep his lieutenants happy. When Hohenwart directed a stiff note to Dunajewski in the summer of 1881, Taaffe protested that it was not wise to leave the ministry weaponless. His letter to the veteran federalist does not disclose what issue really was at stake, but it reveals all too well his determination not to lose Hohenwart's votes. He promised to undertake nothing until he had consulted the recognized *leader* of the majority, and he begged this leader (the use of the singular is instructive) not to allow a breach to develop. The German journalists were a fearsome group when united. He could fend them off only if he had strong counter-weapons—obviously, Hohenwart's strong support.[1]

Dissidence within the Iron Ring was easier to compose than the growing enmity between Taaffe and the German Liberals. The latter had gone into irreconcilable opposition, it seemed by late 1881, and within the government the conviction grew that modifications of the highly privileged electoral system were in order. The Liberals still had a near monopoly of those seats in the curia of the chambers of commerce wherever German-speaking businessmen were active. A sizable number of the great landed proprietors were *verfassungstreu,* and the requirement for the franchise in the city districts, namely, ten gulden in direct taxes, guaranteed a numerous German Liberal representation in the urban curia. If the tax requirement was lowered, persons of quite moderate means, particularly small businessmen, industrious but modestly propertied farmers, and the more prosperous artisans, would have the right to vote. Such strata were likely to despise the intrepid financiers and tough-fisted plutocrats who mingled with the professional classes and "emancipated" aristocrats in the Liberal salons and society of Vienna. The German Ambassador was of the opinion that

[1] Verwaltungsarchiv, Vienna, Nachlass Hohenwart, Karton 12, letter of July 16, 1881.

Taaffe embraced electoral reform to win friends for himself among the "bulk of the people." Moreover, Taaffe seemed definitely to feel that the Liberals might well carry out later what his cabinet failed to accomplish.[2] And the Emperor made no secret of his distaste for dealing with the Liberals.

The sentiment for electoral reform upon which Taaffe capitalized had developed in many sectors. Non-Germans wanted to close the gap which separated their demography from their actual parliamentary representation. Clericals were reasonably sure that enfranchising more farmers would sustain their objectives, though the prospect of urban "radicialism" had some deterrent value. Most vociferous of all the voices for electoral reform were those of the "Democratic Left," a tiny fraction of deputies whose better-known members were Georg von Schönerer, formerly a Liberal but in effect quite jaundiced over the Liberals' "errors," particularly their ties with big business and their too tolerant cosmopolitanism, and Ferdinand Kronawetter, the archetype of a Viennese radical of the 1880s, who moved steadily from a shrewd understanding of the needs of the lower bourgeoisie and artisans to full-fledged espousal of socialism later in his career.

In December, 1880, Schönerer, Kronawetter, Heinrich Fürnkranz, and Johann Steudel proposed fundamental changes in the constitutional provisions for parliamentary representation. Every Austrian male twenty-four years old would enjoy the right to vote, and electoral districts would be nationally demarcated whenever possible, with a special law to determine the number of deputies from each crownland. In the last provision, of course, Germans might hope to continue to preponderate over the non-Germans.

Schönerer's defense of universal manhood suffrage was a blend of extreme German nationalism and concern for the neglected lower middle classes, artisans, and independent peasantry. Truly loyal Germans were no longer willing to be the scapegoats of the "power-mad privileged classes," for the exist-

---

[2] See Reuss's dispatch No. 110, A 1422, March 10, 1882, UC-1, reel 214, frame 650.

ing electoral system and the cabinet which thrived upon it were prima-facie evidence of the delivering up of the Germans to the Slavs. Schönerer fully realized what would happen to the actual German minority (when balanced against all non-Germans) should Austria adopt universal suffrage, so he added verbally to his bill's specifications a demand for special status for Galicia. Unless this relatively populous province were cut off from the jurisdiction of the central parliament, its deputies would have greater influence than ever. Schönerer was even more disturbed by the political power wielded by the rich in the 1880s. He denied that the preceding Liberal regime was German, since it had linked Germanism with injustice, violence, class egoism, Bourse-style free enterprise, and "Semitic jobbery." Hence there had been filibustering and delay in factory legislation, in the reform of direct taxes that would make the rich pay their due share, in laws controlling stock exchanges and securities transactions, and in full-scale regulation of credit operations.[3]

Rudolf Auspitz, factory owner and power in Liberal circles, virulently castigated Schönerer. Why recommend what was inexcusably naïve in 1848? An incapacity to learn seemed to be a characteristic of Austrian radicals. The two Napoleonic despotisms boasted of universal manhood suffrage, and Schönerer might reflect upon the relations between this system, governmental corruption, and the stock exchange in France under the Bonapartes. In Germany universal suffrage was quite compatible with ministerial arbitrariness and a "personal" regime. And where in the world was there a closer connection between politics and filthy lucre than in America?[4] Thoroughly uncowed, the irrepressible four, with a new recruit, Franz Löblich, a master coppersmith from Vienna, introduced a slightly changed substitute motion. In effect, it granted the ballot to every man who paid a direct tax.

Lienbacher meanwhile introduced a reform of more restricted scope. In essence, he reduced the direct tax from 10 to 5 gulden for voting in the town and rural curias, a change which would

[3] *SPA*, IX Session, pp. 3770, 3772–73, Jan. 28, 1881.
[4] *Ibid.*, pp. 3777–78, Jan. 28, 1881.

require approval by a mere majority.[5] Not eager for sudden
leaps, this German Clerical nevertheless expressed shock over
what seemed to be a total absence of artisans and small businessmen among his parliamentary confreres. Was this not an abnor-
mality? Some day labor would stride through the portals of the
Lower House, and it would be wise to invite the petty bourgeoisie first.[6]

The committee elected to consider both bills was blue-
ribbon. The German Right provided Hohenwart, Lienbacher,
and Alois Liechtenstein. The Liberals boasted of Chlumecky,
Herbst, Weeber, Sturm, and Tomaszczuk. The outstanding Pole
was Grocholski, and the Czechs sent Heinrich Clam Martinič,
Rieger, and Ottokar Zeithammer. The remaining committeemen were only slightly less prominent.[7] Czechs and Poles speed-
ily accepted the idea of a reduction in the tax requirement, and
the German Liberals, fearful of being labeled "enemies of the
people," concurred. Zeithammer then proposed a partition of
the landed curia of Bohemia into a *fideikommissarisch* section in
which the Feudalist element would dominate and a *nichtfidei-
kommissarisch* section to be subdivided among the electoral
districts of Karolinenthal (Karlín), Budweis, Pilsen, Jungbunzlau (Mladá Boleslav), and Chrudim.[8]

When Zeithammer asked the Lower House to send his proposition to the electoral reform committee, he minimized its importance. The Czechs had many complaints over the curia of the
chambers of commerce, but his request was their first in regard
to electoral arrangements. It would not disturb existing constitutional provisions, and it would eliminate the need to work out
compromises in future elections in the Bohemian landed curia.
The Left did not hear his explanation. Miffed by the Right's
decision to nullify the Reichsgericht's pro-Liberal verdict in a

[5] *Ibid.,* Beilagen, III, No. 265.
[6] *Ibid.,* pp. 3991, 3993, Feb. 18, 1881.
[7] *Ibid.,* p. 4059, Feb. 22, 1881.
[8] Gustav Kolmer, *Parlament und Verfassung in Oesterreich* (Vienna
and Leipzig, 1902–14), III, 142.

disputed election, its members had temporarily deserted the sessions.[9] The Right without further ado unanimously acceded to Zeithammer's request.

The full committee's consideration of all three programs led to an interesting schism on the German Right. Disappointed with Hohenwart's less than solicitous representation of conservative German desires in the offices of the ministers, Lienbacher and Alfred Liechtenstein seceded from the "Hohenwart Club" to create a Centrums Club. The rebels feared that the Right was interested only in Zeithammer's plan, and, as Germans, they were unwilling to accept responsibility for an obvious Czech maneuver unless guaranteed full support by the Right of the reduction in tax qualifications. The coincidence of this split with the decision of the Progressive and Liberal Clubs to unite as the Club of the United Left occasioned some twinges of anxiety in high places. Taaffe admitted to a reporter from *Národní Listy* that the secession, while not intrinsically dangerous, gave the inspirited Liberal bloc an opportunity to circulate reports of an imminent fall of the cabinet. Unfortunately, said Taaffe, the Right's majority was very small, and it needed to "strengthen its position" by quick approval of revenue measures. Since *Národní Listy* typified ultrademocratic Czech sentiment, its reporter accented Taaffe's reaction to electoral reform. The Minister-President had no opposition in principle to an extension of the franchise, but he declared that he had to consider the effect of voting changes in all crownlands, Dalmatia and Galicia as well as Salzburg.[10]

The committee, as usual, had a majority and minority opinion. To outdo the "democratic" allure of Lienbacher's plan, the Left unsuccessfully proposed the franchise in rural communes for any male citizen paying two gulden in direct taxes. It disapproved of Lienbacher's bill and offered as a possible counterweight an increase in the representation of the rapidly growing suburbs of Vienna by three mandates. As expected,

[9] *SPA*, pp. 5722–23, May 20, 1881.
[10] Cited in *Neue Freie Presse*, Nov. 28, 1881, *Abendblatt*.

Taaffe preferred the majority's decision to combine the Lienbacher and Zeithammer bills into one general "reform."[11] Reuss
was most impressed by the public's apathy. He assured Bismarck that the general disinterest was a good clue to the parliamentary situation, for even the interjection of the "local" Vienna
issue by the Liberals did not shake up the citizens.[12]

In the face of general indifference, the Liberal orators tried to
revive an old bogey, "the feudal menace." Max Menger
doubted that even Lord North in England would have recommended that less than a dozen voters control one mandate,
especially when many of the same voters already had seats in a
House of Lords. He was confident, however, that the Germans
would outlast and overcome those incumbents of abbacies
founded by the Babenbergers who voted against German interests.[13] Professor Eduard Suess emphasized the changing role of
the landed aristocracy, who had increasingly become city renti-
ers. Did not his own Viennese constituency pay more in direct
taxes than the entire Czech *Fideicommissen,* to whom five mandates were being offered?[14]

In reply, the Czechs underlined the continuing Liberal hegemony in the curia of the chambers of commerce. Rieger ominously asked where, in the entire world, a parliamentary system
accorded seats to chambers of commerce. He freely admitted
that a number of the voters in the Bohemian landed estate
collaborated with whatever cabinet was in power. But the aristocrats who had Czech sympathies had reason to resent their past
representation by professors, tenants, and "God knows what
kind of people." Because a man was of the noble caste in
Austria, should custom or law forbid his social equals the right to
be deputies?[15] Clam Martinič insisted loftily upon the continuing
significance of the landed nobility to the state. The *Fideicom-
miss* was the unchanging element as time went by. Small as it

[11] Kolmer, *Parlament,* III, 143–44.
[12] See Reuss's dispatch No. 110, A 1422, March 10, 1882, UC-1, reel
214, frame 650.
[13] *SPA,* pp. 7525–27, March 18, 1882.
[14] *Ibid.,* pp. 7546, 7549, March 18, 1882.
[15] *Ibid.,* pp. 7552, 7554–55, March 18, 1882.

was, it did not deserve being swamped by the lesser proprietors in a general assembly.[16]

German Liberal and Democratic strategy called for a campaign to persuade Taaffe to agree to three new mandates for Viennese suburbs, which actually were still part of the rural curia. Menger estimated the population of these suburbs at 300,000. Was it right to push Germans out of positions they had occupied for five hundred years and yet deny them compensation in Währing, Hernals, and similar "Viennese" districts?[17]

When Taaffe announced to the Lower House the cabinet's reaction to the various suggestions, he underlined above all else its desire for the modifications within the Bohemian landed curia. He reminded the Liberals that the conditions in and around Vienna existed in 1873, when they were at the helm and in charge of writing the electoral reform of that year. While not interposing an absolute negative to requests for more urban deputies for Vienna, he rejected the idea of absolute justice in apportionment as utopian. He also implied that concessions to other areas might accompany a better deal for the capital.[18] A motion to increase the deputies in the Lower House from 353 to 359, with the new seats to go to Greater Vienna, failed to pass, 157 to 138, but another motion requesting the cabinet to lay before parliament as soon as possible a bill to increase representation for Vienna and its suburbs passed on March 23.[19]

Reducing the tax qualifications no doubt frightened the Liberals, but they avoided a direct attack on a bill that had distinct popular appeal. Sturm hoped that the new voters would be "progressive" and foil the Right's ambitions.[20] Julius Magg, yet another Viennese lawyer, carefully explained that he had no personal feeling against allowing a literate taxpayer of fixed domicile to vote. But this did not mean that he was an adherent of democracy and a foe of privilege. Austria was a monarchy, not a republic. Experience in nearly all lands taught that parliaments elected on the broadest possible basis rarely demonstrated

---

[16] *Ibid.*, p. 7522, March 18, 1882.   [17] *Ibid.*, p. 7528, March 18, 1882.
[18] *Ibid.*, pp. 7528–30, March 18, 1882.
[19] *Ibid.*, p. 7686, March 23, 1882.   [20] *Ibid.*, p. 7570, March 20, 1882.

the insight and intelligence of those whose mode of election gave plenty of room for criticism.[21]

When the ballots were cast, the cabinet-favored Lienbacher-Zeithammer revisions triumphed. A roll-call tally of 165 to 145 on March 21 approved the redrawing of the Bohemian landed curia, while the enfranchisement of the "five-gulden men" followed on March 22. The United German Left in caucus decided to vote against the bill should its own motion for a two-gulden requirement fail. A handful of Styrian deputies, including Wurmbrand and Robert von Walterskirchen, refused to follow such "party" discipline, no doubt concerned over the effect on their constituents should they vote against any changes.

The Upper House naturally scrutinized the shift in the Bohemian landed curia when it debated the Lower House's bill. Schmerling and Carlos Auersperg denounced the new partition as a capitulation to federalism.[22] Taaffe retorted with a reference to the constant defeats suffered by the minority in this curia and their consequent abstention from political activity. Such a defeatist attitude was a bad sign in a constitutional state, and he begged the peers to accept the remedy arrived at in the Lower House. It would be fine to abolish inequities everywhere, he readily agreed, but that was beyond human strength. One could only attack the most crying abuses.[23]

Enfranchising the lesser taxpayers stimulated less complaint from the peers. Piqued over the Bohemian proposal, Schmerling recommended either universal suffrage as the only sincere "equality" or a special curia whose voters would not harm the rights of previously enfranchised citizens.[24] Count Richard Belcredi rejoined that the "five-gulden men" would be of consequence only in Vienna, Prague, Graz, and Brünn. Elsewhere the new qualification would do no more than equalize certain incongruities.[25] The motion to table the Lower House's bill lost,

[21] *Ibid.*, pp. 7651–52, March 22, 1882.
[22] *SPH*, IX Session, pp. 1000, 1009, May 24, 1882.
[23] *Ibid.*, pp. 1006–7, May 24, 1882.
[24] *Ibid.*, pp. 995, 1010, May 24, 1882.
[25] *Ibid.*, p. 998, May 24, 1882.

68 to 53, and at the end of the relatively brief debate on May 24, the Upper House voted its approval of electoral reform.

In June, Taaffe informed the cabinet that the reform more than ever required a modification of the rules for elections to the Bohemian Diet. He expected the German majority to table the cabinet's suggested changes, as before, but at least such action would permit him to dissolve the obdurate body. Then he surveyed other advantages deriving from the passage of imperial electoral reform. The cabinet might order new general elections, if such were desired. Taaffe's tone reflected serious concern over such a step. Though he invited his colleagues to reflect upon the possibilities, he noted that new elections would not have to take place if he delayed until September asking the Emperor to sign the electoral reform bill.[26]

In fact, he followed the latter procedure. Though the electoral reform was expected to fortify the progovernment coalition in the next election, the Minister-President evidently needed more time to "prepare" the elections. He eventually asked the cabinet to approve his decision to secure the imperial signature on September 26, and the Emperor complied on October 4, 1882.[27] Berchem reported to Berlin that Franz Joseph's approval corresponded to the political pressure of the moment. "Old Austrian" circles viewed the law with gravity, but if cabinet or crown had refused to countenance reform, the cabinet could not have survived.[28]

Ernst Plener was in Prague when the news of the imperial sanction was published, and he wrote his father that the Emperor had given another proof of his determination to proceed "against us." Incredibly, the younger Plener would have allied the Liberals with the German Clericals, if only the latter had been agreeable.[29] In a calmer mood some days later he admitted that such an alliance would embarrass the Liberals of Upper Austria,

---

[26] MRP 52, June 9, 1882.   [27] MRP 73, Sept. 26, 1882.
[28] See Berchem's dispatch No. 384, A 6250, Oct. 7, 1882, UC-1, reel 214, frames 741–43.
[29] Nachlass Plener, Karton 17, Nos. 83–84, letter of Oct. 8, 1882.

who had long before embarked upon a war to the death with
Bishop Rudigier of Linz. But the Czechs lived in fear of a
general German rapprochement, and *Národní Listy* wrote of
Ernst Plener's relations with Alfred Liechtenstein as a symptom
of such a realignment.[30] Later in the same month, October,
1882, the Liberal chieftain saw Crown Prince Rudolf at 8:30 in
the morning, bloated and flabby of mien and smoking a strong,
thick cigar. The heir to the throne roundly denounced the
Czechs, middle class and aristocratic, and he especially complained that Cardinal Schwarzenberg criticized him for his Sunday hunts. Other Clericals found fault with the Crown Princess' less than regular attendance at mass, and Rudolf was
violent over such intrusions upon his "private affairs." But he
did not expect his father to change the complexion of the cabinet, for that august personage was personally committed to its
retention and success.

In a very black humor, he refused to credit Plener's theory
that Franz Joseph and the army put up with Taaffe and his
coalition because they feared a war with Russia. Rudolf was
most opposed to any steps which might bring such a war, for he
expected the South Slavs and probably the Italians to attack once
Austria was engaged with Russia. Nor would the pessimistic
Habsburg count on help from the German Empire in such a
crisis.[31]

If the Crown Prince disliked the Clericals, Plener still toyed
with the idea of combining forces with them. In Budapest in
November he broached the matter of an alliance with the German Clericals with Chlumecky, Suess, and Sturm, but only
Sturm encouraged him. The idea of a grand German alliance
against Taaffe's Slavicizing tendencies died quickly.[32] In retrospect, it is amazing that the younger Plener dreamed of such a
union, for the ideological differences were profound. Lienbacher was more sensitive to the ethnic loyalties of his Salzburg-
ers than was Hohenwart, but the idea of a Liberal-Clerical bloc

[30] *Ibid.,* Karton 16, Nos. 1–2, letter of Oct. 14, 1882.
[31] *Ibid.,* Karton 17, Nos. 85–86, letter of Oct. 20, 1882.
[32] *Ibid.,* Karton 16, Nos. 359–360, letter of Nov. 16, 1882.

in 1882 was most unrealistic. Plener had to console himself by observing the chilly reception the Magyars gave Rieger in their capital and in listening to Andrássy's characterization of Taaffe's regime as a stupidity. The former Minister of Foreign Affairs did not think it was yet time for the Liberals to take over again, however.[33]

The German Embassy, despite its dependence upon Liberal sources for much of its political reporting, discerned an improvement in Taaffe's position after the sanction of the franchise bill. Reuss emphatically denied rumors that Kálnoky and Taaffe would step down late in 1882, and he confidently predicted that the latter, who had deliberately put off the Emperor's approval of the electoral changes, would move ruthlessly against the troublesome German Liberal majority in the Bohemian Diet.[34] The Crown Prince was beside himself with frustration and rage when he weighed the chances of further Liberal humiliations. Dismissing Taaffe as a mere tool of the crafty bosses of the Iron Ring, he wrote Moriz Szeps that these confederates wanted to further their own power and to deny the claims of modern culture. Fanatic, stupid, unpatriotic, and characterless, they had invoked the help of elements which never again would disperse. "A great and powerful reaction must come, social upheavals, from which an entirely new Europe will arise after long sickness."[35]

The German Liberals among the Bohemian aristocracy refused to agree to the "compromise" which the Feudalists insisted upon. Later in October, 1882, Carlos Auersperg sent the Diet home with a significant, "Adieu, gentlemen," and Taaffe formally dissolved the body in the following May. New elections, thanks to the "reform" in the landed curia, provided the Czechs with a majority. Thereafter the Diet's composition was more in harmony with actual demography, and the Germans turned with

[33] *Ibid.*, Karton 16, Nos. 364–65, letter of Nov. 22, [1882].
[34] See Reuss's dispatch No. 490, A 7613, Dec. 26, 1882, UC-1, reel 215, frames 40–43.
[35] Letter of Nov. 24, 1882, in *Kronprinz Rudolf: Politische Briefe an einen Freund, 1882–1889,* ed. Julius Szeps (Vienna, Munich, and Leipzig, 1922), pp. 20–21.

alacrity to the idea of partitioning the crownland between the
two nationalities. Overwhelmed by the reversal of control in
the province's legislature, there was little else they could do.[36]

Taaffe ignored their new strategy as best he could, just as he
decided there was no need to dissolve the Reichsrat before the
end of its term to get a more reliable working majority there.
Such a decision demanded careful management of his majority
parties, and he was quick to remind Conrad that it was not
prudent to arouse the Czechs. The latter had secured the appointment of a man to Conrad's ministry, and subsequently
Conrad heard of the appointee's unbridled hatred of Germans.
Could the troublemaker be denied his appointment? Taaffe
sternly reminded his colleague that he had given his promise to
the leaders of the Czech Club. If Conrad now should renege, the
cabinet's very existence would be in question. Moreover, when
Zeithammer complained to Conrad that various schools promised the Czechs by the cabinet were not being built, Taaffe
promptly and politely gave reasons for delay. Significantly,
Taaffe did not repeat Conrad's protest that the Czechs wanted a
trade school when some of the greatest industrial centers did not
possess one.[37] The votes were still too close.

In April, 1885, it was the appointed time to send the Lower
House home to face the voters. Taaffe informed the Emperor
that he would schedule the weeks of electioneering and balloting
for spring rather than for summer. Hot weather was too ideal
for agitators. More important, field and harvest chores were
heavier in the summer, and the Minister-President was counting
on rural votes to support majority candidates.[38] Instead of the
usual six weeks, the election campaign lasted only from May 20
to June 13.

Franz Joseph told the cabinet that he expected the government to use pressure up to a certain point to make the majority
stronger than it had been. In reply, Taaffe assured the ruler that
the Right would not have to face the phalanx which the opposi-

[36] Kolmer, *Parlament,* III, 474–75.
[37] *Politischer Nachlass,* pp. 429–36.
[38] Kabinetts-Kanzlei, Vortrag 1372, April 13, 1885.

tion had mustered in the outgoing parliament, even if it did not pick up all of the seats which the Left should lose. A few extremists like Schönerer and Alfred Knotz might win mandates, but they would be few. When pressed by some colleagues to deal with bureaucrats who voted against the government's parties, Taaffe pleaded that he could not order an investigation of such employees. Obviously annoyed by the thought of "Liberal" officials casting ballots against the ministry, the Emperor insisted on German Conservative victories. It simply would not do, he said, to have the cabinet depend solely on "other nationalities."

Dunajewski wanted governmental pressure applied in Galicia to prevent the election of undesirable elements, but Ziemialkowski countered with a promise that the Polish Club's solidarity would take care of dissentients. Possibly a larger number of Ruthenes would get seats, but they would not be extremists. The cabinet might well see to it that they did not develop a radical leader once they were in parliament. The thought of violent nationalists stirred the Emperor to a vigorous statement of what he expected of the majority's parties. The cabinet would have to work on the coalition to secure the new *Ausgleich* with Hungary, the Landsturm bill, and the new version of the Defense Law. And he did not wish to pay for these accomplishments with a series of concessions. The ministers should prescribe a clear-cut policy and refuse to give way to demands that went too far.

Obviously exercised by the problem of ruling with any kind of coalition, Franz Joseph directly attacked his Polish and Czech supporters by lamenting the rapid decline of the knowledge of the German language in Bohemia and Galicia. Young educated persons no longer were of any use to the army, for they and their parents assiduously avoided learning German. Exasperated by the ambiguous comments which the ministers made in reply, he urged some clarification of the language problem, either by imperial legislation or otherwise.[39] The veteran ruler did not choose to see that the issue of imperial versus provincial regula-

[39] MRP 35, April 16, 1885.

tion of the language question was a matter which Taaffe would
have clarified gladly had he dared. Taaffe knew, if the Emperor
did not, that a Czech majority in the Bohemian Diet was not
likely to prescribe sufficient training in German to guarantee a
steady stream of bilingual Czechs to serve as officers and noncoms
in the imperial forces.

During the final preparations for elections, Taaffe advised the
Statthalter of the Tirol to avoid using pressure upon state
officials while simultaneously having them informed orally that it
would be highly improper to vote for candidates whose primary
goal was the cabinet's downfall. When the obedient Baron
Widmann asked if such "directions" also should go to state
railway employees, Taaffe immediately wired in the affirmative.
Such telegrams, of course, were encoded.[40]

Again, the Slovene politician Josef Tonkli complained that a
Hofrat in Trieste was working for a candidate who at best would
join the Coronini Club. Could the Minister-President graciously
take the necessary steps to end such a threat to a candidate who
would join the Hohenwart Club and assuredly support the cabinet? Upon receipt of Tonkli's solicitation, Taaffe wrote privately
to the *Statthalter* of Trieste to end the *Hofrat's* agitation.
Obviously, every race counted. Pretis, the *Statthalter* of the
great port, replied with some spirit that both candidates were
equally conservative and that a man favored by Slavs would
repel non-Slavic voters and increase the chances of the Italian
Nationalists' nominee. Taaffe insisted that a man who would
bolster the majority was preferable to one who would weaken the
Left, and Pretis soon assured him that the *Hofrat* would do no
more politicking for the less-favored candidate.[41]

When the elections were over, the German Left had lost a
total of 15 mandates to the parties of the Right, who re-entered
the Lower House 151 strong. Liberal commentators were quick
to note that governmental interference and "compromises" in
the landed curia in Bohemia and the Tirol, not the new five-
gulden voters, were involved in the Left's decline. Anti-Semitic
"Christians" sent the foul-mouthed Ernst Schneider into Bohe-

[40] *Politischer Nachlass*, pp. 313–14.   [41] *Ibid.*, pp. 314–19.

mia and even into the Leopoldstadt district of Vienna to play on lower middle-class prejudice, but in both cases the new voters did not yield in sufficient numbers to his unpleasantries. Lueger and Kronawetter won in Viennese wards, as did a master tailor named Anton Kreuzig, also a Democrat. Schönerer's German Nationalists were also but three in number. There were no upsets or drastic surprises in the contests among Czechs, Slovenes, Poles, Italians, Ruthenes, and Rumanians.[42]

Taaffe's reluctance to make immediate use of the five-gulden men by ordering new elections in 1882 was justified by events. The change in the Bohemian landed curia had been the major break with past procedures, and it would lead eventually to a German boycott of the Diet in Prague. In the Tirol the Italians discovered they could make a better bargain with German Clericals than with German Liberals. From these two areas came the dozen or so votes which would give Taaffe greater security after 1885. His gains were minimal, but the fact that few truly radical candidates succeeded with the newly enfranchised farmers and lower middle-class made conferences with the Emperor more pleasant.

Within the general Liberal spectrum, Eduard Sturm tried quietly to arrange for the expulsion of the radically nationalist "left wing." Plener was displeased with the maneuver, for he suspected that Sturm and Chlumecky essentially wanted to weaken the Liberal opposition to the "Emperor's cabinet." Furthermore, he was sure that an obvious antinational reorganization would strip the purged party of substantial popular support. It would be better to vote on a new name for a Liberal club, and Plener expected the modifying words to be "German Austrian" rather than "German." Then, if dissatisfied, the radical nationalists could secede. In time, most of the politicians from North Bohemia would quit a "German-Austrian Club," but it would be preferable to postpone secession as long as possible.[43]

Dunajewski provided a surprising epilogue to the election campaign. In late June or July he submitted his resignation to

[42] Kolmer, *Parlament,* IV, 1–5.
[43] Nachlass Plener, Karton 18, No. 249, letter of July 13, 1885.

the Emperor, pleading poor health. The able Pole already had
made his mark as a self-possessed spokesman for the cabinet in
tense parliamentary encounters, and his standing as "the arch-
foe of the Germans" guaranteed continuation of the anti-Liberal
Iron Ring. Undoubtedly Taaffe was alarmed at the thought of
losing his alter ego, and what is left of the minutes of a cabinet
meeting of July 3, 1885, indicates rather well that ill health was
but part of the story. By conviction a classical economist,
Dunajewski was resolved to balance the Austrian budget after
years of deficits. His colleagues often thwarted him by requesting supplementary credits, and he had decided either to force
them to plan more carefully or to retire from his post.

He also had demanded a more vigorous leadership in internal
affairs. With a tinge of resentment, Taaffe asserted that he
already was following a stronger line. Within the limits of what
was possible, he promised even greater forcefulness. Not surprisingly the irate Minister of Finance had also complained of
inadequate briefing in foreign affairs, and here, too, Taaffe promised redress. By the time the cabinet had met on July 3, the
Emperor had prevailed upon Dunajewski to withdraw his resignation. Taaffe's obvious relief was mixed with a degree of
defensiveness, which the rest of the cabinet probably shared.
Conrad was gratified that Dunajewski would remain, but he
reminded the Pole that certain ministries, especially his own,
required unpredictable sums.[44]

Dunajewski's insistence upon greater vigor in the direction of
internal affairs and Conrad's reminder that the educational budget could never be inelastic epitomized the continuing tension
under which Taaffe labored. The electoral reform of 1882
delivered a fairly safe majority to the Iron Ring and, rather self-
consciously, its sponsors deferred to the ever more insistent
European cry for more democracy in elections. Taaffe certainly
was no democrat in 1882, and the limited changes in representation and eligibility did nothing to impugn the principle of
the four-class system. Sentimental aristocrats and driving businessmen could still rejoice that blood and tax contributions out-

[44] MRP 48, July 3, 1885.

weighed mere numbers. But the slight advantages which the non-Germans derived from the drop in the tax qualification whetted their appetites for a further reduction in German preponderance, while the less radical socialists of the 1880s discerned in the issue of parliamentary representation a valuable weapon to arouse the masses without completely antagonizing the forces of order. Though the changes were minimal, the new electoral procedure was still an essential step in the general European evolution toward democracy.

France had enjoyed the blessings of unlimited suffrage for males since 1848, and Bismarck's espousal of the principle in 1867 was but one of his daring moves. Great Britain had enfranchised most urban workers in 1867 and had accepted the secret ballot in 1872. In 1884 and 1885 the British would extend the vote to rural workers and redraw the lines of the constituencies. In such "advanced" countries as the Netherlands, Italy, Sweden, and Denmark the percentage of persons allowed to vote was still quite small in the 1880s, however, and the German federal system always was tempered by restrictive Prussian regulations. Hungarian elections were notoriously undemocratic, while tsar and sultan impassively dismissed all thoughts of decision through popular referendum.

In the context of "democratic progress," Austria was neither neglectful nor doctrinaire. The reform of 1882 answered specific questions of power for a cabinet that could not risk incessant crises. In the larger sense, it also recognized the fact that the Austrian state could no longer deny the lower bourgeoisie and independent farmers participation in political life. The workers remained. Another decade would show whether or not social legislation would be an adequate substitute for the vote which they were calling for.

7 The Public Schools under Fire

European liberalism in the second half of the nineteenth century often put into effect policies which reflected its deep suspicion of the alliance of altar and throne that followed Napoleon's downfall. The Habsburg state, heir to the spirit of medieval Germanic missionary zeal and to the robust inspirations of the Catholic Reformation, was inevitably the scene of unbridgeable conflict between those who were determined to limit or abolish the ancient Church's rights and influence and those who saw damnation, temporal as well as eternal, in a divorcement of Church and state.

The latter won a triumph in 1855 when Austria and the Papacy concluded a concordat which promised the curia unrestricted rights of communication with the Austrian clergy, the settlement of marital disputes by church courts, a limiting of civil jurisdiction over the clergy, and sweeping concessions to the Church in the education of young Austrians. Such ultramontanism was a sore trial for the Austrian Liberals, whose overwhelming victory in the elections of 1867 presaged some amendment of the agreement of 1855. There was no doubt of the Emperor's reluctance to approve of changes, but in May, 1868, he finally sanctioned three laws which severely curtailed the Church's power. The new regulations opened up the *possibility* of dissolution of marriages by civil authority, established a new educational system in which the religious would care only for doctrinal instruction, and allowed every person who reached the age of fourteen to declare his own religious affiliation. Loyal to his ministers, Franz Joseph had dispatched his *Obersthofmeister* to the Upper House, where this official's ostentatious vote for the controversial bills was enough to swing some wavering peers to the government's side. The hierarchy received a significant note from the sovereign. They should remain assured that he knew how to protect the Church. They should also be mindful of the duty he had to fulfill as constitutional monarch.

All of the Catholic powers were exercised by the Vatican Council of 1869–70, thanks to the consideration and acceptance of the doctrine of papal infallibility. Austria in the summer of 1870 had a "federalist," somewhat "clerical" cabinet, but this did not prevent an abrupt announcement to the curia that the concordat was no longer in force. The Emperor wrote his pious mother that he, too, was affected by such a grave step. But it was the mildest and most correct reply to the unhappy decisions reached in Rome, and it would change the rights and the position of the Church in Austria not at all.[1]

Austria's Kulturkampf never approached Bismarck's in intensity, but Austrian citizens who were devout vowed to reverse the decisions of 1868, particularly the new School Law. Their deputies in the Lower House described themselves as "conservative" and did not usually bother to deny the Liberal epithet, "clerical." In the 1870s there was a loose confederation of such Conservative Clericals in both houses of parliament, and, with the announcement of Falkenhayn's appointment as Minister of Agriculture, they penetrated the inner council of the government.

The alliance of countryside and clergy was an axiom of European politics, and a large part of the Clerical attack upon the school system which the Liberals had created confined itself to

[1] Hugo Hantsch, *Die Geschichte Österreichs* (2d ed.; Graz, Vienna, and Cologne, 1953), II, 371–72, 408; Fritz Fellner, "Kaiser Franz Joseph und das Parlament," *Mitteilungen des österreichischen Staatsarchivs,* 9.Band (1956), 310–19; Anton Chroust, *Aufsätze und Vorträge zur fränkischen, deutschen und allgemeinen Geschichte* (Leipzig, 1939), p. 184.

the "noxious" economic workings of the system. Farmers
needed their healthy lads for the unending toil of the agricultural
routine, while their wives needed the girls of the family for
household chores. Why distract these plain but honest children
with a medley of academic subjects of no further use to them
after they had arrived at their twelfth birthday? Sooner or later
Taaffe would find himself attempting to answer these questions,
and it was no coincidence that he fended off the Clerical attack
on the school system as long as he commanded some rapport
with the Liberals, if only through colleagues who saw their
Liberal friends. Once the breach between Taaffe and his prede-
cessors was complete, he listened more carefully to Clerical
expostulations. That the essential structure of the educational
system remained intact was tribute to his honest desire to hold on
to what was generally worth while and also a sign that his Iron
Ring included elements which were quite akin to German Liberalism in looking askance at the Church's overseeing of education.

Prince Alfred Liechtenstein early in Taaffe's regime stated the
case for revision of the system of public schools. Sure that the
Austrian organization of the educational process violated the
natural rights of parent, of nationality, and of Church, he
detected in its workings a plot to denationalize and to dechris-
tianize the children of the realm. Austria had to reverse this
dangerous course by outright repeal, not by winking at infringement and nonenforcement of the law on the books. At worst,
the vanity of the legislators responsible for the original law
would suffer.[2]

Several months later the bishops of Bohemia petitioned Stremayr, one of the founders of the Liberal school system, to restore
the confessional character of the schools. Petty concessions,
they warned, would not avert moral ruin. If the ministry failed
to reply or to give a definite prospect of "betterment," the
bishops would cease all cooperation in executing the School
Law. The clergy would no longer collaborate with school autho-

[2] *SPA*, IX Session, p. 165, Oct. 29, 1879.

rities and would warn their parishioners of the dangers involved when their children attended such compulsory schools.[3]

Alois Liechtenstein and Lienbacher introduced bills in the Lower House aimed at a "rectification" of the Liberal system's "abuses" two days after the publication of the ultimatum, which had sorely irritated the Emperor. The Prince shrewdly called upon the cabinet to restore the rights of the provincial diets over educational affairs, particularly since school costs were overwhelming some communes and crownlands.[4] Lienbacher demanded an explicit modification of the Act of 1869. Obligatory attendance should begin when a child was six and end when he was twelve. The diets would have the right to extend compulsory schooling or to limit it to the completion of the fourteenth year. Only the student who demonstrated the legally prescribed knowledge of reading, writing, and arithmetic would graduate.[5]

In February, 1880, Taaffe relieved Stremayr of the Ministry of Education without having to replace him with the candidate advanced by the Clerical Conservatives. The "neutral" Conrad took over, to give the Liberals some comfort, while the Minister-President judiciously promised a full review of the workings of the School Law since 1869. Placated by such a pledge, Alois Liechtenstein immediately withdrew his motion.[6]

Lienbacher on the other hand sturdily defended his bill in the Lower House. When he reminded his listeners that the rule on eight years of compulsory schooling did not apply to Galicia, the Bukowina, Dalmatia, Istria, Carniola, Gorizia, and Gradisca, he made a strong point for the right of the diets to establish the number of years of compulsory attendance. He was less convincing in dilating upon the chances of immoral conduct when boys and girls of 13 and 14 years went home together after school through meadows and woods and in recalling the half-

---

[3] Gustav Kolmer, *Parlament und Verfassung in Oesterreich* (Vienna and Leipzig, 1902–14), III, 102.
[4] *SPA*, Beilagen, II, No. 134.   [5] *Ibid.*, No. 135.
[6] *SPA*, pp. 1379, 1412, Feb. 18, 1880.

frozen toes and fingers he wept over after a weary trudge to a distant school in his childhood. His curricular concepts were distinctly obscurantist. Why inflict constitutional history on farmers' offspring? Why employ a city lady to teach home economics to a girl who could learn better from her dear mother? Was there a greater misfortune than having all citizens become doctors of law, philosophy, and medicine?[7]

The reception was cool. Jaromír Čelakovský, a Young Czech, had the kindest of words for the eight years of compulsory universal education. But the diets should settle educational details, and Lienbacher's motion failed to define such competence.[8] The German Liberals were generally opposed, as expected. Victor Russ, who represented Karlsbad, contemptuously declared that a peasant's point of view should not be decisive in a state filled with rich cities of great culture. Did fingers freeze more at 13 and 14 than at 10 and 12? Before the era of compulsory schooling children had frequented dance halls, often with their parents, to be sure. Was this less likely to give rise to immorality than the exaggerated picture of young persons of both sexes going home together? Lienbacher forgot that many mothers worked, leaving half-grown daughters at home without protection.[9]

Responding for the government, Conrad had no objection to a parliamentary survey of the school question as long as there was no plan to give provincial diets the power to control the limits of compulsory attendance. Nor would he commit the cabinet to an approval of a reduction of compulsory schooling to six years.[10] Faced with these prohibitions, Lienbacher rewrote his bill. In the crownlands in which the eight-year rule had obtained, provincial legislation would in the future determine the nature of the curriculum of the last two years. Vocational training or "repeat" courses would be possible substitutes for previous academic programs. Adequacy in religion, reading, writing, and arithmetic was still the requirement for graduation. In deter-

---

[7] *Ibid.,* pp. 1417–18, 1420–21, 1423, Feb. 20, 1880.
[8] *Ibid.,* pp. 1428, 1430, Feb. 20, 1880.
[9] *Ibid.,* p. 1436, Feb. 20, 1880.   [10] *Ibid.,* p. 1439, Feb. 20, 1880.

mining the number of teachers to employ (and the covering budget), school authorities were not to count the enrollment in vocational and supplementary work.

For almost a year the controversies over language regulations, the Czech university, and electoral reform pushed aside the issue of compulsory schooling. Occasionally forensic lightning reminded the deputies that the Clericals expected a degree of satisfaction. On the very day of the publication of Stremayr's Language Ordinances, Alois Liechtenstein lambasted the Germans of Bohemia as no German ordinarily dared. He accused them of using their overwhelming majority in the province's Schulrat to injure the Czechs at every opportunity. They ignored the rule which prescribed a school for every forty children when Czechs were involved. They ordered district inspectors to prevent the failure of Czech pupils, and they always spent more from common funds for German schools and German students than for Czech. Liechtenstein was equally wrathful over spectral analysis, polarization of light, telescopes, microscopes, and scientific theories and hypotheses which the teachers themselves did not understand. He accused the schools of abbreviating religious instruction and of deliberately hindering children from making confession and attending mass.[11]

Late in 1880 Conrad issued an order which provided for at least one day free of regular academic work per week so Catholic students could participate in the sacraments of penance and of the Holy Eucharist, and in February, 1881, the Clerical Conservatives finally brought Lienbacher's bill to debate. Disgruntled by Conrad's firm insistence upon an amendment of the first bill, they made no effort to hide their dislike of the entire school system. *Das Vaterland* thundered that "our people" would not permit their children to be "drilled in accord with the recipe of Semitic-plutocratic-ideological liberalism."[12] Johann Oberndorfer, the Clerical representative of a Lower Austrian rural district, accused the public schools of producing youngsters who frequented skittle alleys, played cards, and swaggered about the streets smoking cigars instead of going to church and learning

---

[11] *Ibid.*, pp. 2684–85, April 26, 1880.   [12] Feb. 13, 1881.

the precepts of Christianity. The school libraries were full of
brochures glorifying revolution and Protestantism and depicting
the Catholic clergy as instigators of murder.[13]

The Liberals, as defendants, trotted out constitutional and
moral arguments. If there was a different educational system in
every province, would it not limit a citizen's right to move about
freely? Was not education a better check on usury and alcoho-
lism than mere laws? Would children assigned to watch livestock
be less immune to temptation than those walking home from
school?[14] Professor Eduard Suess satirized his foes, winning the
gallery's wild applause in return. He likened Lienbacher and his
friends to Alpine flora, pretty and fragrant, which never grew
alongside rice, grain, or other sustenance for the millions. The
deputies from the mountains likewise offered the masses nothing. As for the cabinet, it did not rule, it retailed—the prerogative of the empire and its own authority.[15] The gallery's sympathies were ineffective, for the Right carried the bill by a dozen
votes on February 25, 1881.

The Upper House, the abode of more than a few of the
former cabinet members and bureaucrats who had instituted the
state's school system, offered distinct resistance to Lienbacher's
bill. A majority continued to recommend compulsory schooling
to age fourteen in all crownlands other than Dalmatia, Galicia,
Carniola, the Bukowina, Istria, and Gorizia. In the last two
years the Minister of Education might lighten the obligations of
girls and children of the poorer classes in cities and market towns
by limiting instruction to a half-year, to half-day schooling, to
evening schools, or in other appropriate ways.[16] Conrad cautiously admitted that modifications in the existing compulsory
system were necessary and expressed his hope that the peers
would weigh both proposals well.[17] Confronted with such studied disinterest, the Upper House voted for its majority's bill.

[13] *SPA*, p. 3981, Feb. 15, 1881.
[14] Speeches of Adolf Promber, *ibid.*, pp. 3940, 3942, Feb. 11, 1881, and
of Anton Tausche, *ibid.*, pp. 4045–48, Feb. 22, 1881.
[15] *SPA*, pp. 4104–05, Feb. 24, 1881.
[16] *SPH*, IX Session, Beilagen, II, No. 132.
[17] *Ibid.*, p. 441, April 8, 1881.

The *Neue Freie Presse* humorously predicted that all of Conrad's rhetorical acrobatics would not save him from the wrath of the defeated Right, while *Politik* threatened that the Iron Ring would meditate upon "these and similar trifles" during the coming budget debate.[18] Though Lienbacher publicly blamed Conrad for the reverse, he realistically went to work on a compromise.[19]

The new formula prescribed compulsory schooling up to the age of fourteen, with graduation for proficiency in religion, reading, writing, and arithmetic. A country child, however, if his parents or guardians so requested, might attend supplementary or vocational school for a maximum of four hours weekly after a satisfactory completion of six years of schooling. For weighty reasons city pupils might secure the same modification. In short, parents would replace diets as the determining agents for compulsory education between ages twelve and fourteen.[20] In a series of caucuses, the German Clerical Conservatives swore they would vote for no more increases in taxation as long as there was no Minister of Education who agreed with their principles and was ready to support their limitations on compulsory schooling. Nor would they vote for the Galician *Transversalbahn* or for the Czech university until their school bill passed the parliament and received imperial sanction.[21]

What would be the Czech reaction, for it had been the Czechs who were most unhappy about encouraging a "personal" option in the matter of reducing the number of years a child had to attend school full time? On May 19 the Czech Club had a tumultuous meeting, in which Young and Old Czechs freely voiced their vexation with Liechtenstein's "little group of twenty who terrorized the entire Right." But *Pokrok* authoritatively announced that the new bill would have the backing of the entire Polish Club, the Club of Right Center, and all save three of the Czech Club.[22] Only a month before, the Emperor had directed

[18] *Neue Freie Presse,* April 9 and 13, 1881.
[19] *Ibid.,* April 23, 1881, *Abendblatt.*　　　[20] *SPA,* Beilagen, IV, No. 348.
[21] *Briefe zur deutschen Politik in Österreich von 1848 bis 1918,* ed. Paul Molisch (Vienna and Leipzig, 1934), pp. 275–76.
[22] Quoted in *Neue Freie Presse,* May 21, 1881, *Abendblatt.*

Conrad to prepare the changes at the University of Prague, and the Czechs might have needed the obstinate twenty.

Lienbacher's revised bill suffered the same fate as its predecessor, and the embarrassed cabinet, to prevent serious schism within the Iron Ring, was compelled to bring in its own version of a "reformed" educational system. The Lower House had accepted Lienbacher's bill by only 10 votes, and the peers had rejected it by only 9 votes. But the Czechs were conspicuously uncomfortable as they cast their ballots for the Clerical Conservative bill, while the Right in the Upper House was beginning to talk of forcing Conrad out of office.[23] To avert disaster, Taaffe had to move.

On January 23, 1882, Conrad laid before the Upper House a bill which preserved the established school system, with certain definite concessions to its avowed enemies. First, the Clericals noted with pleasure that the formula of 1869, "The public school has as its task the training of children, morally and religiously" now reversed the order of the modifying adverbs. Second, the bill permitted parents or communes to substitute half-day or part-time schooling for regular obligatory classes for children twelve to fourteen years of age. Third, a teacher had to prove special competence in instructing his students in the religious faith a majority of them professed. The last provision was a direct recognition of the complaints that Protestants and Jews often presided over predominantly Roman Catholic classes. The government carefully used the test of competence, not necessarily of allegiance, for the constitution would have been a hindrance to a rule that only Catholics could teach Catholics.[24]

The Liberals in the Upper House used every parliamentary device to delay full consideration of Conrad's proposal, but in the end their final weapon, abstention from the Special Commission's deliberations, permitted the Right to specify that school authorities were to pick teachers whose denominational affiliations definitely enabled them to direct the religious training of their students. To pacify the Poles, who dared not turn over the

[23] *Briefe,* ed. Molisch, pp. 276–77.   [24] *SPH,* Beilagen, III, No. 189.

Greek Catholic Ruthenes to non-Polish teachers, the Right exempted Galicia from this regulation, as it also exempted Dalmatia.[25]

Conrad had already told Berchem of the German Embassy that the stiffening of the regulation on the teacher's religious ties was an attempt to decrease the large number of Jewish public school teachers in Lower Austria. The Poles, knowing that teachers of their nationality and faith were active in most of the 1,800 Ruthene schools in Galicia, refused to comply with such a program, and, had Galicia not been exempted, they would have prevented the bill's passage.[26] The Czechs, according to *Politik,* were unhappy on another score. In view of the extraordinary differences in school conditions from one crownland to another, they condemned a revision of the School Law which failed to give the control of "fundamental principles," as well as of the practical implementation of these principles, to the diets.[27]

In the Upper House's debate the redoubtable Cardinal Schwarzenberg, speaking for the bishops of the realm, unenthusiastically endorsed the bill. Though the Church never could accept anything short of the confessional school, its prelates saw some improvements in the government's revisions and would not endanger their passage by resistance. Prince Adam Sapieha defended the special provisions for Galicia by stressing the large number of Jewish children in many Galician towns, for he made no attempt to hide the Polish disinclination to employ Jewish teachers for such youngsters. Count Friedrich Schönborn completed the Right's case by asserting that the religious test prescribed for teachers limited a Catholic pedagogue's freedom to move from one school to another as much as it did a Protestant's. Despite able Liberal rejoinders, the government's bill won the support of a majority of the peers.[28]

Just before the Lower House turned its attention to the sug-

[25] Kolmer, *Parlament,* III, 287–89.
[26] See Berchem's dispatch No. 442, A 6802, Nov. 8, 1882, UC-1, reel 215, frame 17.
[27] Quoted in *Neue Freie Presse,* Jan. 26, 1883.
[28] Kolmer, *Parlament,* III, 289–90.

gested changes, some members of the *Mittelpartei* of the Upper House, a generally reliable prop for the ministry's program in that House, submitted an interpellation for the cabinet's approval. Very briefly, they requested the ministers to issue a statement of the principles which the regime would follow in the future. The petitioners admitted the difficulty of composing such a credo, but they believed they could second the cabinet in such a program, which in the long run should have a soothing effect on the Reichsrat. Otherwise, indecision, misunderstanding, and bitterness would increase until passion became the ruling element in political life.

Taaffe assured the cabinet that the last sentence of the petitioners' message indicated their willingness to drop the interpellation if the government so desired, but his colleagues, obviously under much tension thanks to the coming tussle over the new school bill, reacted in interestingly partisan fashion. Ziemialkowski, the Pole, tartly declared that the gentlemen wanted to learn what they already knew. They should drop the matter or schedule it at a time less embarrassing to the regime. Falkenhayn, the Clerical, was quite sure that the interpellants merely wished to disconcert the cabinet, while Pražak, the Czech, feared that the posing of such an interpellation would indicate a great lack of confidence on the part of the *Mittelpartei* in the ministry. Dunajewski shared Pražak's fear of public and press reaction. A full reply would require a book, while a brief statement would encourage people to accuse the cabinet of not knowing how to answer.

Conrad and Welsersheimb attempted to mitigate their associates' displeasure. The Minister of Education reasoned that a governmental pronouncement might clear the air and destroy the honest doubts of its friends. The Minister of Defense reiterated his conviction that the cabinet had to state its views, though postponement of an answer to the interpellation would be the better course. Pino, the third German, counseled a very general reply to what he called a conglomerate of phrases, and Conrad, almost eagerly, suggested a promise that the government would not go beyond action already taken in national, constitutional, and religious affairs. Concretely, there should be a guarantee of no action leading to a concordat with the Church. Dunajewski quickly countered that such an answer would arouse the non-German nationalities and the Clericals against the cabinet, and his authoritative tone secured a unanimous decision to ask the *Mittelpartei* to desist from introducing its interpellation.[29]

If saved from a probing inquiry by its friends, the government experienced a heavy bombardment from the Left in the Lower House's debates on Conrad's version of a school law. There was no surprise when a few Ruthenes added their voices to the Liberal complaints, but the refusal of Professor František Tilšer to go along with the Czech Club's politic collaboration with the Clericals encouraged the Left's orators to hammer away at stricken Czech consciences, though the chief objective was always the Church and its devout adherents.

Tomaszczuk defied the teachers of the future to give a confessional slant to arithmetic, writing, geography, and natural science, though he soberly admitted that they could falsify history by injecting religious prejudice. What would happen in schools where three or four different denominations sat together in almost equal proportions? At the very least the new changes would spread religious hatreds.[30] Adolf Promber alleged that it was clericalism which had lost Austria Europe's sympathy in the disastrous post-1850 struggles. Certain circles still wanted to keep the peasants ignorant of the true nature of comets and other phenomena. But they would not accomplish this aim by putting the teacher's daily life under the control of the clergy.[31] Professor Suess, whose speech of April 18 was the most polished of the entire Liberal offensive, acidly condemned the bill's makers for plotting a "Vendée of ignorance" and mocked those who believed that adding hours to the public school's curriculum would cure religious indifferentism. One unresolved doubt occasioned by a simple Biblical text might affect a young person forever.[32]

---

[29] MRP 28, April 6, 1883.   [30] *SPA*, p. 10181, April 16, 1883.
[31] *Ibid.*, pp. 10191–92, April 16, 1883.
[32] *Ibid.*, p. 10266, April 18, 1883.

Closely allied to the Liberal fear of clericalism in the public schools was their concern over the teacher's academic and personal freedom and the content of the curriculum. How could Conrad brazenly claim that the new rules on the personal behavior expected of teachers raised the status of such teachers? demanded Suess. No real friend of pedagogy could have created such a degrading paragraph.[33] The sometimes derided Wurmbrand, quite alert and aroused in these debates, insisted that the priest would become a vigilante, checking closely on all the teacher did. In no time the Church would have the power to decide who could and who could not teach.[34]

The latitude given the commune in substituting half-day classes and "adult education" programs for the regular curriculum of the seventh and eighth years naturally infuriated the party which stood for a maximum of centralization and of educational opportunity. In tune with the era's accent on unblushing nationalism, Professor Wenzel Lustkandl asked why a teacher should not represent the state's point of view, rather than the family's or the Church's, in making moral conquests among his pupils. Was the state so insignificant and faulty that it had no power to educate? The Church might be satisfied with mere piety, but the state required men who worked as well as prayed. Again, those who recommended a widening of the franchise should not simultaneously endeavor to reduce educational opportunities, for greater popular participation in government automatically followed higher educational standards.[35] Early in the debate Hermann Hallwich invoked the inevitable shadow of the Prussian schoolmaster, triumphant at Königgrätz. Had not school attendance increased from 58 per cent to 87 per cent since 1869? The percentage of those liable to military duty who could read and write rose from 45 per cent to 67 per cent in the same period, but in 1883 the anguished demands of 1866 for better schools were forgotten in the campaign for confessionalism.[36]

[33] Ibid., p. 10263, April 18, 1883.
[34] Ibid., p. 10377, April 21, 1883.
[35] Ibid., pp. 10335–36, April 20, 1883.
[36] Ibid., pp. 10131–32, 10135, April 14, 1883.

Other Liberals underscored the public school's opportunity to meet the "social question," the ramifications of which certainly commanded the rapt attention of the Austrian public. Moritz Weitlof predicted that resentment would pervade the laboring class if school opportunities were reduced despite the generous contributions which big business and large landed interests made to education through taxes. Though he did not "flirt" with labor groups as others did, he had some idea of their reaction if the only hope they possessed, decent schooling for their children, were shattered.[37] Denying that existing agricultural and trade schools were adequate substitutes for the seventh and eighth years of the regular public schools, Professor Wilhelm Exner of Vienna's Hochschule für Bodencultur was particularly caustic about the conditions of apprenticeship. He invited his colleagues to drop in on Vienna's largest hospital for a look at the injuries boys under fourteen had suffered in trying to learn a trade. The state should prevent such sacrifice of the immature to a system which treated them unreasonably. The safeguards prescribed for factories should also apply to the shops owned by the masters of trades.[38]

The Polish refusal to accept for Galicia the provision which made the teacher's religion a test of his employment especially angered the Liberals. Promber contrasted Sobieski's gallant defense of Vienna two hundred years before with the contemporary Polish drive for *Unkultur*.[39] Bartholomäus von Carneri ruefully wondered how the Poles squared their resentment of Prussian oppressions and Germanization with their own Polonization of Galicia, but the Polish Club did not yield a single vote to the reproachful German Liberals.[40]

The Czechs were more vulnerable, for Richard Clam Martinič's stolid acquiescence in the new bill on the first day of debate inspired Tilšer to break party discipline. Defending the right of the poor to eight years of school, he insisted that the last

---

[37] *Ibid.,* p. 10246, April 17, 1883.
[38] *Ibid.,* pp. 10495, 10497, April 24, 1883.
[39] *Ibid.,* pp. 10194–95, April 16, 1883.
[40] *Ibid.,* p. 10207, April 17, 1883.

two years were especially valuable, whether a boy went into
business, handicrafts, a trade, or the army. If Czechs agreed to
allow communes to substitute special schools for the last two
years, the Germans would accuse them of pushing Germans to a
lower level of culture against the Germans' will. Friendship
between these two nationalities could exist only through a proper
school system, for it certainly would not flourish thanks to "deals
from above." Though he vigorously resented the "fact" that
schools for Czechs were not as good as those for Germans, he
well knew that the Czechs could secure the equality they needed
to compete with their German neighbors only through the public
schools.[41]

It was Rieger who undertook the onerous task of reducing
Tilšer's damaging statements to understandable proportions.
Cognizant of the abuse which the Young Czechs would hurl at
the Czech Club should it continue to collaborate on the school
bill, he first questioned the right of the Reichsrat to consider such
a bill. Since details of curriculum were at stake, not broad
principles, the central parliament's competence was dubious.
Since the new law, like the old law, would not apply to the entire
empire, as it should, he argued that autonomists like himself who
challenged both versions were the genuine *verfassungstreu* deputies. Having made this bow to theory, which gave the Liberals
an excellent chance to question his logic in voting for what he
deemed unconstitutional, Rieger then ticked off his reasons for
voting to please his allies and to make changes that were "good
for the people."

On the tricky question of the supervision of teachers' conduct,
he saw no reason for teachers to complain. They were officials,
all of whom were under discipline, and he was sure that their
superiors would not use political pressure upon them. The new
rules on compulsory schooling did not violate the principle of
eight years of attendance, and its backers wanted only to give the
poor a break. Already dispensations and violations had seriously impaired the hopes of the original law's framers, and there

[41] *Ibid.,* pp. 10145–47, 10149, April 14, 1883.

was an increasing awareness of the waste involved in keeping most children in classes until they were fourteen. A large number would never go further with formal education, and to keep them at twelve and thirteen from helping on Alpine farms and in Bohemian beet fields was an infringement of parental rights. A basic command of reading, writing, and arithmetic was enough for a Franklin, so deputies had no reason to worry about "degrading" the general level of knowledge. Since the Liberals did not demand the *removal* of the term "moral-religious" or even "religious-moral" from the general description of the law's purposes, he saw no logical reason to criticize the new rule concerning religious affiliation. A Jew or a confession-less person could not give Catholics moral and religious guidance.[42]

If Tilšer was an embarrassing exception to the government's united front, Schönerer balanced the score by promising to vote for most of the new provisions. Though he was anathema ordinarily to any coalition, the anticipation of a very close vote made him temporarily acceptable to the bill's friends. He vowed opposition to the proviso on the teacher's religious affiliation, for he wanted Christians to be the teachers even where Jews were in the majority in classes. Significantly proximate to this statement was his promise to fight all alien elements that might injure "practical Christianity," in particular that *vaterlandslose Speculantenthum* which aimed at the corruption of the German race. The great virtue of the changes was the opportunities the rural people would have to cut the expenses of local schools and to make use of their adolescent offspring in farm chores. Best of all, Galicia and Dalmatia would enjoy complete right to order their own school systems. He fervently hoped that such a special arrangement would lead to the political separation of these crownlands from the "one-time German Austrian lands of the Bund."[43]

Most audacious of the explanations of Galicia's special treatment was Count Adalbert Dzieduszycki's. Sarcastic references

[42] *Ibid.*, pp. 10150–57, April 14, 1883.
[43] *Ibid.*, pp. 10185–87, April 16, 1883.

to his youth (he was under forty) and to his aristocratic hauteur testified to the distaste he aroused among the German Liberals when he dismissed the bill as rather unimportant and certainly sometimes irrelevant and impractical for Galicia. The large number of non-Catholics there, notably in the towns, where the division was often 50–50, was sufficient reason to omit the rule on religious affiliation in this crownland. While his German Clerical friends shifted uneasily at their desks, Dzieduszycki pontificated against any religious clause which might estrange schoolmates of differing allegiances. With much disdain he asked the Liberal benches how Galicians could possibly fight to retain the eight-year rule when Galicia had only six years of compulsory schooling. And, with what must be reckoned supreme self-confidence, he referred only obliquely and complacently to the Ruthene protests that the bill would continue the tyranny of the Poles.[44]

Lienbacher, so closely identified with all German Clerical assaults upon the Liberal school system, and Conrad, whose continuing tenure in the cabinet no doubt depended upon a judicious steering of the government's bill, completed the Iron Ring's case. The Minister of Education made no effort to hide the cabinet's worry over the intensity of feeling which the proposals had aroused. Obviously irked by accusations of inconsistency, he spoke of the many studies and reports which had proved the advisability of modifications. Sternly denying that Taaffe's regime ever would surrender the supervision of education to the Church, Conrad played up the rural population's desire for an education they could afford. The original law's guiding principles remained, but the teachers in the future would have greater responsibility for the moral and religious training of the young.[45] Lienbacher, unusually restrained after several years of trying to persuade the government and its chief cohorts to "improve" state schooling, rather sensibly argued that there were not enough priests to give home instruction to Austria's growing number of children. When Liberals asserted that ser-

[44] *Ibid.,* pp. 10223, 10225–26, April 17, 1883.
[45] *Ibid.,* pp. 10211–12, 10217, 10219, April 17, 1883.

mons should inculcate religious conviction in the children, did they really believe that sermons destined for younger ears would hold the interest of the rest of the assembled faithful? Teachers who were loyal adherents of the creeds they professed had to substitute for overworked priests.[46]

The highly dramatic vote of April 19, on the question of going into special debate, was an eloquent foretaste of the final result. Of the actual members at that juncture, 349, no fewer than 339 were present. One failed to vote, but the Right, joined by Schönerer, his close associate Fürnkranz, and five ministers, won this first decisive engagement, 174 to 164. The gallery, packed with friends of the eight-year rule, hissed the future Pan-German leader and his ally, and the parliamentary stenographer dutifully recorded Ritter Georg's disdainful, "That bothers me just as little as the vulgar insults of the Judaized Viennese newspapers."[47] Voting on specific portions of Conrad's bill varied. Closest was the contest over the religious "test" for the teacher, which passed by a count of 169 to 163. Finally, on April 27, the Lower House accepted the bill *in toto* in a second reading.[48]

The German Clerical Conservative victory was a modest one, but it was the best obtainable under the circumstances. Neither bourgeois Czechs nor ministry relished the prospect of more sweeping changes that might inspire broad sectors of public opinion to an all-out struggle for "free," that is religiously neutral schools. Austria was indeed not France, but the reserves of power represented by the Liberal press, the not inconsiderable corps of lay teachers, the vociferous Young Czechs, and a bureaucracy still crowded with Liberal-oriented centralists were formidable. For the moment, discretion was indicated. Crown Prince Rudolf was recklessly anticlerical in his comments to German Embassy attachés who went hunting with him.[49] To Szeps he wrote sorrowfully of the change that had overtaken "this proud, liberal, hopefully developing Austria in a few

[46] *Ibid.*, p. 10384, April 21, 1883.
[47] *Neue Freie Presse*, April 20, 1883.
[48] Kolmer, *Parlament*, III, 297–98.
[49] See dispatch No. 50, A 7394, Dec. 10, 1882, UC-1, reel 215, frame 36.

years." The days of the Concordat would return. At least the
men of the Left had behaved magnificently in their desperate
attempts to head off reaction.[50] In more veiled manner he
opened an electrical exhibit at the Prater in the summer of 1883
with the profound hope that a sea of light might again illumine
the capital and that its progress would resume.[51] Yet somehow
the impatient young heir resented Taaffe's frank desire to skip
these opening ceremonies, and he suspected that Pražak and
Archduke Albrecht were hatching some sort of revenge upon
him for what he had said. Convinced that the "Slavicizing"
policy was driving Austria to ruin, he passionately declared to
Szeps his preference for Liberal Hungary. If Hungary, the
bulwark against complete reaction, should experience Austrian
intervention, then revolution and total imperial collapse would
be the well-deserved outcome.[52]

The Emperor kept his own counsel, but his constant worry
over the decline of German as a universally known and utilized
language in the empire was guarantee that relaxations of compulsory schooling had their limits. Taaffe finally had paid an
installment upon his debt to the German Clerical Conservatives. Without this token of gratitude he might well have lost
their constant allegiance. Until and unless he arrived at an
understanding with their deadly antagonists, the Liberals, they
would have to be satisfied. The ever-present chance of such a
rapprochement kept them in line. They had already learned that
in every coalition someone gets only the crumbs.

---

[50] Letter of April 22, 1883, in *Kronprinz Rudolf: Politische Briefe an
einen Freund, 1882–1889*, ed. Julius Szeps (Vienna, Munich, and Leipzig,
1922), p. 46.

[51] Kolmer, *Parlament*, III, 302.

[52] Letters of Aug. 16 and 29, 1883, in *Kronprinz Rudolf: Politische
Briefe*, pp. 54–55, 57–59.

8 The Nordbahn Controversy

Roman Catholic ardor for confessional education and Czech importunacy in linguistic affairs had their counterpart in the 1880s in a radical German nationalism whose chief prophet was Georg von Schönerer. In the early part of the decade he had collaborated with Heinrich Friedjung, a historian who had lost his post at the Handelsakademie in Vienna because of his political agitation, with Victor Adler, a well-fixed physician with a heart for the underdog, and with such pronounced German nationalists as Engelbert Pernerstorfer and Otto Steinwender in constructing a political statement that blended social consciousness with pride in the "Teutonic mission." In 1882, the year of the formulation of this Linz Program, Schönerer saw no harm in sitting down with men of Jewish antecedents such as Friedjung and Adler, for these young intellectuals were so thoroughly assimilated that they were critical of Christian German Austrians who neglected their ethnic ancestry. He was of quite another mind, however, in fearing the economic competition of Jewish refugees from Russia and in concluding that big business and high finance benefited Jewish entrepreneurs at the cost of hard-working German Austrians.

The Linz Program was German nationalist in its willingness to sever Galicia, the Bukowina, and Dalmatia from the Austrian complex of crownlands. It would have made German the official *Staatssprache,* taught as a compulsory subject in all secondary schools. It was anti-laisser-faire in stressing social security, nationalization of railroads, a progressive income tax, a tax on Bourse transactions, effective factory inspection, a normal workday, and limits on woman and child labor. As democratic ballast, it demanded a progressive extension of the franchise and true freedom of press, association, and meeting.

The authors of the program sincerely believed that peasants, artisans, and small businessmen were increasingly helpless in the face of developing industrialism and finance capitalism. The internationalism of the Viennese moneyed circles intensified their anger over the undoubted misery of thousands of German Austrians who through little fault of their own no longer were proudly self-reliant. Economic insecurity and unsettling social mobility in German Austria coincided with the triumph of Teutonic ingenuity and might in Hohenzollern Germany. If peasants and workers also had their problems under Bismarck, at least he seemed to be moving toward their relief. Schönerer and men who thought as he did needed but one controversial issue to convince the resentful and frustrated that Taaffe and his confederates were as insensible to social justice as they were to the "just" claims of Germanism. As if made to order, the question of renewing the franchise of the great Kaiser Ferdinand-Nordbahn in 1884–85 afforded Schönerer and an incongruous following of anti-Semites, anti-Liberals, and sincere democrats a fine chance to try Taaffe's resourcefulness to the uttermost.

This historic railway had secured its franchise on March 4, 1836, for a line between Vienna and Bochnia in Galicia, including the necessary spurs and a special connection to the salt mines at Wieliczka. The work gangs reached Olmütz by October, 1841, though the costs of construction kept earnings in this year to 1.48 per cent. The entrepreneurs begged to be allowed to relinquish their rights to proceed from Leipnik (Lipník nad Bečvou) to Bochnia, embarrassed as they were over disappointing dividends and by depression, but the firm refusal of the government plus a cash advance of 8,000,000 gulden from the Rothschild banking house revived their spirits.

By 1855 earnings had reached 15.55 per cent, and the company petitioned for the right to extend their concession to Kraków and Przemyśl. They quickly regretted this step, and the state did relieve them to the extent of requiring the line to go only as far as Kraków. The company eventually controlled 1,312.367 kilometers of track, and the fat income its stockholders derived from their shares excited the general public to demand an end to the franchise, which was to run out in March, 1886.[1]

After some public and press discussion of the chances of the state's assumption of the Nordbahn, the cabinet addressed itself to the general problems in a session of May 19, 1883. Pino told his colleagues that the company had asked for a renewal of the franchise or for talks which might lead to this. A ministerial commission meanwhile had decided that the government's right to expropriate the line was legally incontestable, and Pino was sure that the directors knew quite well that their only chance lay in a new but considerably restricted concession. As Minister of Commerce, Pino was definitely in favor of nationalizing the Nordbahn, insisting that annual income would exceed the amortized costs by 3,000,000 gulden. Such a favorable situation would permit rate decreases, to say nothing of the authority the state would win by taking over such a strategically important line. Possibly realizing that the Nordbahn's directorate was not without influence, Pino ended his comments with a lengthy list of guarantees the company should make if a new concession was granted. He stressed the need to force the Nordbahn's tariffs into line with the state-operated railways, and he was rather crisp in underlining the Nordbahn's failure in the past to serve public interests.

Dunajewski, the increasingly influential Finance Minister, wanted merely to tell the Nordbahn that a governmental commission would study its future. It was obvious that this eloquent Pole was fearful that the state would pay too high a price for the line, since the price would be based upon an annual income

[1] Aloys von Czedik, *Der Weg von und zu den österreichischen Staatsbahnen* (Teschen, Vienna, and Leipzig, 1913), I, 29–33, 419.

derived from tariffs which the state would be compelled to lower once it assumed control. He consequently recommended that the regime keep strongly in mind the possibility of granting a new concession. To reinforce his case, he reported that the company, to get a new franchise, would immediately refund 10,000,000 gulden in guaranteed advances and interest thereon. Should parliament deny a concession, the receipt of this sum would be dubious.

Taaffe set the tone for further deliberations by declaring that clearly there could be no renewal of the franchise in its original form. Conrad wanted the government's experts to act as if nationalization were the expressed goal when they negotiated with the line. Falkenhayn opposed such a prejudicing procedure, though he personally seemed to feel that military reasons and the past tradition of nationalizing railroads pointed to the state's acquisition of the Nordbahn sooner or later. The cabinet finally agreed to have its experts go into all of the issues fully, with no particular solution in mind, save for the decision not to renew the old franchise as such.[2] That Dunajewski had made a distinct impression is borne out by the agenda of the cabinet meeting of June 2, 1883, at which the ministers discussed the initiation of negotiations with the Nordbahn for a new agreement.[3]

Pino still was a proponent of nationalization at this meeting, but circumstances already were dictating the granting of a new concession. Presumably it was agreed that the concession would last fifty years, since such an offer on the part of the government would force the Nordbahn into surrender on other points. Furthermore, a longer period of amortization would eventually work out for the good of the state. As re-insurance, however, the ministers subscribed in principle to the idea of dating the state's right to redeem the line from January 1, 1896.[4]

In Prague in the late summer of 1883 Herbst and Ernst Plener

[2] MRP 37, May 19, 1883.
[3] According to the *Tagesordnungen* of the MRP. The protocol itself has been destroyed.
[4] These decisions are gleaned from the references to the cabinet meeting of June 2, 1883, which are found in MRP 69, Nov. 6, 7, 8, 1883.

gossiped over the future of the Nordbahn, and the former confided that he thought he would sell what shares he owned. The current quotation was not too disadvantageous, and then one could never predict what would happen when public opinion, notoriously anti-Nordbahn, was compounded with the regime's inscrutable resolves. Very unfavorable decisions might well win the support of the Lower House. Already there was a rumor that the Emperor had sold his shares to buy a domain. Herbst believed that the state should buy out the company, and the younger Plener wrote his father that he generally agreed with this opinion.[5]

A full-scale cabinet discussion of the nature of the new concession took place on November 6, 7, and 8, 1883. Pino continued to champion nationalization. If the state bought all of the stock at 140 gulden a share, it could finance the operation through 5 per cent bonds payable in ninety years. Judging by the line's recent surpluses, he estimated that the government eventually would have 15,000,000 gulden to help wipe out the imperial deficit. Dunajewski was resolutely opposed to such "interference" with private initiative. State control would inevitably mean reduction in rates, and the margin of loss might be made up only after the passage of years. The government also would assume a debt of 34,206,050 gulden in taking over the Nordbahn.

Pino's preference for nationalization evidently was not deeply rooted, for he acquiesced, almost eagerly, in what Dunajewski had said. Taaffe briefly informed the rest of the cabinet that confidential discussions of a new franchise were already under way with representatives of the Nordbahn, and the ministers then voted their approval of such negotiations. Despite Welsersheimb's advocacy of a maximum term of fifty years, the cabinet set a new terminal date at May 5, 1966, to coincide with the expiration of the concession for the Moravian-Silesian Nordbahn.[6]

The Liberal deputy Michael Matscheko of Vienna interpel-

[5] Nachlass Plener, Karton 16, Nos. 297–298.
[6] MRP 69, Nov. 6, 7, 8, 1883.

lated the government on February 29, 1884, as to what it was
doing about the approaching expiration of the Nordbahn's concession. He asserted that the high rates on transporting coal
were hampering industry, that the exorbitant freight rates were
injuring commerce, and that Vienna especially was suffering
from the tariffs levied upon the meat and produce brought in by
the Nordbahn.[7]

Next day Taaffe told his colleagues that this interpellation
forced the government to come to a speedy conclusion of the
question. Interestingly enough, previous cabinet discussions, to
judge from the protocols, never reckoned with public reaction or
with the possibilities of a fight in the Reichsrat. Suddenly Taaffe
was impatient to get the new concession into effect, no doubt
because he knew from the beginning that expert politicians with
a lust for notoriety would appreciate the chance to scrutinize the
Nordbahn and its lush earnings.[8]

On March 3 and 5, 1884, the cabinet worked out the final
details of the new agreement. The state would have the right to
acquire the Nordbahn only on and after May 5, 1904. If the state
did not terminate the franchise before it ran out in 1966, the
entire property would go to the state without any compensation
to the stockholders. The Nordbahn promised to pay back in
cash all state subsidies, plus interest, which had been received to
forward the creation of the Moravian-Silesian Nordbahn, a concession which Alois von Czedik valued at 22,440,000 gulden.[9]
In addition the Nordbahn was to make substantial reductions in
its rates and to construct certain new stretches desired by the
government.

Taaffe spent some time discussing the possibility of renewing
the concession administratively. A commission had considered
the constitutionality of such a move, and it finally had recommended submitting the franchise to the Reichsrat. The cabinet
also decided that it would be more politic, leaving constitutional

---

[7] Gustav Kolmer, *Parlament und Verfassung in Oesterreich* (Vienna
and Leipzig, 1902–14), III, 393.
[8] MRP 16, March 1, 1884.   [9] Czedik, *Staatsbahnen,* I, 419.

interpretations aside, to allow the Reichsrat to deal with the new arrangements for the Nordbahn.[10]

Meanwhile the Reichsrat faced a flood of petitions demanding state assumption of the Nordbahn. On April 2, Schönerer presented a plea from the German National Association of Vienna, which attainted the house of Rothschild as the guiding genius behind the "Vampire of the Austrian March." In his speech the future Pan-German idol accused the press of being silent because they were "bought."[11] Again, on the evening of April 21 about 1,500 persons assembled in the Volkshalle of Vienna's new Rathaus to listen to Karl Lueger evaluate the recently published text of the new franchise. Lueger was the epitome of bluntness in his attack on what the regime had done, alleging that the state, because of its need for credits, had become the pawn of international capitalism and the press it controlled. Why should the government take over unprofitable lines and at the same time leave an enterprise bringing in 13,000,000 gulden in net profits every year to a private corporation?[12]

The *Neue Freie Presse* did its best to disparage Lueger and Schönerer, the spirits behind the popular resentment against the governmental proposal. Lueger was the "hero of ward democracy" whose speeches always resembled Zola's novels, "where every woman was a Hetaira, every girl a whore, every bourgeois 'on the make,' the world a hell of crime and hypocrisy." Schönerer compared unfavorably with his father, who had won fame and wealth during the climactic years of railroad construction. The son of the man who had surveyed the route of the Nordbahn for S. M. von Rothschild was the current apostle of anti-Semitism, the challenger of the doctrine of equal rights for all citizens.

These two men had indicated how imperative it was to note well the line between socialism and bourgeois society. Many had stepped over the line without realizing what they were doing,

---

[10] MRP 17, March 3 and 5, 1884.
[11] Kolmer, *Parlament*, III, 393–94.
[12] *Neue Freie Presse*, April 22, 1884; *Das Vaterland*, April 22, 1884.

and communism, unconsciously picked up and practiced, could become a real danger for Austria. The agreement with the Nordbahn was a compromise, warned the powerful Liberal paper, and the discussion that followed should not degenerate into an inflammatory campaign against capitalism and property.[13]

In securing the Emperor's formal consent to submit the agreement to the Reichsrat, Pino repeated his conviction that state assumption of the line would be the best solution. But other circumstances forced the new concession. Prospects for raising a loan to cover expropriation were poor, and the state, by compromising, would receive substantial material advantages. Best of all, the new bargain afforded the state a breathing spell in which the increasingly powerful state lines could work competitively against the Nordbahn and its artful stockholders.[14]

Meanwhile the avowed anti-Semitic elements in the rowdy political life of the capital were stressing the tie between the Rothschilds and the Nordbahn. On April 29 they met to crow over the resignation of Josef Kopp as deputy from the Mariahilf ward in Vienna. This "lackey" of Magyar cattle barons, of the Rothschilds, and of the "Jewish press" had refused to heed the demands of his voters to fight for nationalization. The police official who was necessarily present at this hate session warned one of the demogogues only when the latter asserted that freedom in Hungary meant freedom to murder Christian maidens.[15] Undoubtedly the years of smoldering resentment against the prosperous Nordbahn played directly into the hands of the strident anti-Semites and thus colored the entire controversy with extraneous but eventually potent propaganda. Viennese anti-Semitism originally fed on economic discontent, and the disputes over the Nordbahn's franchise were landmarks in the disheartening background of prejudice into which Hitler was born.

Strong disapproval of the new agreement was not limited to

[13] April 23, 1884.
[14] Kabinetts-Kanzlei, Vortrag 1484, April 23, 1884.
[15] *Neue Freie Presse,* April 29, *Abendblatt,* and 30, 1884.

Vienna. The provinces also exerted great pressure upon their parliamentary representatives, so that there never was any real chance of the first proposal's being accepted. In the first reading Max Menger caustically declared that the big capitalists of the empire could do no better for themselves were they personally sitting in the cabinet and asked why Taaffe continued to pose as the friend of the "little man." Schönerer continued to call for nationalization on the basis of physical values alone and read a great series of petitions supporting his solution.[16] The Club of Right Center and the Centrums Club, which usually cooperated with Taaffe, unanimously agreed to reject the cabinet's transaction with the Nordbahn just as the bill was referred to the Railway Committee. Lueger's prophecy of a general disaffection was coming to pass.[17]

A special subcommittee of the Lower House asked the government to undertake new negotiations on May 22, and a chastened cabinet met to consider this total rebuff on May 31. Pino suggested the renewal of *pourparlers,* with the idea of working out a concession which the ministry could promulgate administratively, but Dunajewski declared that such flouting of public opinion was no longer possible. Other members of the cabinet endorsed the idea of moving toward nationalization, and Falkenhayn reported that the overwhelming majority in the Lower House would accept nothing else. The entire cabinet then directed Pino to renew his conversations with the Nordbahn, the objective being state assumption of the line.[18]

As insurance against unpleasant surprises, Taaffe suggested asking the Oberste Gerichtshof for a clarification of the rights of both state and Nordbahn, since he understood that the railway was asking a foreign university for such a legal opinion. The Minister-President had first pointed out that an opinion had not been needed for a mere concession. Nationalization, he implied, made such expert counsel of especial importance, and the cabinet concurred on June 14.[19]

Yet Pino reported on October 8 that his negotiations with the

[16] *Das Vaterland,* May 3, 1884.   [17] *Ibid.,* May 4 and 6, 1884.
[18] MRP 39, May 31, 1884.   [19] MRP 43, June 14, 1884.

representatives of the Nordbahn had convinced him that nationalization could not take place. The *Tagesordnungen* of the
cabinet meetings between June 14 and October 8 give no hint of
this distinct change in procedure, and Pino's announcement of
what he had been doing during the summer presumably did not
arouse comment or questioning by any member of the cabinet.
Taaffe merely added that the business should end before Easter,
1885, unless, of course, the state had to initiate expropriation
proceedings.[20]

It is not clear what had changed Pino's mind or what had in
effect persuaded his colleagues again to brave parliamentary
tempers with a concession rather than with a bill for nationalization. It is singular that the minutes of the meeting of October
8 give no hint of disagreement with what amounted to Pino's
disobedience to a mandate from the cabinet. One can only
surmise that Dunajewski continued to express concern over the
preliminary costs of assuming control or that the majority of the
cabinet was hopeful that the deputies would accept, as many had
said or implied, a concession that encouraged private enterprise
without damaging the rights of the public.

On October 31 Taaffe acquainted the cabinet with Schmerling's answer to the questions posed by the cabinet during the
previous summer. The president of the Oberste Gerichtshof
declared that the Nordbahn did indeed remain owner of the
permanent right of way and of all other properties connected
with its undertaking after its concession expired. After the end
of its franchise, however, it would not transport persons or goods
in return for payment, not even coal from its own collieries.

Schmerling also was of the opinion that the Nordbahn had no
legal right to demand a renewal of its concession or precedence
over other suitors should the government permit a private concern to operate its network. He asserted that the state had the
power to expropriate this railway if the common welfare so
required, but he practically nullified this statement by declaring
that the Reichsrat would have to pass a new law on the subject of
the expropriation of railroads. Previous ordinances and laws in

[20] MRP 57, Oct. 8, 1884.

his opinion were not applicable because of almost total difference in the conditions which had to be appraised.[21]

Taaffe on November 16 apprised his associates of a "supplementary opinion" he had secured from Schmerling in case the
state had to take measures leading to expropriation. The president of the court was absolutely sure that the state had every
right to expropriate property if the common welfare of its citizens so required. But he was just as convinced that a special
law was required to institute proceedings against the Nordbahn.[22]

Two days later Pino reported his latest compromises with the
gentlemen of the Nordbahn. The latter had continued to insist
on a concession lasting sixty years, particularly in view of their
agreement to reduce rates should dividends exceed 8 per cent per
year. Pino was confident that his stubborn opponents eventually
would give in on the length of the concession, particularly since
they had not contested the cabinet's decision to fix the time of the
state's right to purchase at January 1, 1904.[23]

Taaffe and the cabinet then pondered the strategy to adopt in
securing parliamentary approval of the new concession. Dunajewski was rather dubious of preliminary negotiations with the
leaders of the majority before the Nordbahn and the state had
reached accord on all issues, and he reminded his fellow ministers that these leaders had approved the first concession without
being able to secure its acceptance. Ziemialkowski feared that
acquainting deputies with those points on which the Nordbahn
might eventually capitulate would stimulate parliamentary demands for modifications of all decisions heretofore reached by
hard bargaining. Taaffe significantly remarked that the public
might well accuse the regime of weakness should it yield to the

[21] MRP 62, Oct. 31, 1884. The *Neue Freie Presse* published this
Gutachten, Jan. 31, 1885.

[22] MRP 65, Nov. 16, 1884.

[23] The damage suffered by MRP 63, Nov. 3, 1884, leaves uncertain the
cabinet's reaction to Pino's suggestion of the year 1901 as the desired
date for possible redemption. The minutes of the meeting of Nov. 18 indicate that the cabinet agreed with Dunajewski on Nov. 3 to stick to
Jan. 1, 1904, as the date desired.

urgencies of parliamentary leaders before putting its version of a concession before both houses.[24]

Pino reported on November 29 that the Nordbahn continued to insist on a sixty-year concession, promising in return the complete extinction of the debt of the Moravian-Silesian Nord-bahn. He had suggested that the eventual agreement should fix a dividend of 120 gulden as the maximum profit per share before an automatic reduction of rates. Though Welsersheimb contin-ued to voice honest distaste for anything short of nationalization, the cabinet decided to get in touch with the influential leaders of the Reichsrat to attempt to secure their approval of the new agreement.[25]

Just before Christmas Taaffe told the cabinet that he had informed the chiefs of the Lower House's majority of the course of negotiations and that he felt there were better chances for parliamentary approval of a concession. He wanted speedy conclusion of the talks with the Nordbahn, so that the Upper House might consider the provisions exhaustively, and Duna-jewski no doubt added to the cabinet's hope for a quick ending to the bargaining by reporting a conversation he had had with Baron Rothschild and Dr. Mauthner. He pointed out to the powers within the Nordbahn's hierarchy what provisions they still had to compromise and he gained from this impromptu exchange the impression that the Nordbahn would give in.[26]

The destruction and heavy damage suffered by the protocols of cabinet meetings held in 1885 prevent a description of the reaction of Taaffe's colleagues to the stiff battle which even a modified concession brought on in that year. The *Tagesord-nungen* reveal that on January 5 and 7 the cabinet decided upon the definitive text of an agreement with the Nordbahn and that Taaffe reported on January 19 as to the measures he had taken, with the president of the Lower House, to facilitate parlia-mentary handling of the new franchise, which was introduced the following day.

The *Neue Freie Presse* singled out the salient changes from

[24] MRP 66, Nov. 18, 1884.   [25] MRP 70, Nov. 29, 1884.
[26] MRP 79, Dec. 22, 1884.

the first proposal. The new concession would expire at the end of 1940, and this clause specifically included the Moravian-Silesian Nordbahn. The state's right to redeem the line would go into effect in 1904, but the Nordbahn's directors would have the right to refuse such a redemption were it offered in terms of imperial bonds. Rates could never drop below those set by the western lines, unless the Nordbahn itself decided to reduce them. The government's right to fix tariffs would be exercised only as long as dividends on a share currently worth 1,050 gulden did not fall below 112 gulden.[27]

In the general debate Taaffe was present, flanked by Pino, Dunajewski, Pražak, Falkenhayn, and Ziemialkowski, for *Národní Listy* had reported that seven Clericals would vote contra and that six Poles and six Czechs were going to abstain. *Politik* gave somewhat differing estimates, but it was clear that the Iron Ring was in trouble.[28]

The Left prepared a trap by deciding to insist on a roll-call vote. The cabinet riposted with rumors to the effect that the Emperor wanted a settlement of the Nordbahn affair before the new elections. Dr. Rieger complained bitterly of the reckless attacks on the deputies by "political trash," who dared question the probity of any parliamentarian who considered voting to renew the agreement. The German Clerical Conservatives were highly vulnerable to demagogic fire, for they had castigated high finance for years in their campaign to rescue the "little man" from his tormentors. Alois Liechtenstein went after the house of Rothschild in his attempt to avert accusations of double-dealing. Whatever profits the state might make from the revised arrangements the Rothschilds would recover in the next loan they floated for the state, he declared. Franz von Zallinger of Bozen denounced the Right for supporting the government in a sellout of the peasants and lower middle class. With penetrating sarcasm he attributed the cabinet's lame justifications to the state's dependence upon the Rothschilds. Eternally reduced to sycophantic attendance upon the great banking house, the min-

---

[27] Jan. 20, 1885, *Abendblatt*.
[28] Quoted, *ibid.,* March 21, 1885, *Abendblatt*.

istry should have paraded under its true colors, "The Dunajewski cabinet, called Taaffe's."

Since Liberals joined in the chorus against vested interests and
vied with German Clericals and Nationalists in their sympathy
for all who were not stockholders in the Nordbahn, the cabinet
had to exert maximum pressure upon its whips in the Lower
House to salvage the bill. Like sans-culottes jeering at staid
bourgeois tribunes, ultranationalist students in the galleries
shouted abuse at all who seemed to admit that the government
and Nordbahn deserved a hearing. Anti-Semitism tinged their
remarks, and there can be no doubt that popular agitation linked
the prosperous line with the opulent Rothschilds and with Jewish
lawyers who were integral cogs in the Liberal political organization. The House's sergeant at arms could order the firemen to
eject Schönerer's noisy young friends from the galleries.[29] It was
quite another matter to erase from many rural and lower middle
class minds a growing conviction that the Jews had the government in an unbreakable vise.

Though Rieger and Clam Martinič worked hard to keep the
Czech Club in line, it was clear that the bill would pass only if a
proposal from the Coronini Club met with the cabinet's approval. This proposal required the Nordbahn to duplicate the
rates charged by the western lines and to cut rates when the latter
did unless its dividends dropped below 100 gulden per share.
As for the hotly debated coal rates, these were to match the
levels of the western lines as long as the Nordbahn was able to
pay more than 100 gulden in dividends.[30]

Pino wryly assured the Lower House that a state-controlled
Nordbahn would not be able to offer lower rates than the ones
suggested by the Coronini Club, and he defended the new coal
rates with a promise to be mindful of the interests of all big
industry. A handful of important Liberals absented themselves
from the vote on going into special debate, a gesture which
justified the government's acquiescence in the amendments

[29] Kolmer, *Parlament,* III, 400–4.
[30] *Neue Freie Presse,* March 23, 1885, *Abendblatt.*

submitted.[31] On March 27, after the defeat of a motion which would have saddled the next Reichsrat with the onus of deciding on the agreement, the deputies accepted the new concession for the Nordbahn, 159 to 148.

The Nordbahn still had to agree, and Pino, after the Upper House signified its approval of the Lower House's bill, spent most of the summer haggling over a few last details. In July he told his colleagues he expected the Nordbahn to give in on coal rates and on an issue of preferred stock which the directors had suggested.[32] On August 3 Baron Rothschild had a conference with Taaffe in which he declared that the new agreement badly hurt his interests, though he promised to secure its quick approval by the stockholders at a January meeting. In addition, he guaranteed the election of an obvious government choice to the Nordbahn's administrative council. The news was conveyed, significantly, to Dunajewski, momentarily at Ischl.[33] Rothschild was as good as his word, so that Franz Joseph was able to sign the agreement on September 6, 1885.

The Nordbahn controversy had revived in Franz Joseph's consciousness all of the resentments of 1866. Extremely sensitive to manifestations of devotion to Bismarck and the Hohenzollerns, he was thoroughly aroused by the raucous student demonstrations in Vienna as the young ultranationalists swarmed to Schönerer's anti-Nordbahn banners. For some years he had distrusted the Deutsche Schulverein, founded in 1880 to "defend" Germanism in Austrian educational affairs. Refusing to believe that its members were nonpolitical, he condemned university students who helped multiply its branches and worried over the ties it had "abroad." Taaffe tried to calm Franz Joseph's fears, though he realized that the organization's propaganda was a threat to eventual peace in Bohemia. In the South Tirol he welcomed its thrusts against Italian irredentism, and probably he was secretly glad that a poll of provincial governors, undertaken to satisfy the sovereign, discouraged the inauguration of tough measures against a German society.

[31] *Ibid.*, March 24 and 25, 1885.   [32] MRP 52, July 11, 1885.
[33] *Politischer Nachlass*, pp. 262–63.

What was found to be subversive in a German club might also be subversive in a non-German organization, and Taaffe was not eager, as Minister of the Interior, to outrage foes and friends alike by adding to the state's array of investigators and spies.[34]

The controversy over the Nordbahn also deflected the Crown Prince's attention from the Minister-President's iniquities to the challenge of German irredentism. He found the worst of the Sudeten agitators nauseating, and he admitted that the existence of the Dual Alliance did not moderate the unpleasantness of their appeals to Bismarck's Germans. He solemnly warned Szeps that he would reveal wondrous things to him concerning the same Alliance. Was it secure? What if it dissolved? For once Rudolf lost sight of "Slavicization" in his obvious trepidation over the basic loyalties of German Austrians.[35]

If incipient Pan-Germanism outraged the chief personalities of the regnant house, it was the state's financial embarrassment and the agonizingly close balance of power in the Lower House which engaged the ministry's attention in devising the ultimate compromise. It is ironic that Pino, who at first was enthusiastic for nationalization, had to take the lead in securing approval of the franchise, limited though it was. Dunajewski's stubborn insistence on a limited continuation of private direction had its reward in Zallinger's contemptuous phrase. Nonetheless, the entire operation, if far from fully revealed in what is left of the ministerial minutes, was typical of the skill which Taaffe and his confederates often mustered in tight spots. Though the *Neue Freie Presse* scornfully described the"Coronini men" as opportunists who surged from Right to Left in search of honey, it had to admit that their votes carried the day. And though it showered unpleasantness upon Pino—Herbst's review of the Commerce Minister's exposé was likened to a surgeon's laying open "every sick muscle with his scalpel"—Pino's cautious manner and his

[34] Paul Molisch, *Geschichte der deutschnationalen Bewegung in Oesterreich* (Jena, 1926), pp. 137–39.

[35] Letter of Oct. 25, 1885, in *Kronprinz Rudolf: Politische Briefe an einen Freund, 1882–1889,* ed. Julius Szeps (Vienna, Munich, and Leipzig, 1922), pp. 125–27.

refusal to rush or antagonize any possible supporters formed a classic example of the Taaffe technique. For all of the ugliness which the Nordbahn issue aroused, the cabinet's calm direction of the negotiations with company and with parliament ended in a compromise that paved the way for an eventual nationalization whose consummation caused scarcely a syllable of comment in 1906. Taaffe and Dunajewski had to live with the realities of a deficit, which certainly colored the government's relations with the great banking interests and the corporations they controlled. The Minister-President was aware of the dangers which his coalition faced when its members voted for an unpopular measure. The imminence of new elections hardly diminished the worries which some of the most loyal adherents felt. Yet he saved the bill by a shrewd compromise that netted enough Liberal abstentions to offset defections on the Right. The resolution of the Nordbahn crisis was a first-class parliamentary operation. It goes far to explain Franz Joseph's continuing dependence upon Taaffe, who had saved state funds for more important military matters despite popular uproar. The Emperor admired such victories over the mob, especially when "defense" was at stake.

9 Social Radicalism at the Gates

The historian who sifts through what remains of the reports that came to Taaffe in his capacity as Minister of the Interior is left with the feeling that social radicalism preoccupied the thought of all of the empire's chief executives and police. From Trieste, Lemberg, Innsbruck, Steyr, Cattaro, Brünn—the brief biographies of suspects poured in. If the Paris Commune had been the prelude, the fanatical revolutionary movement in Alexander II's Russia and the resilient Social Democratic resistance to Bismarck in Germany provided full-stage dressing for the worried concern of men responsible for a state as ill assorted as Austria. Potocki wrote from Galicia that his officials and his people would do their duty against the nihilists in neighboring "Congress Poland," though of course there always were hotheads in the land. Almost resignedly, he repeated an earlier opinion. Unless nihilism became firmly established on the other side of Galician frontiers, his crownland would be safe.[1] In another report the watchful police of Vienna guardedly described the relations between the Lower House's Ferdinand Kronawetter and the radical wing of the socialists, who seemingly feared that their eloquent friend was using them for his own political pur-

[1] Verwaltungsarchiv, Vienna, Innern-Präsidiale, 22, Karton 821, No. 237, Jan. 9, 1880.

poses.[2] More ominously, the police in Prague retailed the news that Julius Grégr, owner of the *Národní Listy,* was listening favorably to socialist offers of support in return for publicizing their ideas in his columns.[3] Other informers followed Karl Kautsky's railroad trips, evaluated the degree of anti-Semitism in the socialist movement, or looked in on radical conspirators in Zurich, Geneva, and London. Crown Prince Rudolf kept up with fashion by commenting on socialist activity in Bohemia, but his estimate was for Szeps's eyes and not for the Minister-President's. Not surprisingly Rudolf noted the great progress which the Marxians had made, and he particularly relished the fact that within the party Czechs and Germans worked for a common end, despite national differences.[4]

How had Marxian socialism and anarchism developed in Austria? Contending with antistrike laws in the 1850s and with the rivalry of "self-help" and "state help" factions in the 1860s, the laborers of Austria came into their own with the establishment of Dualism in 1867. Guaranteed the rights of association and meeting, they formed some unions and initiated work stoppages to secure their objectives. Under pressure from a monster demonstration of December 13, 1869, the Austrian cabinet promised a law to permit labor to organize and to strike as long as there was no use of intimidation or force. Alarmed by such coercion and by the founding of a Social Democratic Party in 1869 in Germany, the same ministry decided to arrest the demonstrators' leaders on charges of treason. The sensational trial of July, 1870, ended in fairly stiff sentences, but a Conservative ministry of 1871 amnestied the prisoners.

One of the "martyrs," Heinrich Oberwinder, felt no gratitude for the "feudalistic" Conservatives who had freed him, and he rather perversely advocated cooperation with the Liberals, who were most alarmed by socialism. His great antagonist in the movement was Andreas Scheu, who abhorred collaboration with

[2] *Ibid.,* Karton 822, No. 1520, March 11, 1882.
[3] *Ibid.,* Karton 823, No. 3774, July 14, 1882.
[4] Letter of Nov. 19, 1882, in *Kronprinz Rudolf: Politische Briefe an einen Freund, 1882–1889,* ed. Julius Szeps (Vienna, Munich, and Leipzig, 1922), p. 18.

the bourgeoisie. Neither had much success in winning masses of converts, and it was not until Bismarck drove his Social Democratic critics into exile during 1878 that propaganda in the German language began to penetrate the Austrian lower classes. From London a tough-minded core of zealots dispatched copies of *Freiheit*. The editor was Johann Most, a veteran of the trial of 1870 and of Austrian jails who had embraced anarchism. In 1881 the London cell deputized Josef Peukert to gain control of the amorphous Austrian workers' movement, and by the end of 1882 this disciple of direct action was directing the editorials in *Die Zukunft,* the voice of Austrian socialism. Peukert indubitably plotted violent actions, and Taaffe's police were happy to round up the disseminators of the radical journals and pamphlets. Within the ranks of labor there were moderates who distrusted the uncompromising ways of the doctrinaires, but it took some shocking incidents to clarify the issues for workers and parliamentarians alike.

On July 4, 1882, two carpenter's helpers murdered a shoe manufacturer and admitted, when caught, that they had decided to donate the money they took from their victim to the anarchist cause. Despite raids and rounds of interrogations, the police could not pin a charge of complicity upon Peukert, who gained enough public attention to qualify as a witness in a parliamentary hearing on the "social question." There his arrogance and unconcealed hatred for self-appointed social reformers gave color to bourgeois conviction that Austrian workers were moving toward absolute intransigence. In the western suburbs of Vienna in November, 1882, police clashed with laborers, and arsonists destroyed a huge wood yard in the ninth ward on September 3 of the following year. It almost seemed as if the red glow, silhouetting the nearby Palais Liechtenstein and a host of middle-class apartment buildings, foreshadowed a violent social upheaval.[5] Taaffe told his colleagues a few days later that arson and illegal meetings were so much on the increase that the police force's capacity to withstand the pressure was in ques-

[5] Gustav Kolmer, *Parlament und Verfassung in Oesterreich* (Vienna and Leipzig, 1902–14), III, 380.

tion. He personally wanted to wait a few more days for affairs to quiet down. If the workers continued to assemble despite official veto, then the government would have to decree temporary and partial suspension of the rights of association and meeting.[6]

At the end of 1883 and early in 1884 a wave of terrorism forced Taaffe to institute more rigid controls. A police observer was shot down after leaving a workers' meeting in Floridsdorf, another met a similar fate on his way to work, and on January 10, 1884, a money-changer lost his life to assassins who did not hesitate to murder the chief witnesses to their crime, the victim's sons, aged nine and eleven. Investigators picked up Heinrich Stellmacher and Anton Kammerer as suspects, and their connections with extremist circles in Germany and Switzerland sufficed to send them to the gallows.[7]

These sensational murders persuaded Taaffe early in 1884 that public security required extraordinary measures, at least in the areas of maximum extremist activity. A governmental commission had been at work, debating whether or not to invoke martial law, and both Taaffe and these experts decided against such a measure. A law of May 9, 1869, provided for "milder" remedies. It permitted a cabinet to abridge the rights of personal freedom, of association, assembly, and press, as well as the sanctity of home and mail, if the cabinet then secured the approval of the Lower House. Should the deputies not be sitting, they were to consider the exceptional measures at their first reconvening. If they agreed, the government then turned to the peers for their ratification.

Such safety devices bespoke the anguish of the Liberals who wanted order without social repression in the first few years of Austrian constitutionalism. It seems clear that Taaffe and his associates were quite aware of the distaste which exceptional decrees would arouse, and the cabinet was notably unenthusiastic about its ultimate recommendations. Nevertheless, the gov-

[6] MRP 56, Sept. 7, 1883.
[7] Ludwig Brügel, *Geschichte der österreichischen Sozialdemokratie* (Vienna, 1922), III, 263, 312–14.

ernment decided to authorize the suspension of the rights of association and assembly, the expulsion of dangerous individuals from their places of residence, and the opening and reading of mail in the court districts of Vienna, Korneuburg, and Wiener-Neustadt. In the first two districts named, jury trials also were suspended. Since Austrian jurors were nearly always the settled and prosperous members of society, they tended to be unsympathetic to the underprivileged or subject to intimidation by terrorist cells. The government later would consequently maintain that judges were likely to be more efficient dispensers of justice than were these jurymen.

What kind of radicalism was envisioned by the ministers as they moved reluctantly to suspensions of normal civil rights? Pino was relieved that St. Pölten and Krems were exempted, for he believed they were free of "socialistic" agitation. A great number of laborers had nothing to do with "socialism," he declared. Other comments made in the decisive cabinet meeting of January 27, 1884, indicate that "socialism" was indeed the adversary in the ministers' minds.[8] The terminology was important, for later the Liberals would resist measures which did not explicitly name anarchism as the enemy. Inspired by memories of the years of bureaucratic absolutism, they exhibited much alarm over what might be included under the rubric of "socialism." Rudolf, their bright hope, wrote Szeps that the bad times of the fifties had returned. Little would happen to the true socialists, who were hard to track down, but respectable people would be plagued without letup.[9]

The Crown Prince easily divined that his Liberal friends would feel somewhat menaced by the special ordinances. Before the matter went to the Lower House, Taaffe summoned a British journalist to acquaint the world with the cabinet's thinking. He and his colleagues had never dreamed of using the exceptional decrees against Liberalism or the press. Moreover, he was "too proud" to use the ordinances as a screen for political

[8] MRP 8, Jan. 27, 1884; Brügel, *Geschichte,* III, 324.
[9] Letter of Jan. 31, 1884, in *Kronprinz Rudolf: Politische Briefe,* pp. 80–81.

maneuvering.[10] In a rather restrained commentary Josef Kopp, a Liberal lawyer representing the sixth Viennese ward, was not so sure about the clauses which might be used against the press. A printer might innocently accept and turn out some subversive material, and, with one blow, the new regulations would beggar him. Might not a regime equipped with extraordinary powers silence a critical paper for "offenses" which no state prosecutor ordinarily would dare investigate? As for "socialism," Liberals might consider the activities of the Socialist Laborers' Party to be childish, utopian, and dangerous, but they nonetheless believed that it was entitled to exist and to express its erroneous opinions.[11]

Other Liberals were perplexed as to what their attitude should be. Eduard Suess pungently asserted that Austrian laws already in existence were stricter than Bismarck's anti-Socialist laws, and August Weeber doubted that anarchists would follow up threats they might make against jurors. The fact that citizens were asking to be excused from jury duty meant little, for they tended to beg off all kinds of cases.[12]

Taaffe had effective rebuttals. The Oberste Gerichtshof, a citadel of Liberal legal talent, had recommended the lifting of jury trial in Vienna and Korneuburg. He was scrupulously following the letter of the Liberal law of 1869, and no one could deny there had been frightening incidents. Furthermore, the Liberal mayor of Wiener-Neustadt publicly sought his party's endorsement of the new precautions. Before they were issued, his city officials declined to prosecute an imprisoned laborer and his police reported "sick" if asked to track one down.[13] Even so, no fewer than 137 deputies voted against the emergency decrees on February 15, 1884, and it was no secret that some Poles and Czechs secretly sympathized with the Liberal attitude.

Three months later Taaffe glumly predicted to his associates that both Right and Left would hotly contest the privilege of

[10] *Neue Freie Presse,* Feb. 4, 1884, *Abendblatt.*
[11] *SPA,* IX Session, pp. 11403–10, Feb. 5, 1884.
[12] *Ibid.,* pp. 11542–45, Feb. 14, 1884; pp. 11574–76, Feb. 15, 1884.
[13] Kolmer, *Parlament,* III, 381–83, 386.

denying the government a renewal of *Ausnahmszustand.* To
avert such a painful situation, he wanted the responsible ministers to prepare an antisocialist bill, based on Germany's, during
the summer. He had decided that a frontal attack on socialism
was the only way to keep radicals from exploiting the clamor
over civil liberties to mask their own subversive activities, and
Pražak energetically backed the idea of a specifically antisocialist action.[14]

Securing the Lower House's approval of an antisocialist
measure would take time. Meanwhile the suspension of jury
trial in Vienna and Korneuburg would end on December 31,
1884, unless the cabinet could persuade the deputies to extend
the restrictions for another year. The Minister of Justice proposed this extension in the cabinet meeting of November 28 and
recommended that trial by jury for serious offenses also cease in
the court district of Wiener-Neustadt. In Vienna and Korneuburg anarchistic terrorism had declined, but in Wiener-Neustadt
such activity had all the characteristics of a thoroughly planned
reign of intimidation. Dynamiters who had stolen their sticks
from the magazine attempted to blow up the Pfarrkirche's
steeple. The burgomaster received death threats, and witnesses
in anarchist trials had their homes set on fire or broken into.
Under such conditions the government could not trust juries
to give independent verdicts against persons accused of anarchism.[15]

Pražak repeated such justifications in the usual *mémoire* to the
Emperor, but he was astute enough to report that the executions
of Stellmacher and Kammerer had stemmed the worst of the
disorders. Franz Joseph needed reassurance that his officials
could contain anarchism, while the Reichsrat required proof of
continuing jeopardy. Taaffe implied in his report to the monarch that getting a general law against anarchism and a formal
measure to limit the use and possession of explosives would be
no easy task. Unless the leaders of the majority were agreeable,

[14] Brügel, *Geschichte,* III, 337 (little is left of the actual MRP 37,
May 23, 1884).
[15] MRP 68, Nov. 28, 1884.

he would not undertake the introduction of such bills.[16] For the moment the cabinet would concentrate on extension of the ordinances of January 30, 1884.

The usual recourse to the Oberste Gerichtshof for an opinion to strengthen the government's arguments did not turn out as well as Pražak had hoped. Schmerling, the presiding justice, courteously reported that a *majority* of the court did feel, in view of official evidence submitted by the ministry, that another year's suspension of jury trial was indicated—for Wiener-Neustadt as well as Vienna and Korneuburg. But two justices had voted otherwise, and Pražak told his colleagues that lack of unanimity in the court spelled opportunity for the opposition in the Lower House. Could he, to save his bill on suspension of jury trial, hint to the deputies that the government intended to modify this decree as soon as an antisocialist law passed? Since the cabinet was already hard at work debating the exact terminology and extent of such a bill, it approved the course Pražak planned to follow.[17]

In the brief debate on continuing the suspension of jury trial in Vienna and Korneuburg, Eduard Sturm perfunctorily reviewed the "official" Liberal position. They had wanted to apply emergency measures only against anarchists and only in the sense of restrictions upon personal movement, justified searches of private homes, and the opening of mail. The few months of arbitrary governmental action in the three court districts affected had convinced them that checks on association, meeting, and press had gone too far. They continued their opposition to any suspension of jury trials. Taaffe should bring in a comprehensive special bill to deal with the situation. Otherwise they anticipated far greater danger in the form of a scared press during the general elections of 1885.[18] Interestingly enough, the man in whom the Liberals put their fondest hopes, the Crown Prince, was writing to Szeps that he was more and more convinced that bloody days were coming. Only the army, the last

[16] Kabinetts-Kanzlei, Vortrag 4298, Nov. 30, 1884 (Pražak); Vortrag 4314, Nov. 30, 1884 (Taaffe).
[17] MRP 71, Dec. 2, 1884.   [18] *SPA*, pp. 13315–17, Dec. 15, 1884.

guardian of order and of loyalty to the state, would be able to
save the citizenry with its iron might. Clearly Rudolf did not
fear the socialists. As always, he despised the reigning system
and sympathized with those who struggled for "our modern
civilization."[19]

Despite his laments, the Lower House on December 17 approved the regime's decision to prolong the ordinances on trials
of radicals for another year, followed by the Upper House on
December 19. Pražak then issued the decree applying the same
conditions to Wiener-Neustadt, which the Lower House "took
cognizance of" on February 21, 1885, the Upper House on
March 28, 1885.

Taaffe had expected opposition to the suspension of jury trials
in Wiener-Neustadt, and he was relieved when a spate of incidents in December attested to increased radical activity in the
area. Such recurrences, he wrote the Emperor, should expedite
passage of comprehensive laws against socialism. (In early
1885 Taaffe was not precise in his use of terms to describe the
plottings of enemies of existing society.[20])

The higher bureaucrats in the Ministries of Interior and Justice who elaborated the bill against socialistic endeavors which
would be injurious to the common weal and against a similarly
noxious use of explosives underlined their satisfaction with the
term "socialistic." They did not feel that the German law's
more comprehensive "socialistic, communistic, and Social Democratic" fitted Austrian conditions. Their first paragraph consequently forbade the creation of *Vereinen* which would serve
socialistic endeavors to overthrow the existing order in state and
society. Conrad, who did not always contribute the maximum
of perception in his contributions to cabinet deliberations, immediately pounced on the terms "socialistic" and *Vereinen*. The
latter word was too narrow, and it was used to describe workers'
welfare associations as well as profit-making partnerships. He
wanted to add the phrase, *und Verbindungen jeder Art,* so that

[19] Letter of Nov. 19, 1884, in *Kronprinz Rudolf: Politische Briefe,*
p. 105.
[20] Kabinetts-Kanzlei, Vortrag 13, Jan. 2, 1884.

there would be plenty of range for state prosecutor and police. It would be advisable also to strengthen the words "socialistic endeavor" with the more precise "Social Democratic." Socialism in the purely intellectual meaning of the word was not suspicious, for a movement such as the Old Catholic had a socialistic character throughout, in his opinion. The subversive movements that grew out of socialism were the perils. Sektionschef Gustav von Kubin tersely replied there was no need to add to or to amplify the term *Vereinen*. No one had ever perceived in the activities of religious communities a bias toward socialistic endeavors. Kubin, of course, worked directly for Taaffe in the Ministry of Interior, and his chances of tenure in his post were far greater than a mere minister's.

Conrad's dissatisfaction with "socialistic" nonetheless met with some response among his colleagues. Pražak insisted that there were justified movements in the sphere of what was socialistic, and he urged the substitution of the word "anarchistic." Dunajewski likewise noted the tendency to interchange "social" and "socialistic." There were perfectly appropriate efforts to better society, and certainly there was a social science. Welsersheimb, Minister of Defense, disliked the expression, "socialistic," and Taaffe finally had to come to the rescue of the authors of the bill. It was clear, he asserted, that there had to be limitations on the civil rights of those groups which were guilty of especially pernicious socialistic revoluntionary action. If the government did not compose the bill as a special, exceptional law against socialistic agitation, it would have no justification for bringing it before parliament. Taaffe's tough line sufficed, for the cabinet unanimously opted for "socialistic."[21]

For tactical reasons the Emperor's chief advisers and their aides decided upon a "Dynamite Bill" as their first move against socialism.[22] Restrictions upon the utilization of explosives were not new, but these regulations would forbid the manufacture, transport, or possession of such materials without official permission. Simple violations would incur fines as high as 300 gulden

[21] MRP 69, Nov. 28, 1884.   [22] MRP 79, Dec. 22, 1884.

and sentences up to six months. If the accused was found guilty of
an unpremeditated threat against the life, health, or property of
another, he might receive a maximum imprisonment of three
years and a maximum fine of 1,000 gulden. Those convicted of
premeditated property damage could receive twenty years in
jail. If they killed others through explosives, they were subject
to the death penalty.[23] No deputy seriously contested the bill,
which passed the Lower House on March 27, the Upper House
on April 16.

The antisocialist bill proper, which a committee of the Lower
House first discussed on January 31, 1885, called for strict
supervision of all associations, the destruction of secret societies,
controls over socialistic printed materials, and an end to the
importation of already illegal incendiary literature. The key
phrase was "socialistic endeavors aimed at the overthrow of
order in state and society," which the Liberals found entirely too
expansive. Quite tellingly the *Neue Freie Presse* wrote: "Nothing nowadays is more common than criticism of the existing
order in state and society; in this field Prince Bismarck meets
Herr Bebel, Prince von Liechtenstein Herr Peukert. But who
decided with surety whether this criticism aims at legal reformation or violent overthrow?"[24]

Press comments from Prague and Kraków hinted at delay, if
not defeat, of the cabinet's phrases. *Politik* said that any police
official would be able to throttle attacks on the government or
attempts to reform society by declaring them to be revolutionary. *Pokrok* reaffirmed its trust in the probity of the Taaffe
regime, but it doubted that a future cabinet would move only
against anarchists if endowed with such checks on civil liberties.
Some socialists could be good people when they wanted to better
conditions through legal processes.[25] In Austrian Poland the
Gazeta Narodowa superciliously declared that existing powers in
Galicia had been quite sufficient so far and doubted that measures such as those proposed ever choked off anarchist propa-

---

[23] *SPA*, IX Session, Beilagen 1096.   [24] Jan. 24, 1885.
[25] Quoted, *ibid.*, Jan. 22, 1885, *Morgen- und Abendblatt;* Jan. 23, 1885,
Abendblatt.

ganda. The *Reforma* resented the five-year term requested and questioned the justice of checks on freedom where socialism did not even exist.[26]

Such obvious reservations outside the Liberal camp compelled Taaffe to mark time on his antisocialist bill and yet go through the misery of securing a prolongation of the suspension of jury trial in Vienna, Korneuburg, and Wiener-Neustadt until June 30, 1886. Georg Lienbacher was the Iron Ring's sturdiest advocate as the Liberals, more energetically than before, tried to envelop the government's position. Frankly admitting no enthusiasm for the whole idea of jury trials, he insisted that in his thirty-nine years in court as magistrate and functionary he had seen many witnesses tremble as they gave testimony against ruthless men. Viennese men were brave, but could they be if their wives and children were in danger? Who could really say what anarchism was or when it left off being socialism? The Liberals should realize that suspension of jury trials left the cases in the hands of judges, not of the state. These judges were independent and had tenure, and he thought they would remain so.[27] When Professor Alois Zucker of the Czech Club also asked why juries were indispensable, Schönerer intemperately called upon his followers to witness that "a Jew here today publicly and very provocatively stood up for an exceptional law."[28] The Liberals were displeased to have Schönerer on their side and embarrassed that the slight losses they had suffered in the elections of 1885 enabled the government to secure the renewal of the prohibition of juries, 162 to 126. On October 26, 1885, the Upper House gave its consent without debate.

When the major bill aimed at socialism went to a twenty-four-man committee of the Lower House on February 9, 1886, it underwent virtual emasculation. Taaffe was quite unprepared for such treatment, for he had just assured the Emperor that he had arrived at a compromise with parliamentary advisers that would maintain the principles and purposes of the cabinet's

[26] Quoted, *ibid.,* Jan. 24 and 25, 1885.
[27] *SPA,* X Session, pp. 432, 434–35, Oct. 23, 1885.
[28] *Ibid.,* pp. 416, 421, Oct. 23, 1885.

original bill.[29] As a result of the full committee's action, however, the formal debate of June, 1886, merely concerned a general prohibition of jury trial in cases involving socialistic endeavors to overthrow state and society by violence. The committee's majority did honor the regime's request for a five-year term, but the opposition promised a hot reception for such a protracted legalization of exceptional courts throughout Austria.

Permission to suspend jury trial entailed a two-thirds favorable vote in the Lower House, and the regime's slight success in the general elections of 1885 did not come close to guaranteeing such a majority. It was obvious, however, that Right and Liberal Left would settle for a mutually satisfactory law. The Economic Section of the Czech Club had already gone on record against press restrictions.[30] The Liberals, on the other hand, were sufficiently pleased with the regime's shrewd avoidance of trouble with Liberal editors to chance an extension and enlargement of the suspension of jury trial.

Under these circumstances it was up to fiery extremists such as Grégr and Kronawetter to lament the coming of the antisocialist law, however limited. The Young Czech orator disliked most the cabinet's employment of the term "socialistic." Why belabor anarchism's greatest enemy? After all, whoever believed in trying to rid the world of misery and poverty was already a socialist, "and we even have a duty to be a socialist." What was being recommended would lame the moderates in the socialist movement but give the criminal anarchists unlimited opportunity to exploit labor's resentment. In Germany the socialists always had a tribune in the Reichstag. Austrian radicals did not have such a safety valve, and, if banished from the cities, they would stir up the agrarian proletariat with catastrophic results. Universal manhood suffrage should be the point of departure for social reform, not abridgments of rights and neomedieval, so-called Christian Social remedies.[31]

[29] Kabinetts-Kanzlei, Vortrag 390, Jan. 25, 1886.
[30] *Neue Freie Presse,* March 2, 1886, *Abendblatt.*
[31] *SPA,* pp. 2881–82, 2884–85, June 5, 1886.

Kronawetter emphasized police "brutalities" in his plea against the continuation of emergency rules. In the first eight days of a prisoner's incarceration, they questioned and held his relatives, resorted to night interrogations to induce confession, and secured signatures to statements which the accused never made. Throwing a suspect into a cell with the scum of society also speeded up confessions, declared the deputy who, rather surprisingly, represented Vienna's far from radical eighth district. The citizens were not frightened, he argued. Rather, the state wanted to return to absolutism, and it was disgraceful to allege that Austrian jurors had less courage than Belgian, French, British, and American.[32]

Heartened by the signs of a general parliamentary distaste for laws that would make Austria a replica of Bismarck's Germany, the Liberals realistically spelled out the limits of their cooperation with Taaffe. Herbst would permit two years, not five, of the denial of jury trials for anarchists. Kopp moved an amendment that would entitle a court to decide after a preliminary hearing whether or not a case involved revolutionary anarchism. If not, it would immediately renounce its power to act without a jury.[33]

The Right's unpredictable Lienbacher quickly recommended a discussion of these suggestions, since the government did not possess the two-thirds majority necessary to suspend jury trial. Pražak declared that the government could not oppose this move toward compromise, and the responsible committee duly incorporated the Liberal amendments into the general law. The Lower House concurred with decisive majorities, the Upper House unanimously in June, 1886.[34]

Taaffe had protection of sorts from anarchism, and a powerful bloc on the Left seemed to indicate that it would not be too picayune in watching the state ascertain a radical's true colors. Actually it was the circle which hoped to re-establish social harmony despite Marxist prediction and action which had serious

[32] Ibid., pp. 2909–10, 2912, 2915, June 7, 1886.
[33] Ibid., p. 2904, June 7, 1886; p. 2944, June 8, 1886.
[34] Ibid., pp. 2944–52, June 8, 1886; pp. 2963–70, June 9, 1886; SPH, X Session, p. 218, June 23, 1886.

doubts about the laws against anarchism. *Das Vaterland* queru-
lously complained of highly colored journalistic accounts of
anarchistic plots. An unbelievably unworthy "Jewish press"
had corrupted the people's minds with such fantasies. The
Clerical Conservative daily was equally sharp with General
Grant and those who shared his second-hand belief that asphalt
pavements and the Gatling gun were the best preventatives
against social revolution. Very pointedly Vogelsang chided
those who believed that the police could save society from its
deep moral, social, and economic corruption. Only a moral
revival from within, an individual regeneration, could effect its
salvation.[35]

Up to the end of 1887 the government initiated charges
against thirty-nine radicals, with thirteen trials actually taking
place. It was at this time that Victor Adler, converted from
German nationalism to Marxian socialism, was winning more
workers to moderatism, to be sure, but the relatively small
number of governmental actions also indicates that Taaffe had
no great taste for proscription. It seemed best, however, to
retain the right to suspend jury trial. As Pražak told the
Emperor in the customary request for imperial permission to
take the matter to parliament, the socialists still had some followers with criminal tendencies, and the anarchists were always
trying to extend their propagandistic efforts. The cabinet had
been forced to accept a two-year limit in the law of 1886 solely
because of the parliamentary situation at that time. Pražak
seemed to feel that a request for a three-year extension had
better prospects.[36] When the regime asked for such an extension
in April, 1888, however, strong resistance in the Lower House
lowered the term to two years. Indeed, the deputies went home
in June without acting on the measure, forcing Pražak to invoke
the ever-reliable Article 19 of the Fundamental Laws.[37] This
permitted legislation by ordinance until legislators reassembled,

[35] Oct. 12 and 16, 1886.
[36] Kabinetts-Kanzlei, Vortrag 1285, April 9, 1888.
[37] Walter Knarr, "Das Ministerium des Grafen Taaffe und die soziale
Frage" (unpubl. diss., Vienna, 1948), pp. 84–85.

and on August 1 the government suspended jury trials in cases linked with revolutionary anarchism in the court districts of Vienna, Korneuburg, Wiener-Neustadt, Wels, Prague, Brüx (Most), Jičín, Jungbunzlau, Reichenberg, Brünn, Olmütz, Neutitschein (Nový Jičín), Graz, Leoben, and Klagenfurt for a period of a year.

Schönborn meanwhile had assumed the Justice portfolio, and his relative newness and his often convincing frankness were decisive in persuading the skeptics that the ordinance had merit. Again the Oberste Gerichtshof had found that there was sufficient agitation to warrant an extension, and the ordinance, unlike the antisocialist law of 1886, specifically listed the offenses which, if linked with revolutionary anarchism, would not receive a hearing before a jury.[38] After a bureaucratic "expert" emphasized the continuing flow of propaganda from Swiss sources and warned that jurors often were employers whose laborers read such provocative literature, Schönborn simply asked if a juror could know the difference between anarchism and socialism when a state, with all of its imposing apparatus, was not entirely clear as to the line of separation. He could honestly say that here and there the anarchist movement had declined and still bring in documentary evidence of its adherents' determination to fight on. For every court district named in the ordinance the regime had first secured the affirmative advice of an Oberlandesgerichtspräsidium. Finally, he and his colleagues well knew that their request for approval would not help them politically or make their ordinance popular.[39]

The Left proposed the restoration of jury trial in every district in which it had been suspended, but the motion failed, 142 to 122. With the German and Italian Liberals voted Young Czechs, German Nationalists, and the still somewhat uncommitted Lueger and Ernst Vergani. Had it not been for Coronini and his fraction, the Lower House would not have recognized the validity of the ordinance of August 1.[40] Without debate the

[38] *SPA,* X Session, Beilagen 698.
[39] *Ibid.,* pp. 10366–68, 10377–78, Dec. 19, 1888.
[40] *Ibid.,* p. 10401, Dec. 19, 1888.

Upper House had already agreed to Taaffe's measure a month before.

It was the government's hapless duty to begin work on renewal of permission from the Reichsrat almost as soon as the two houses had acted on a standing ordinance. In January, 1889, Schönborn formally asked Taaffe in a letter if he should begin action to continue the suspension of jury trial in anarchistic cases. The Minister of Justice discerned no real change in the situation, and Taaffe indirectly charged him with the task of securing a renewal by sending him the annual report of the Vienna police on socialistic and anarchistic activity. When Schönborn turned to his vitally important provincial superior courts and state attorneys for convincing backing, he discovered that only the courts of Vienna and Prague recommended a continuance of the ordinance for a few court districts. Among the deputies of the Right there never had been a great love for the suspension of jury trial, which affronted the sense of aristocratic obligation to the masses and threatened one of the basic civil rights which the non-German nationalities had reason to treasure. Taaffe instructed Schönborn not to press for renewal.[41] For the moment the regime could do no more than hang on to its right to abridge personal freedom and exile agitators from Vienna, Korneuburg, and Wiener-Neustadt.

The widely publicized founding of the Second International in Paris in 1889 and the decision of world socialism to demonstrate its solidarity on May 1, 1890, renewed the apprehensions of the Austrian government and the more timid members of the bourgeoisie. The most doctrinaire of all Liberals, Herbst, a master of impolitic timing, turned with some of his old-time fire upon Taaffe and Schönborn a week before May Day and demanded the lifting of the government's exceptional powers in Vienna. Freely granting that there had been a serious crisis posed by anarchistic criminals in 1884, he declared that the danger was long past and that the government should once again justify its confiscation of a newspaper or its refusal to permit a meeting. With wonted sarcasm he declared that Bismarck's laws against social-

41 Brügel, *Geschichte,* IV, 19.

ism, which had so signally failed, were equal in their prohibitions only to the normal powers of an Austrian cabinet over association, meeting, and press. One new argument: there was a time when people could say that Vienna had no mob. That was no longer the case, and the city could enjoy no increase in tourism as long as potential visitors heard of "exceptional conditions."[42] Herbst's actual motion to deny the regime special powers lost by the rather interesting vote of 112 to 93.[43] The large number of abstentions indicated the end of the road for special governmental privileges against radicalism.

Herbst had a surprising ally of sorts in the master of the Hofburg, at least in the matter of estimating the change in Viennese tempers. Though he admitted that security forces had properly handled the demonstrations in the capital on May 1, the Emperor was displeased that previous excesses had surprised these forces and caused them a loss in prestige. The once obedient and correct Viennese now made obstinacy one of their public pleasures, and he practically ordered his ministers on May 27 to revive popular respect for law and order in the city. Franz Joseph's comments in cabinet meetings were ordinarily brief and predictable, and he probably surprised no one with his clichés about restoration of calm and dutifulness. On this occasion, however, he shook his immediate advisers in Austria with some unanticipated philosophizing on the "labor question." In line with his fatalism he remarked that one could not hope for a complete abolition of the social evils which were basic to the war against society. He was most struck by the intense bitterness between employers and employees, and here and there, apart from the influence of agitators, he got the impression that the way laborers were handled was quite unsuitable. Labor's conviction that no one cared about its justified claims also generated ill feeling. Sensing their ruler's unusual perturbation, the ministers hastened to recite what had been done and what was being planned for labor's benefit. In the end they seemed to succeed, for, in the spirit of 1849, Franz Joseph emphatically excoriated

---

[42] *SPA*, pp. 14545–46, 14548–49, April 24, 1890.
[43] Kolmer, *Parlament*, IV, 344.

the "peaceful high treason" implicit in the ultra-German, the Italian Pro-Patria, and the ultra-Slavic associations. Nor was he happy over the exultant celebrations of anniversaries of a political character in Galicia. The security forces of the empire should be militarized, for then the regime could prove its authority everywhere.[44]

No minister dared tell the Emperor that the time for such militarization of the police was long past. The cabinet was already hard pressed on the issue of its right to curtail civil liberties in three court districts, and the composed demeanor of the laborers who marched in the second May Day (1891) celebration added to the Reichsrat's growing conviction that it was neither necessary nor politic to maintain the suspension of jury trials in areas with a large concentration of workers. In June, 1891, the "Socialist" Committee of the Lower House asked Taaffe to surrender his ordinances. In reply, the government asked for the passage of the bill it had prepared against revolutionary socialism in 1886. What an unimpressed Lower House did not grant in 1886 was impossible to get in 1891, and the government's quick retreat was as graceless as its counterproposal. By June 26 the game was over. A resolution passed the House calling for an end to all exceptional conditions, even the police surveillance of expelled workers. The government rescinded the ordinances, and only a brief and hopeless attempt to get the committee to ponder an anarchist bill reminded the public of the years of anxiety in high places.[45]

The Reichsrat's disinclination to countenance antiradical measures in Taaffe's last years reflected a general Austrian feeling that socialists were not implacable enemies of law and order. After 1886 Victor Adler slowly gained control of both moderate and radical wings, despite his bourgeois origins and previous German nationalist affectations, and a Social Democratic Workers' Party emerged from a large congress that met in Hainfeld at the very end of 1888. The statement of principles which the delegates adopted stressed universal suffrage, the full

[44] Brügel, *Geschichte*, IV, 127–29.
[45] Kolmer, *Parlament*, V, 232–33.

right of labor to organize, equality for all individuals and nationalities, and separation of church and state. The word "revolution" was conspicuously absent, though an Austrian delegation did go to Paris in 1889 to help found the Second International, whose very name should have inspired a variety of states to take repressive action.

The relatively good reputation which the Second International's founding fathers enjoyed in their homelands and the orderly celebration of labor's first May Day in 1890 lessened the fears of the more easily alarmed citizens. The very fact that anarchists continued their *attentats* also enhanced socialism's chance to work for peaceful solutions in most European areas. The "oppressors" almost welcomed labor leaders who might talk of general strikes and the coming society of equals but who were fairly effective in diminishing the attractiveness of direct action among discontented wage earners. Adler breezily dismissed Taaffe's Austria as a "despotism tempered by slovenliness," whose inefficiency aided socialism's organizational work. In time, capitalism and the feudalistic superstructure that was an Austrian specialty would collapse of their inner contradictions, according to theory, but meanwhile the Social Democrats propagandized for a truly democratic suffrage and amplification of the social legislation which Taaffe had initiated. The *Arbeiter-Zeitung* solemnly balanced ponderous dialectics with down-to-earth surveys of wretched living and working conditions. The cabinet ordered its confiscation when the editorials became too strident, but in this respect the Marxist daily suffered no more than did the bourgeois papers. There were strikes and occasional ugliness, but the party's membership rose from 15,498 in 1888 to 47,166 in 1891. It was too early to expect aristocrats and academicians to see in socialism a reasonable, if unorthodox, weapon against corrosive nationalisms, but the Crown Prince had not been alone in noting that Germans and Czechs would collaborate for Marxist ends.

Certainly Adler and his associates regarded Taaffe's social insurance schemes as palliatives, and they never ceased to resent the special attention which the Austrian police conferred upon

every form of socialist activity. They despised the titled gentlemen who lent a feudal aura to Taaffe's social politics, just as they
feared the ultramontanes and "misguided" nationalists who
completed the regime's array of forces. But the German Liberals, accommodating themselves so reluctantly to the demands of
the new industrial proletariat, offered little hope of amity or
alliance. The complexity of Austrian politics created great opportunities for a movement that was resolute and informed.
Armed with impeccable doctrine and a sense of mission, Socialism could dispense with the crude tactics which the anarchists
had employed, and there was an obvious connection between the
lapse of Taaffe's exceptional laws and the rise of self-assured and
moderate Social Democracy. The deputies from country, town,
and splendid castle no longer believed that repression was necessary or effective. Rather, they asked how they might better
undercut all radical successes with the workers by expanding the
system of social legislation.

10 Social Reform: The First Steps

Franz Joseph's address from the throne of October 7, 1879, unmistakably committed the Taaffe ministry to social reform. In contrast to the law of 1859, which generally proclaimed the freedom of citizens to make their own contracts as employers and employed, the Austrian government now pledged itself to a reinvigoration of small business and the crafts and a regulation of labor-capital relationships. Twenty years of laisser faire, limited only by token restrictions on child labor, had paralleled the rise of big industry, with its shattering competitive effect upon time-honored skills ignorant of complex machinery and of rigorous mass discipline. The peasant's freedom to divide his land by bequest inevitably added to the labor force needed by the new industry, for the partition of a modest holding among a half-dozen sons left all in distress.[1] The development of the railroad net expedited the quick disposal of ready-made goods, often by peddlers whose profitable circuits inspired curses from artisans whose products they easily undersold.

Handicraftsmen and small businessmen added to their own plight by sticking to old techniques, to tired fashions, and to unimaginative merchandising habits. Like the guilds of old, which no practicing politician sincerely counted on restoring,

[1] Walter Knarr, "Das Ministerium des Grafen Taaffe und die soziale Frage" (unpubl. diss., Vienna, 1948), p. 9.

they represented a stratum of economic activity that bespoke solidity and honesty in an increasingly acquisitive society. Their spiritual links with the concept of the just price and reputable workmanship won them protectors among the socially conscious Catholics, while their especial distress in Vienna inspired a variety of "Democrats" to take up their cause. The decade of the 1870s had begun with the fierce reprisals that attended the founding and the destruction of the Paris Commune and had ended with Bismarck's declaration of war on Marxian socialism. If few Austrian parliamentarians were fully aware of Marx's prophecy concerning the inevitable descent of the less successful members of the bourgeoisie into the ranks of the proletariat, they tended nonetheless to worry over anarchism, socialism, and nihilism to such an extent that the execrations of the hard-pushed artisans and small retailers were having an effect even among doctrinaire Liberals. The "social question" was the dissonant but inescapable theme of the time.

In the autumn of 1879 the cabinet worked out what was to be a still-born reformation of conditions in handicrafts and industry. State inspectors were to enforce rules on child labor and report on factory conditions. Workers in trades and in factories would have to join insurance funds that would provide for them in case of sickness or disability and for their widows and orphans when they died. No one seemed happy over such limited objectives, and the ministers quickly withdrew their bill. Early in 1880 the Lower House voted to entrust a thorough-going reform of the *Gewerbe-Ordnung* (the rules which applied to the conditions of production in workshop and factory) to a special committee.[2]

Constant pressure from workers' meetings, particularly in Vienna, did not appreciably hurry the Lower House's committee's deliberations. The cabinet was curiously undecided as to the scope of social reform, and the election of Count Egbert Belcredi as reporter for the committee in November, 1881, was something of an unpleasant surprise. This aristocrat was close to Vogelsang and the "High Tory" school of social reform, and

[2] *Ibid.*, pp. 15–16.

he had vowed fundamental changes. Before long he and Pino, the Minister of Commerce, had disagreed so frequently that the minister began to absent himself from the committee's conferences.

Clerical Conservatives of Belcredi's stripe in the early 1880s were primarily interested in saving the skilled handicraftsmen from economic ruin. Such honored artisans were the relics of the guild system which these "Social Catholics" constantly apostrophized, and, as settled members of urban society in Austria, they were more frequently seen at mass than the "emancipated" upper middle class and the rootless peasants who drifted from factory to factory. By the spring of 1882 the committee had decided to propose compulsory associations for master artisans in the same calling and the establishment of a competency test for would-be craftsmen. The resemblance to medieval practice was not sufficiently blatant to keep a majority within the Liberal *Klub der Linken* from an endorsement of these remedies in March, 1882.[3]

In the autumn the cabinet debated whether or not to support the committee's bill. Taaffe knowingly reminded his associates of the change in Liberal point of view and stated that the cabinet's position in the Lower House would be untenable if it failed to second the committee's two requirements. Pražak and Ziemialkowski, speaking for the Czechs and Poles, readily assented. Conrad was unhappy that Austrian trade schools were not strong enough to serve as examiners of a craftsman's proficiency, while Dunajewski feared that the government was assuming a heavy moral responsibility in arousing expectations of improvement among these depressed expert workers. Pino, aroused by suggestions that the government should be broadminded in listing enterprises which relied upon factory organization as handicrafts, persuaded his associates to insist upon a narrow definition of "handwork."

Social reformers of the period believed that men who plied the same trade or craft needed organization if they were to survive, but the Lower House's committee had insisted primarily on

[3] *Ibid.*, p. 19.

associations of masters or employers. Special assemblies of
helpers or employees would meet at specified times to protect the
interests of these wage earners. Only in arbitration committees
and in the administration of sick funds was there to be representation of both masters and helpers. Pražak argued that the
union of both elements in the association would develop a *modus
vivendi* otherwise lacking. He also feared that the opposition in
parliament would pose as defenders of the helpers and would
renew demands for labor chambers. Pino retorted that the
helpers would have representation where their interests were
involved. If the opposition seized upon this issue, the government could easily reply that it would investigate the helpers' case
more thoroughly in conjunction with laws establishing liability
for accidents and comprehensive factory inspection. The cabinet finally decided to instruct Pino to support the committee's
proposal for tests of vocational competence. Other portions of
the committee's bill he was simply not to oppose.[4]

The regime's careful avoidance of the more hotly contested
details of the bill resulted from its surmise that the United Left
was not going to offer resistance to thoroughgoing social reform. On December 5 the opposition proposed a committee of
thirty-six to consider bills to decrease child and woman labor, to
enforce healthful and safe factory conditions through inspectors,
to establish obligatory sickness insurance for laborers, and to
elaborate accident insurance that would transcend the older
concept of an employer's liability in such affairs.[5] For the
moment the United Left may be said to have been enthusiastic
for labor and labor's interests if one remembers that the tailor,
the enameler, and the jeweler were as much the objects of this
attention as were factory operatives.

The Lower House debated its committee's bill in early
December, 1882, and the arguments concentrated on the reasons
for the decline of the crafts and on the remedies advanced for
their recovery, namely, qualification tests and compulsory associations. Slavic and Conservative Clerical deputies put the

[4] MRP 92, Nov. 23, 1882.
[5] *Neue Freie Presse,* Dec. 5, 1882, *Abendblatt.*

blame for the artisans' plight squarely on the Liberals. Karel Adámek swore that the trade treaties of the 1860s had delivered the internal market to outside competitors, while outright graft in the 1870s had showered the Liberals with railway concessions and other plums. The much-vaunted free enterprise, introduced by law in 1859, had created anarchy among differing interests. When the crash of 1873 maimed the economy, the Liberals provided millions in state funds for large-scale industry, but they provided the hard-pressed craftsmen with no more than the opportunity to borrow legally at usurious rates.[6] Belcredi bewailed the steady increase in mortgages on land, a sure sign of waxing class hatreds, for the man pushed out of his normal status naturally would be unfriendly toward the society which had dispossessed him. Suicidally blind, the Liberal regime had deliberately weakened the two factors which were indispensable for the restoration of society, the Christian Church and the vocational and professional associations.[7]

Liberals were quick to retort that the bill's most voluble friends were using the craftsmen's admitted troubles as a blind for pure reaction. Typically, Russ stigmatized the Right for attempting to divide society into neat classifications in order to declassify the individual. Thus the federalists would dissolve the modern omnipotent state they so thoroughly hated and rear upon its ruins a corporative state.[8]

Less partisan approaches marked the differing analyses of the decline of the crafts. The Right generally agreed that skilled individualism had to learn to compete with machines and large-scale industrial enterprise. Adámek frankly predicated the survival of the handicrafts upon cooperative employment of raw materials, machines, and merchandising halls.[9] Alois Mikyška was somewhat more buoyant in asserting that the advantages which permitted large-scale enterprise to triumph could just as well help the skilled vocations. They could utilize division of labor, machinery, and new techniques. A dose of the intelli-

[6] *SPA,* IX Session, pp. 8499–8501, Dec. 6, 1882.
[7] *Ibid.,* p. 8584, Dec. 11, 1882.   [8] *Ibid.,* p. 8646, Dec. 12, 1882.
[9] *Ibid.,* p. 8505, Dec. 6, 1882.

gence which big business had demonstrated, when added to the craftsman's native resourcefulness, diligence, and professional know-how, would ensure successful competition.[10] Spokesmen for the bill were convinced, however, that no amount of rejuvenation of the crafts would mean much if peddlers and their ready-made staples continued to circulate throughout Austria. Franz Löblich, the Viennese Democrat, discerned a direct threat to state interest in the ubiquitousness of machine-made goods, hawked from door to door by insubstantial members of society.[11] In melodramatic accents Adámek contrasted the poor master tailor, with hungry family, working for no more than eight gulden a week on piece goods, with the merchandiser of ready-made outfits who had become his master. The white slave and the king of advertising! Could there be a better example of capitalism's degradation of genuine skill?[12]

The heart of the debate concerned the introduction of compulsory tests of competence for a number of handicrafts. Again Adámek played a leading role, arguing that tests would compel the government to improve and expand its system of trade schools, the surest guarantee against an increase of the "extremely dangerous" proletariat. Denying the charge that the proposed test of capacity was but a prelude to a revival of guild regulations and a *numerus clausus* affecting the membership of all trades, he estimated that only 10 per cent of all artisans would be liable to such examination.[13] Löblich estimated that some 60 crafts out of 804 would institute proficiency tests under the proposed law. Obviously nettled by a sentimentalized picture of lamplighters put out of work by the coming of electricity, he asserted that such technologically displaced persons still could turn to many fields of potential employment which did not require proof of skill.[14]

Liberal arguments against proficiency tests were uninspired, and the Left's inclination to avoid a full-scale fight was obvious in one of the last speeches the opposition offered. Josef

[10] *Ibid.*, p. 8526, Dec. 7, 1882.   [11] *Ibid.*, p. 8565, Dec. 9, 1882.
[12] *Ibid.*, p. 8615, Dec. 12, 1882.   [13] *Ibid.*, pp. 8502–3, Dec. 6, 1882.
[14] *Ibid.*, p. 8560, Dec. 9, 1882.

Neuwirth, often a probing critic of the cabinet's activities, blandly admitted that he would vote for the tests, though he saw no immediate panacea in their adoption. They merely created the means to improve standards, a conclusion he had reached without succumbing to pressure from artisans or from his political opponents.[15]

Neuwirth's comments presaged the large majority which the bill received on December 14, when 220 voted in favor, 75 against. The debate in the Upper House resulted only in minor changes, which the deputies accepted. On March 15, 1885, the first step toward social reform became law. To repeat, it concerned the threatened handicrafts and small industry. The workers in large-scale industry still awaited a hearing.

In quite a sensational manner they told the Austrian public later in the spring of 1883 what they expected. Ostensibly the committee entrusted with social reform in the Lower House desired expert opinion on the proper limits of the normal workday, and its members summoned 103 witnesses—deputies, employers, and employees—for information and advice. Crimes against the established order, or at least against members of the possessing classes, had heightened the general public's interest in labor's ultimate objectives, and this *enquête* inevitably energized the cabinet's decision to continue social legislation.[16]

The stars of the hearings were Karl Höger, a moderate socialist, and Josef Peukert, the increasingly feared radical. The former stuck to pronouncements that cheered social reformers. He vigorously espoused the cause of eight years of compulsory schooling as a necessary preparation for a vocation, and he derided the idea that employees needed time off in the morning for religious observances. Workers for the most part were materialists, disbelieving in a future life of rewards and desiring a good life on this earth, he claimed. No one should labor before he was fourteen years old, while girls should refrain from going to work until they had reached puberty. It was useless to try to

[15] *Ibid.*, pp. 8694–700, Dec. 14, 1882.
[16] For a Social Democratic appraisal, see Ludwig Brügel, *Geschichte der österreichischen Sozialdemokratie* (Vienna, 1921), III, 291–96.

differentiate between factory life and life in a workshop. In either routine the workdays should be six hours for persons fourteen to sixteen, no more than eight hours for persons sixteen to eighteen. Such adolescents should be spared nightwork. Pregnant women should not work the six weeks before and after confinement.

Peukert was the picture of cool disdain. The *enquête,* he alleged, was either a scheme to pump information from labor or to win labor's votes. Mass poverty, increasing throughout Austria, demanded consideration of the entire social question, not just the palliative of a maximum workday. How could labor believe that the privileged honestly wanted to help when the spiritual nourishment of an adequate educational system was being steadily reduced? To give hours of Sunday worship in place of hours of schooling was a mockery.[17]

Other testimony reflected a society in which factory procedures were swamping skilled craftsmen, where some workers rather humbly asked for needed protection, and where others declared that the hour was too late for melioration, for compromise. A bit of unconscious humor occasionally relieved the grim recitals and prognoses. A tailor feared that prohibition of Sunday labor would send the relatives of a person who had died on a Saturday to the ready-to-wear merchant. A glovemaker opposed holidays in addition to Sundays because laborers spent too much money if free from regular work. Professor Richard Godeffroy primly testified that the chemical industry did not employ women and children, save for the fabrication of fireworks. In the trickier production of explosives women again were preferred, thanks to their superior manual dexterity and the refusal of males to stop smoking.[18]

The good professor's revelations again focused attention on the need for efficient factory inspection, which the government, the Liberals, and the Right had unanimously supported. The initiative was the committee's, however, as it voted to empower the Minister of Commerce with the right to divide Austria into

[17] *Neue Freie Presse,* May 1, 1883; *Das Vaterland,* May 1, 1883.
[18] *Neue Freie Presse,* May 5, 6, 7, and 8, 1883.

inspection districts, to appoint inspectors in accord with qualifications the ministry itself would set up, and to direct these inspectors to look into conditions in factories and workshops, large and small.

Some argument did develop over the extent and possible nationalistic implication of the new regulations. Liberal spokesmen revealed a degree of self-consciousness by asserting that they had always favored checks on industrial conditions and by stubbornly demanding that artisans' workshops meet the same standards as those expected of large factories. Franz Roser, a physician, was sure that the inspectors would actually protect the interests of the employers, at least if they were doctors or technicians, as they should be. Decent buildings and devices against noxious dust were necessities, and workshops, often worse than factories, required governmental surveillance.[19] Heinrich Reschauer, a writer, stressed the fact that he represented the richest Austrian industrial area, centered at Falkenau in Bohemia, which wanted factory inspection. Abuses and bad working conditions had led to unrest among the workers, but he feared that the area of competence granted the new inspectors was too narrow. Industry was primarily a German affair in Austria, and so the Taaffe regime was anti-industry. Was there not reason to fear that the government would use the inspectors to make life even more uncomfortable for industrialists? Certainly he would demand a "proper" interpretation of the paragraph which prescribed that the inspector know the language of the area to which he was assigned. There was no need to appoint a man conversant with both Czech and German to a purely German area.[20]

Löblich was a rather isolated advocate of the idea of exempting the artisan's shop from inspection. As a Viennese Democrat, he operated on the principle of maximum protection and minimal interference with the distressed handicraftsmen and small industrialists, but the usually sympathetic German Conservative Clericals and pro-Taaffe Slavs felt that a special concession to the hard-pressed small-scale producers would invite

[19] SPA, pp. 10756–58, May 4, 1883.
[20] Ibid., pp. 10810–12, May 5, 1883.

too many injustices. Löblich asserted there were not enough inspectors to check on 350,000 enterprises, that disgruntled neighbors through anonymous notes could bring endless trouble and interruptions to the small operator, and that it simply was not fair to demand the same standards from a small workshop as from a large factory.[21]

The Czech Adámek had already indicated that the government intended to allow no exemptions. Even if the associations of workers in the smaller trades should pick the inspectors, they would be too much under the power of their employers to recommend truly independent men. In smaller establishments a father was likely to exploit his own wife and children, a circumstance which doubly emphasized the need for official checks.[22]

Löblich was as outspoken as the Liberals in assuming that the regime would use factory inspection to undermine the German position in Austria. Unhappy that the Minister of Commerce could name the inspectors without any kind of directive, he urged competitive tests. Otherwise the government might use a hard core of appointees as nationalistic propagandists in "German" areas where Slavic workers would be quick to respond.[23] With such essentially low-pitched disagreements, the leading debaters moved to the vote of May 5, when the Lower House gave its approval. The Upper House followed on May 15, and an ordinance of the Minister of Commerce divided Austria into nine inspection areas on December 30, 1883.[24]

Revision of the law which regulated the crafts and small industries and the institution of inspectors for factories were steps which the most conservative regimes might have taken. Taaffe's full commitment to social reform actually dated from his decision to sponsor a bill aimed at improving conditions in mines, whose workers had already clashed with law-enforcement agents in bloody strikes.

In reality the restriction of working hours in the mines, as well

[21] *Ibid.*, pp. 10813–14, May 5, 1883.
[22] *Ibid.*, p. 10760, May 4, 1883.   [23] *Ibid.*, pp. 10806–7, May 5, 1883.
[24] Gustav Kolmer, *Parlament und Verfassung in Oesterreich* (Vienna and Leipzig, 1902–14), III, 374.

as the new rules regarding the employment of women and younger persons in this highly perilous occupation, met with general approval. In the future, according to the provisions of the projected law, no one could undertake work in the mines while still of school age. Boys between fourteen and sixteen and girls under twenty-one were to do no work which might be hazardous to their health, and no female could engage in mine operations at night. Women who had just borne a child were to abstain from mine employment for six weeks after delivery. No employee was to labor more than ten hours on every twelve-hour shift, and Sunday rest was to begin between 4:00 and 6:00 on Sunday morning for a duration of twenty-four hours.[25]

The Liberal Left revealed a certain disinclination to go along with the far-reaching implications of the proposal in the brief two-day debate of May, 1884, but it succeeded only in redefining the age provision for minors and the rest period prescribed for new mothers. Franz Sprung suggested that children between twelve and fourteen years of age who were not subject to compulsory schooling should work in mines only if the labor was light, if it took place during the day, and if it was requested by parents or guardians and approved specifically by local government officials. Though Falkenhayn tried to show that these "exceptions" were threats to the proposed limitation of child labor, the Lower House accepted Sprung's restrictions.[26] The time needed by a mother to recover from childbirth also aroused a small flurry of debate. Rather sententiously Sprung asserted that the most bitter punishment visited upon industrious women was a refusal to let them work. Falkenhayn rather quickly agreed to a four-week recuperation period if a doctor approved, and, despite Rieger's appeal to Mosaic axioms, the Lower House ratified the compromise.[27]

When the Minister of Agriculture explained the changes to the Emperor, he made it clear that he approved of employing children of twelve who were not subject to public schooling when they obviously were destined for the mines in the future. They

[25] *Ibid.*, III, 372.   [26] *SPA*, pp. 12748–49, 12756, May 9, 1884.
[27] *Ibid.*, pp. 12749, 12752, May 9, 1884.

could thereby add to their family's income. He also repeated Sprung's arguments for speedy re-employment of recent mothers. Falkenhayn, for all of his disclaimers, believed that idleness was a greater threat to society than overwork or potential exhaustion.[28]

Conservative religious reaction against the Liberal legislation of the 1870s also entered into the debates. Victor Fuchs, a Viennese lawyer whose Clerical sympathies earned him a mandate from the great landowners of Salzburg, was quite distressed that the committee's report offered only sanitary and humane reasons for a respite from labor on Sunday. He was sure that a Sabbath that began no earlier than 6:00 on Sunday morning would keep some poor workers from customary weekly service, and he moved that the day of rest and devotion begin at midnight on Saturday.[29] While the clergyman Albert Pflügl predicted that nihilism and socialism would inevitably triumph if a father did not have a midnight-to-midnight Sunday with his family, the Liberals predicted that a miner free at midnight would go the local tavern, stay until dawn, and then go home to sleep, not to church.[30] When Carl Schindler, a member of the Czech Club, kindly but firmly rejected Fuchs's motion as one which could not square with existing mine schedules, the Lower House voted its agreement.[31] Again it was a matter of displeasing a part of the Iron Ring, if only in details, to ensure the success of a crucial governmental decision.

While the Clericals who hoped to get more miners to mass on Sundays were miffed by the outcome, the Liberals closed the debates by collaborating with Rieger, the Czech leader, and the regime in a revision of the proviso dealing with female workers in the mines. Rieger, though admitting that probably no more than 200 women were employed in the pits, pleaded for their complete exclusion from such exhausting and dangerous endeavors. Falkenhayn warmly seconded Rieger's proposal, and

[28] Kabinetts-Kanzlei, Vortrag 2280, June 19, 1884.
[29] *SPA*, pp. 12767–68, May 12, 1884.
[30] *Ibid.*, pp. 12769, 12773–74, May 12, 1884.
[31] *Ibid.*, p. 12775, May 12, 1884.

Rudolf Auspitz, a factory owner himself, moved the prohibition of all female labor in mines after a period of five years. During this interim the mines could hire no new female help.[32] On May 13 the Lower House accepted the bill, with the several minor amendments, and the Upper House added its sanction, without debate, on May 27. The principle of parliamentary control of working hours was established, and in the same month of May, 1884, the Lower House was hotly debating a second bill on conditions in factories and workshops. If conditions in mines compelled instant sympathy even among stanch defenders of economic liberalism, would the somewhat less grim facts of life on workbench or beside a machine inspire similar sentiments?

The cabinet and the Clerical Conservatives who dominated the Lower House's committee on social reform certainly realized that helpers in workshops and laborers in factories also expected relief, particularly in terms of a shorter workday. Belcredi and his associates were particularly intent on guaranteeing Sunday rest, and their general concern for women and minors likewise implied further revisions of the *Gewerbe-Ordnung*.

The ministers by no means controlled the committee, and the latter's first recommendations on child labor in 1883 thoroughly shocked Pino. In the future no child under fourteen years of age could work, and those aged fourteen to sixteen could spend no more than six hours a day at a job. No one could serve full time as a helper before he had reached eighteen. Only states like Denmark and Switzerland had such rigorous controls, complained Pino, and Pražak agreed with him that the existing rule, which permitted full-time activity as a helper at sixteen, was the sensible solution. Taaffe also seemed bothered by the total prohibition of work before fourteen. If young persons could not start learning a vocation before that time, Austria would lose most of the economic advantages expected from the changes in the school laws. Dunajewski then suggested an eight-hour day for boys between fourteen and sixteen, and the cabinet resolved to fight for this compromise.[33]

[32] *Ibid.*, pp. 12778–80, May 12, 1884.   [33] MRP 30, April 9, 1883.

Thanks to the government's representations and to Liberal protests, the committee did amend its original plan by 1884. The new version allowed a boy to begin his training as a future craftsman at twelve, though it barred him from a factory until he was fourteen. Until age fourteen, his day's limit was eight hours. Boys between fourteen and sixteen could spend a maximum of ten hours per day at work, and no girl could work in industry or workshop until she reached the age of twenty-one. Adult workers thereafter would enjoy an eleven-hour day.[34]

The Liberals hoped only to amend the bill in details, but this modest aspiration did not prevent them from a general assault on the premises assumed by the bill's framers. Rudolf Auspitz, beneficent in the matter of female miners, was less accommodating in regard to changes which he, as a factory owner, would help subsidize. Challenging the proposal's basic assumptions, he asserted that Austria suffered from a dearth of capital, which was the basic reason for low wages. The spirit of enterprise was slack in Austria, and those who honestly desired a wise social policy should do something to stimulate it. The Liberals had not promised a maximum workday, for they did not wish to seem less than earnest when it became clear how hard it would be to fulfill such a promise.[35] Michael Matscheko, a Viennese rentier, warned against the adoption of a limited workday before Austria's great competitors settled on one. Foreign capital had not poured into Austria because industry could not count on cheap labor. In remote areas industry had attempted to utilize the cheaper labor there, but if labor costs increased, such isolated enterprises would shut down and whole communities would lose their last loaf of bread.[36]

Adámek, a Czech always to the fore in discussions of social legislation, defended the new *Gewerbe-Ordnung*. When economic egoists ignored society's needs, said Adámek, the state alone possessed the power to force their subordination to the common welfare. The protection of the interests of all, he added heavily, was the vocation of true liberalism. Absolute economic

[34] Knarr, "Das Ministerium des Grafen Taaffe," p. 38.
[35] *SPA*, pp. 12903, 12907–11, May 17, 1884.
[36] *Ibid.*, p. 12946, May 19, 1884.

freedom forwarded the sickness of a society, for the state actually had to defend wives and children from ruthless exploitation by the male head of the family. Tariffs had eliminated the old argument that labor dared not work fewer hours in the face of foreign competition. Indeed, it was lack of taste in the production of goods, lack of progress in the purely technical aspects of manufacturing, and unreliability of exporters which menaced business far more than labor's just demands.[37]

Once the general preliminaries had been completed (and the Liberals did not hide their conviction that their principles were likely to suffer reverses), the government and its opposition wrangled conscientiously over details. With a trace of mischievousness, Menger remarked that a strict Sabbath had been particularly an Anglo-Saxon Puritan phenomenon. The Clericals had better not deny their peasant supporters the right to order a drink after mass or to make some necessary purchases at the retail store. Anyway, was not Sunday in Austria traditionally a time for a bit of frolic? What a tragic comedy if a stern law to the contrary could not be enforced![38] The Lower House nonetheless refused to accept any modification of Sunday rest, save in cases where management could not interrupt operations. Here the central government, through the cabinet, would decide what enterprises merited such a classification.

The only Liberal success was the result of the veteran Chlumecky's persuasiveness. The committee's bill did empower the Minister of Commerce to allow certain factories to operate on the basis of a twelve-hour day if the Minister felt that such factories otherwise would suffer serious harm. Such relaxations of the rule were subject to an annual review, however, and Chlumecky feared that such evaluations would overburden the minister and promote socialist agitation at the end of every year. Certain that the Austrian textile industry would fail without a twelve-hour day, he declared that the mills had to work overtime because of the uncontrollable world market and seasonal demand. Their regular employees wanted to earn the extra sums which such periods paid, and so it was not politic, or

[37] *Ibid.*, pp. 12916–20, May 17, 1884.
[38] *Ibid.*, pp. 12970–71, May 19, 1884.

even easy, to bring in substitute laborers. As a result, he moved that the Ministers of Commerce and Interior grant special dispensations of three years' validity to factories which could demonstrate an absolute need for a twelve-hour day.[39]

Leon Biliński, the Polish spokesman for the parties which pressed for the eleven-hour day, insisted that annual permission for a twelve-hour day was enough. He did agree with Chlumecky and the Liberals that, in cases of emergency, local officials might give individual factories the right to work twelve hours a day for no more than three weeks at a time.[40] Pino quickly declared that he would welcome the Lower House's acceptance of either plan. It was good to give industry a fair break, as long as the law adequately protected labor. The committee's original systematization of the procedures which officials would follow in making exceptions called for a great expenditure of energy, and he was happy that both amendments left more discretion in the hands of local administrators.[41] By the very close vote of 142 to 141, Chlumecky's provision for a three-year review passed. Among the vanquished were four cabinet members and such an unlikely pair as Rieger and Schönerer. Had it not been for the support of some deputies from Galicia and Lienbacher, the Liberals might easily have lost their fight for the textile industry.[42]

There was one last flurry in the Lower House over hours for minors, both male and female. Matscheko offered an amendment which would have permitted some employment of women before they reached eighteen years of age. Modern times demanded some female participation in factory production, particularly when the settled married man needed extra money to rear his children. For some branches of work, women's hands were more agile and more careful of details. France and Germany did not prohibit nightwork for women, and it would be wise to remember the competition they offered.[43] Gustav Pacher, direc-

---

[39] *Ibid.,* pp. 13030–35, May 21, 1884.
[40] *Ibid.,* p. 13043, May 21, 1884.　　[41] *Ibid.,* p. 13044, May 21, 1884.
[42] Roll-call vote, *ibid.,* p. 13069, May 21, 1884.
[43] *SPA,* pp. 13087–88, May 23, 1884.

tor of a famous cotton-yarn firm in Vienna and the representative of the Klagenfurt Chamber of Commerce, bewailed the
rude awakening that would come to thousands of poor families
on New Year's Day of 1885. At that time the new law would
expel 11,000 workers' children from factories because they were
under fourteen. What did the prophets of religious and moral
revival think would happen to children between twelve and
fourteen who were neither in school nor in factory? Moral
bewilderment, vagabondage, and running in unemployed gangs
would be their fate. To underscore his distaste for the "prophets" on the Right, who tended to favor crafts and small
enterprise over large-scale industry, he suggested a limitation of
work by minors in artisans' shops to a maximum of six hours of
light work during daylight hours.[44] Both proposals met defeat,
but the Liberals in the Upper House eight months later also tried
to keep the factories open for twelve-year-old boys. Rather
surprisingly their spokesman was a Taaffe appointee, Baron
Bezecny, who openly declared that to forbid a person to work as
long as he liked was a limitation of human freedom. He realized
that the industrialists of North Bohemia did not want employees
under fourteen, for they wanted to maintain eight years of
compulsory schooling there. But why hinder employers in the
southern parts of Austria from hiring children who naturally
matured more quickly than those in the northern regions and
who could leave school at twelve? He proposed allowing factories the right to hire such school-exempt boys for six hours a day
if a medical doctor agreed.[45] Pino absolutely refused to countenance Bezecny's amendment, and, under direct pressure from
the government to put the bill through before the new elections,
the usually tractable lords voted to accept the new *Gewerbe-
Ordnung* unchanged on February 24, 1885. Taaffe's first parliament had formally approved the principle of a maximum day
and had further limited the employment of women and minors.
It would be the task of the new parliament to create a comprehensive system of insurance for labor.

[44] *Ibid.*, pp. 13089–94, May 23, 1884.
[45] *SPH*, IX Session, pp. 1592, 1610–11, Feb. 25, 1885.

11 Accident and Sickness Insurance Programs

The alliance signed by Austria-Hungary and the German Empire in 1879 inevitably riveted Austrian eyes upon the policies of the great Chancellor in Berlin, whether he warred on the socialists, allowed the breach with Rome to heal, or shrewdly neutralized the Habsburg-Romanov rivalry in the Balkans. In his last decade of power, Bismarck played the role of guardian of the peace as never before, and his manipulation of German internal politics seemed no less magical to a variety of governments which were hypnotized by his astuteness. If it is fashionable today to scoff at his "control" of international policy and to question his ultimate expertise in managing the parties of the Reichstag, it was far from fashionable in the 1880s to doubt his near-infallibility.

As early as 1879 he had persuaded William I to recommend "a positive advancement of the welfare of the working classes" following the passage of the laws against socialism in Germany. The Reichstag's subsequent consideration of accident and sickness insurance for workingmen inspired European countries from Spain to Russia to try such positive weapons against social radicalism. In most states it was conservative or clerical parties which wrote the laws that recognized the insecurities that haunted labor, to be sure, and their long-time emphasis on *noblesse oblige* and Christian fraternalism meant as much as Bismarck's example.

Taaffe was peculiarly fortunate in profiting from the German example. His allies, the Clerical Conservatives, had actually outstripped the cabinet in revising the ordering of factory and workshop disciplines. Though the German Liberals of Austria were very much aware of Bismarck's contempt for their obduracy over Bosnia and Austrian military preparedness, they could not withhold their admiration from a man who had placed German power and Kultur in such a dazzling light. They had reason to fear socialism, yet they wanted to destroy its influence without sacrificing the basic human rights they long had championed. In the 1880s Austrian industry was largely German in ownership and direction, and its directors were convinced that it was good business to conciliate the labor force.

In earlier times medieval guilds had established varying types of funds to care for sick and disabled brother craftsmen or for their families in case of a member's death. Postmedieval governments often were suspicious of such protective associations, for beneath the charitable surface there might be activity subversive of good mercantilistic policy. The French Revolution's suspicion of guilds and corporative action was but the climax of several centuries of governmental surveillance. For many in Europe for whom "liberty, equality, and fraternity" were hateful words, the guilds or similar brotherhoods of men in the same vocation suddenly became symbols of the organic development of European society. They represented the unchanging strata of an ordered world, and even Metternich's and Kolowrat's prying bureaucrats in the Austrian Empire looked with tolerance upon corporative protection of masters, journeymen, and helpers during the placid early Biedermeier days. The oldest of the relief funds were those which tried to meet the miners' needs, the Bruderladen or Knappschaftskassen.

With the *Gewerbe-Ordnung* of December 20, 1859, the government ostensibly encouraged the formation of sickness and accident funds to which employers would contribute an amount equal to half of the sums turned in by the workers. The worker's premium was 3 per cent of his wages, but only a few of the associations founded after 1859 had more than a paper existence.[1]

The cabinet first considered arguments for a comprehensive workers' accident law in early December, 1882, the year in which it was constantly engaged in the planning of social reforms. In this preliminary meeting, Pražak, the Minister of Justice, had responsibility for obtaining the opinions of his colleagues before completing the draft of a law. Aiding him was the dedicated and influential *Sectionsrat* Emil Steinbach, one of the most creative and controversial of the figures of the Taaffe era. For the following five years these two were on permanent call to defend, modify, and trim their original ideas before the Fabians of both houses. And, in this first cabinet meeting, the ministers raised some of the issues which the Reichsrat would most strenuously dispute.

Pražak assured his colleagues that proper financial care for accident cases was first on the list of labor's demands, and he hinted that he preferred a separate accident insurance law to a comprehensive social insurance code. Only Falkenhayn demurred, and he simply raised the issue of combining invalidity insurance with accident coverage. As representative of the socially oriented Catholic circles of the early 1880s, however, he warmly recommended using the organization followed by the Bruderladen as a pattern for the government's program. Several factories could combine their labor forces into one Bruderladen, and a principle of reciprocity among all such funds would enable a worker to move from one area to another without damaging his right to future claims. Since workers would be in charge of the funds, they would personally prevent fraud and peculation. Steinbach pointedly rejected such a scheme. The Bruderladen were all right "for conservative elements such as miners," but the rest of industrial labor was hostile to the idea of using them as

[1] Walter Knarr, "Das Ministerium des Grafen Taaffe und die soziale Frage" (unpubl. diss., Vienna, 1948), p. 40.

models. Falkenhayn did not deign to reply, but his silence did not connote agreement.

Rather tentatively Pino expressed his partiality for insurance funds whose contributors would belong to the same vocation. If funds represented territorial units, mere "labor districts," they would enroll quite disparate types of workers and skills. Vocational arrangements would expedite insurance against diseases common to, or developing out of, a specific pursuit.[2] The cabinet's first exchange of views was restrained, but its consideration of a bill which experts from the Ministries of Justice, Interior, Agriculture, and Commerce elaborated in the next two months revealed a serious split between Falkenhayn and his colleagues.

This draft established compulsory accident insurance for industrial workers and for those agricultural workers who were active as operators of potentially dangerous machinery. The worker would pay 10 per cent of the premium established by the insurance institute in which he was enrolled, his employer paid 90 per cent. These institutes were to be organized territorially, not vocationally, and their administration was to be in the hands of representatives of the employees and of the employers, plus delegates chosen by the government from knowledgeable persons resident in the general area of jurisdiction. Each institute would build up a reserve fund by anticipating through actuarial methods the expected disbursements for a number of years in advance. A common reserve fund, contributed to by all the institutes, would serve as a reservoir for future institutes or as a source of emergency financing. A person who had an accident would have to wait four weeks before his insurance payments began. A worker permanently disabled would receive 60 per cent of his usual wages. If partially disabled, he would draw up to 50 per cent for the period of enforced inactivity. Should a worker suffer a mortal accident, his widow would receive 20 per cent of his wages until she remarried, while a legitimate orphan would receive 10 per cent of his parent's wages until he reached

[2] MRP 96, Dec. 4, 1882.

the age of fifteen. A legitimate child bereft of both parents would receive 20 per cent of one parent's pay if that parent had been killed in an accident. Illegitimate children under fifteen could only claim 10 per cent of the deceased parent's salary. A maximum of 25 gulden was available for funeral expenses. The total income of widow and orphans could not exceed 50 per cent of the deceased's wages.

Obviously this project ignored Falkenhayn's recommendation to use the Bruderladen organization as a prototype, and Steinbach even dared to ask if mineworkers should be included in the general plan. The Minister of Agriculture promptly launched into a filibuster against the entire draft, arguing that it would extinguish the spirit and very existence of the "centuries-old" Bruderladen. He resented the "excessive power" of the central government manifested in the bill. Why not permit factories "of the same category" to form their own funds, which would correspond to local conditions? Imperial law should merely state guiding principles. Until the government assembled more data to clarify the whole question of social insurance, he proposed postponement of the accident bill.

Pražak abruptly rejected the Bruderladen as possible models, and Taaffe unhesitatingly asked all present to pass on Falkenhayn's motion to delay action. With no attempt at subtlety, he reminded the cabinet that it had already commissioned Dunajewski to tell the Lower House that such a bill was in preparation. Urgent political necessity forbade procrastination. Pino and Conrad backed the Minister-President's plea, but Falkenhayn stubbornly refused to withdraw his motion. The embarrassed ministers then voted unanimously against him.[3]

A month later Steinbach raised the question of excluding miners and workers in the salt pits from the provisions of the accident insurance bill. Would it not be odd to deprive a very dangerous occupation of a financial protection greater than that offered by the Bruderladen? Pražak and Taaffe agreed that the law would be but halfway effective without miners, but Falkenhayn replied that he would resign if anything was done to allow

[3] MRP 19, Feb. 25, 1883.

the Bruderladen to conform to the general levels established in the bill. Behind the doughty Minister stood an undetermined number of Clerical Conservative deputies, many of whom identified the miners' protective associations with the valiant spirit of medieval self-help. Pino gently provided for Taaffe's retreat by declaring that, though he wanted to include the miners, such an inclusion would destroy the bill's chances to pass. His colleagues assented, and the Minister-President could only acquiesce, with great regret.[4]

In the autumn of 1883 the Minister-President informed the cabinet that the Emperor desired a reconsideration of the exclusion of miners and saltworkers. Although it was clear that Falkenhayn stood isolated in his continuing fight for the Bruderladen, he agreed only to a rephrasing of the draft bill that would allow the members of a miners' relief fund either to convert their particular organization into part of the new arrangements or to remain as they had been. Taaffe was worried that this option substantially weakened the whole force of the bill, but he and his colleagues accepted Falkenhayn's slight concession.[5] Pražak's report to the Emperor anent the change did not omit sarcastic references to Falkenhayn, his "extreme desire" to exclude the miners, and his "fear" that the accident insurance plan would work against the projected reform of the Bruderladen. Although the majority of the cabinet did not share his concern, noted Pražak rather primly, they had agreed to further changes that would safeguard the Bruderladen without putting undue burdens on mine owners.[6]

In December, 1884, the bill went to the Lower House, where the Liberals raised major objections. They wanted to excuse the insured workers from contributing any of their wages to the accident funds. They were disturbed that many agricultural and forestry workers would not come under the new law. Finally, they insisted that a sickness insurance bill precede an accident insurance bill, or that the Reichsrat consider both types simultaneously. Alois Liechtenstein reported the bill from committee

[4] MRP 25, Mar. 30, 1883.   [5] MRP 61, Oct. 19, 1883.
[6] Kabinetts-Kanzlei, Vortrag 4136, Nov. 9, 1883.

in record time, but the crowded calendar which the outgoing Lower House faced in 1885, plus obvious Liberal determination to contest major points, forced a long delay.[7]

The elections of 1885 eased Taaffe's position in the Lower House, and the speech from the throne stressed the need for accident and sickness insurance, for regulation of the Bruderladen, and for legal checks on radicalism. In the spring of 1886 the deputies finally moved to a distinctly brilliant debate in which the Liberals astounded public opinion with their zeal to outdo the government and the "Social Catholics" in securing the best possible treatment of laborers who had suffered accidents on the job.

Four major conflicts between Right and Left in the decisive debate of late May and early June, 1886, enlisted many of the oratorical stars of the day, and the general tone was worthy of praise. The four pivotal controversies centered about the territorial system of institutes (in which the insured would be enrolled), the liability of the insured to pay part of the premiums, the exclusion of large numbers of workers in agriculture and forestry, and the creation of a strong reserve fund system rather than a system of assessment based on current need.

The plan to assign workers to insurance institutes arranged on a territorial basis inevitably renewed the struggle between federalists and centralists. Josef Bromovsky of Prague alleged that the great differences among the *Länder* in Austria made a vocational organization quite impractical. The larger the sphere of the individual institute, the greater the chance to spread risks.[8] The Polish deputy Biliński made no attempt to deny that men of his beliefs were playing politics in demanding territorial institutes. Were not parliamentarians expected to politick? Did the proponents of vocational institutes plan to pick a *Staatssprache* for the daily business of the insurance funds? How else would the members understand each other?[9] Alois Liechtenstein, whose numerous apologias for the guilds of old put him in an uncom-

---

[7] Knarr, "Das Ministerium des Grafen Taaffe," pp. 42–43.

[8] *SPA*, X Session, pp. 2497–99, 2501–2, May 20, 1886.

[9] *Ibid.,* p. 2574, May 25, 1886.

fortable position, affected considerable gladness that people everywhere recognized the value of vocational associations. Unfortunately, they were unsuitable for accident insurance programs, for they represented the principle of specialization, even splintering, whereas it was necessary to insure the largest possible number of workers.[10]

The German deputies who passionately advocated a vocational organization as a substitute for the "federalistic" scheme advanced by Taaffe and his Iron Ring were Nationalist and Democratic for the most part. Representing the German National Vereinigung, Heinrich Prade, a merchant of Reichenberg in Bohemia, turned some of the government's arguments around to suit his own convictions. If the greatest possible sharing of risks was desirable, what limits were greater than those of the empire itself? If Galicians disapproved of vocational institutes, then the Reichsrat could exclude their crownland. Proclaiming himself a strong German Nationalist and a member of a generation that wanted something greater than "the Liberal ideal," Prade announced that one nationality in a multinational state must lead, one language must rule. He and his party had nothing to lose in the battle to keep Austria an outpost of German culture, for, should the empire fail, there was always the opportunity to return to *Allmutter Germania*.[11] Robert Pattai, an Independent and anti-Semite who represented the economically distressed sixth ward in Vienna, feared that national hatreds and partiality would color the decisions reached within territorial institutes. In a decade the great principle of social security would be swallowed up in the project of dividing the empire into federal crownlands, in which the German would be the oppressed.[12]

Steinbach summarized the case for the regime by denying that the ministers were trying to forward federalism or centralism. Actuarially, the territorial delimitation was preferable, for distance and language problems would add appreciably to the cost

[10] *Ibid.*, pp. 2609–10, May 27, 1886.
[11] *Ibid.*, pp. 2486, 2492–96, May 20, 1886.
[12] *Ibid.*, pp. 2743–45, May 31, 1886.

of vocational arrangements. The German Empire had surrendered the vocational approach when it added agricultural labor
to the accident insurance coverage. If Austria began with the
purely territorial system, it could assign all future insurance
programs to such a system.[13] On May 31 the regime and the
Right carried the principle of territorial institutes.

Less tempestuous was the debate over the duty of the insured
to pay 10 per cent of the premiums due for accident coverage.
Here the Liberals grandiloquently paraded as labor's friend, but
some on the extreme German Left mocked them or simply
disagreed with their simplified approach. Lueger openly hoped
for the extinction of all private insurance firms as he cynically
welcomed Liberalism's new interest in labor. If the industrialists, as the Liberals implied, wanted so desperately to pay all of
the premium, he would not try to dissuade them.[14] Prade
wanted employer, employee, and the state to contribute. The
state always had money for the armed forces, no matter how
ominous the deficit appeared to be. He anticipated the worri-
some burdens for the laboring class when sickness, invalidity,
and survivors' insurance programs were later established.[15]

The parties which supported the government either stressed
the laborer's right to help administer insurance funds or his duty
to help meet the costs of the program by a minimal contribu-
tion. A Czech like Adámek, whose Bohemia was increasingly a
land of ambitious, skilled workers, was likely to emphasize the
laborer's desire to avoid alms, to learn how to share in managing
the institutes' affairs.[16] Biliński, a professor interested in economics and, as a Pole, less personally involved with growing
industrial populations, underlined the laborer's obligation to
share the burden.[17] Steinbach's approval of the idea that the
insured should pay part of the premiums was "correct" rather
than enthusiastic. He admitted that it would be technically
easier to manage the funds if the workers contributed nothing.

[13] *Ibid.*, pp. 2752–54, May 31, 1886.
[14] *Ibid.*, pp. 2535, 2537, May 21, 1886.
[15] *Ibid.*, pp. 2488–89, May 20, 1886.
[16] *Ibid.*, p. 2523, May 21, 1886.   [17] *Ibid.*, p. 2577, May 25, 1886.

But accident insurance no doubt would prepare the way for other insurance programs in which the worker obviously would help to defray costs. To avoid later resentments and disagreements, it would be better to accustom labor to deductions.[18] The roll-call vote was too close for the Right's peace of mind, 133 to 122, and the majority included ballots cast by members of the cabinet. Lueger, true to his pledge, voted with the Liberals to let the employers pay all of the costs of accident insurance.[19]

The Left hammered even more vigorously at the Right's careful exclusion of a majority of agricultural and forestry workers. The rather unexpected championing of rural underdogs by the lawyers, professors, and businessmen of Vienna and the great industrial centers was not much more of a surprise than the failure of the Clerical Conservatives to opt for vocational institutes. It was clear that the Left's attack embarrassed the Right, and no one on the Right attempted to deny that the powerful bloc of Galician landlords was responsible for the studied exclusion of the vast mass of peasants who worked without the blessings of farm machinery. Lueger told the majority that it would do the right thing if it would agree, with proper restrictions, to insuring the greater part of the artisans, the peasants, and the lumberers, whom the present bill excluded.[20] In reply, a Czech like Adámek hinted that farmers could be insured if the Left would accept the diets as the supervisors of such programs. He freely admitted that insuring industrial labor would result in a stream of farm hands leaving the country. Farmers would face ever more crippling strikes, and for these reasons agrarian interests in his land were already planning an adequate insurance program.[21]

Outstanding Liberals did their best to bring the country workers into the coverage. Professor Exner, who represented what were in 1886 the "rural" communes of Hernals, Ottakring, and Währing, was very much exercised over the committee's excision of numerous occupations from the list of those which required

[18] *Ibid.*, pp. 2838–39, June 2, 1886.
[19] *Ibid.*, pp. 2844–45, June 2, 1886.
[20] *Ibid.*, p. 2534, May 21, 1886.   [21] *Ibid.*, pp. 2653–54, May 28, 1886.

accident coverage. What of the very dangerous job of operating
a chaff-cutting engine? Why ignore the lumberjacks who guided
timber down the streams, who were in much greater peril than
the men who operated industry's secondary rail lines? Was it
right to excuse a farmer who rented a machine when in industrial
operations both owner and renter of a machine had to pay
premiums?[22] Neuwirth openly accused the Poles of sabotaging
the hopes of the poor for financial security against accidents on
the rural scene, and he tongue-lashed Biliński quite thoroughly
when the latter pompously described the patriarchal custom of
indemnifying a peasant disabled on a noble's estate with part of a
field or a cottage.[23] Could this cripple in the cottage eat from the
field or could he only till it? asked the representative of Brünn's
business community. Very much put out by the Right's tendency to describe industrial conditions in Brünn as symptomatic
of labor's cruel fate, he alternated harrowing accounts of the lot
of miners in Galicia with stories of starvation wages paid on
Taaffe's estate, Ellischau.[24]

Neuwirth's personal attack on the Minister-President's private
affairs was indicative of the Left's determination to milk the
agricultural-forestry issue as exhaustively as possible. In the
end the Lower House did accept a minority resolution which
called upon the cabinet to prepare a bill that would protect all
workers left out of the draft under discussion.[25] The fact that the
German Empire had very recently drawn farm labor into the
accident insurance program and the admission by the Czechs
that the problem worried them in Bohemia were more reliable
auguries than a resolution that the cabinet might do something.
The fate of resolutions was a subject for jokes in Austrian
circles.

The Left was astute in making strong cases for including farm
and forestry labor and for excusing all the insured from contributing to the general funds. It may have surprised the Right by

[22] *Ibid.,* pp. 2557–58, May 25, 1886.
[23] *Ibid.,* p. 2579, May 25, 1886.
[24] *Ibid.,* pp. 2599–2604, May 27, 1886.
[25] *Ibid.,* p. 2708, May 29, 1886.

such stands. It certainly put the Right on the defensive. The fourth great disagreement between Right and Left revealed the Liberals, as in the case of vocational organization, in more predictable battle dress. Briefly, how should the accident insurance scheme pay for itself? The government acted only as a supervisor, not as a contributor. The employer was to pay almost all the premiums decided upon, the employee a token 10 per cent.

The Left maintained that an assessment system, based upon actual payments to accident victims or their survivors, was the only possible procedure in view of poor business conditions. The government, with the support of the Right, insisted upon the creation of reserve funds by collection of actuarially determined premiums. Each institute would have its own reserve, and there would be a central reserve in Vienna for new institutes or for institutes in temporary difficulties. Both sides generally agreed that the assessment system would be cheaper. A fair number of Liberals, whose orthodox economic tenets no doubt were strained by a "pay now, let the future take care of itself" approach, admitted that in normal times a reserve fund certainly would be the correct mode of financing. With near unanimity the Liberals were swearing that the times were far from normal.

The climax of the Left's attempt to avoid the introduction of reserve funds came on June 1, when Max Mauthner, who represented the capital's chamber of commerce, and Ernst Plener, elected by the chamber in Eger (Cheb), blended specific pleas for the assessment procedure with ringing paeans to industrial capitalism. Neither was intellectually able to defend an assessment system as a permanent solution. Mauthner drew a sharp distinction between private insurance companies, which dared not operate without reserve funds, and the proposed institutes, which were examples of state socialism. He estimated that the projected average premium which employers would pay (1.5 per cent of their payrolls) would be a colossal burden, equal to the incidence of the *Erwerbsteuer,* the general tax on industrial and commercial enterprises. For years anxious voices had urged small industry to introduce machinery. Now those who complied would pay the high costs of accident insurance. In the past the state had gradually increased the sugar tax, the land tax, the tax on income from rents on houses. This orderly process had been good for industry and for the over-all economy. Some older factories would face ruin if they had to meet the new insurance charges at the same time they were modernizing their plants.[26] Steinbach was obviously roiled by Mauthner's speech and by the fact that he made a motion calling for an assessment system "on the German Empire's model." Such a motion had not appeared in the minority's report from committee, complained the *Sectionsrat,* and, to make a decent appraisal of what was requested, the committee would have to postpone the bill until the next parliamentary year. With unwonted curtness Steinbach served notice on the Left that the government could never accept an assessment plan unless it simultaneously guaranteed the financial stability of such a plan. This would benefit certain interests at the cost of the general public, and he could tell the Reichsrat plainly that a state guarantee would not be forthcoming.[27]

Liberalism was extremely sensitive to executive pressure upon legislative persons and processes. The coercion of parliament by English Stuarts was ever vivid in Liberal minds, and Steinbach's abrupt lecturing provoked a scornful reply from Plener, who left little to the imagination in his critique of Steinbach's hectoring manner. Moreover, he took to task his colleagues on the Right who unendingly sniped at successful large-scale enterprise. No matter how many speeches and brochures emanated from reactionary *Sozialpolitiker,* such enterprises furthered civilization. Parliament should give them time to plan for these new responsibilities. It was not unrealistic to believe that the consumer eventually would pay for the resulting higher costs of production, but such a shift came slowly.[28] The Right had the last word. In reply to Plener's lament that "reactionaries" hated

[26] *Ibid.,* pp. 2786–92, June 1, 1886.
[27] *Ibid.,* pp. 2795–96, 2799–2800, June 1, 1886.
[28] *Ibid.,* pp. 2811–14, June 1, 1886.

industry, Alois Liechtenstein wryly assured him that they were
not the people to replace locomotives with droshkies or to cut off
the gas. Wood cost too much.[29]

Speakers for the Right had not stressed the virtues of a reserve
fund to a notable extent in the debates. Steinbach and the
government had primary responsibility for a financially sound
insurance system, or at least for a system which industry and
workers would subsidize without benefit of a state guarantee.
The Liberals usually were the treasury's most devoted watch-
dogs. In face of their temporary desertion, the Right was content merely to vote as Steinbach had directed on June 2. Friends
of the Austrian cabinet could boast that Franz Joseph's ministers
had more concern for fiscal limits than did Bismarck. Cynics
merely uttered the word "necessity."

A few side issues were interesting as commentaries upon the
differing standards of judgment in moral matters. Taaffe's term
of office began the same year that Franz von Suppé's risqué and
irreverent *Boccaccio* had its first performance. In later years
Karl Lueger expressed shock over the low tone of the theater of
his younger days, and Vienna in the 1880s offered, like most
European cities, quite a contrast between precept and practice.
Vital statistics did more than pert operetta lines to reveal the
casual attitudes toward marriage and the family. Very much
bothered by the bill's discrimination against illegitimate children
whose parent had died in an accident, Lueger noted that almost
half the births in Vienna were outside the marriage bond. The
economic woes of the people were more responsible for the
situation than contempt for morality, he felt, and he offered an
amendment which would give illegitimate survivors the same
sums guaranteed legitimate children. No doubt everyone would
like to limit concubinage, he remarked. Could the bill's discrim-
inatory clause do so? Working mothers always made poor
money. Why punish further their illegitimate offspring?[30]
Lueger's future collaborator, Alois Liechtenstein, was downright
volksthümlich in his rebuttal of the young Independent's ideas.
Most illegitimate children were the direct result of a male disin-

[29] *Ibid.,* p. 2828, June 2, 1886.   [30] *Ibid.,* pp. 2733–35, May 31, 1886.

clination to bind one's self for the future, opined the Prince. If women were pressed by economic hardships, they would pursue their lovers and force them to marry. So much the better for morality was this aristocrat's considered judgment.[31] The House brought in a similar verdict by defeating Lueger's amendment.

The campaign for social reform had serious unrest among Austrian laborers as its backdrop. The regime was frankly following a "carrot and whip" policy, and it was not difficult to convince an already frightened bourgeoisie that radicalism was on the march. If sexual immorality got short shrift in the Lower House's treatment of natural children, social immorality in the sense of willful destruction of property gave the deputies a tougher problem to mull over. No one expected deserted women to unite against the existing order. What to do with the obviously disaffected working class was worthier of oratorical fencing.

The committee's bill allowed the survivors of a worker who deliberately caused the accident that ended in his own death to claim the prescribed benefits. Vigorous anarchist propaganda and nihilist action since 1871 made the destruction of machinery and factories a distinct possibility, and Menger, an acknowledged spokesman for industry, moved the denial of benefits for the survivors of a laborer who maliciously caused an industrial accident. Their innocence he granted, but legislators should do nothing to encourage criminal acts.[32] In response, Alois Liechtenstein begged the Lower House to look upon the bill as an olive branch which should calm rather than antagonize the workers. It was very difficult to prove base intent. What could be proved was the death of an individual and the need of his dependents. It would be better to prevent ugly recriminations and bad blood, he advised, by providing for the dependents of one whose actions were misguidedly antisocial.[33] It was Liechtenstein, not Menger, whom the Lower House heeded.

[31] *Ibid.*, p. 2738, May 31, 1886.   [32] *Ibid.*, pp. 2736–37, May 31, 1886.
[33] *Ibid.*, p. 2739, May 31, 1886.

In February, 1887, the Upper House eliminated the paragraph which specifically indemnified the survivors of willful saboteurs and then balanced matters by voting insurance benefits for widowers whose wives had worked and who had legitimate children to rear. The peers also wanted to exclude from accident insurance plans all who made less than one gulden a day, and so there had to be a bargaining session between representatives of the two houses. In the end the elected deputies refused to yield on the issue of contributions from all employees and accepted the exclusion of the relatives of saboteurs from benefits.[34] On December 28, 1887, Franz Joseph finally was able to sign the long-delayed act.

The regime had no reason to congratulate itself on the speed with which the bill had finally become law. Various reasons for the wearisome progress are obvious. First, the Poles were not vitally interested, and the German Clerical Conservatives, to secure minimal Polish support, had to agree to a territorial arrangement of insurance institutes somewhat at variance with their philosophical justifications of a neomedieval vocationalized society. Second, the Liberals were unusually clever in taking advantage of the Right's basic lack of unity. If their numerical strength in the Lower House after the election of 1885 was decisive only in details, their continuing influence in the Upper House was sufficient to force delay and reconsideration, if only again of details. Despite some ugly exchanges of superheated nationalists, both houses had given the bill decent, if unduly long, attention. In 1890 the program indemnified 1,539 workers disabled for a long period of time, 4,600 who suffered from temporary injuries, and the survivors of 548 killed in accidents. In 1900 fatal cases had risen to 1,103, cases of lengthy disability to 5,962, and short-term cases to 16,174.[35]

The delay in agreeing upon a suitable accident insurance program did much to hamper the Reichsrat's discussion of the cabinet's bill for sickness insurance, which actually went to the Lower House in February, 1885. Two years later, after some

---

[34] *Ibid.*, pp. 6479, 6485, 6498, Oct. 26, 1887.
[35] Knarr, "Das Ministerium des Grafen Taaffe," p. 68.

amendment in committee, the regulations underwent the Lower House's scrutiny.

Thanks to the existence of a variety of sickness funds in Austria, it was agreed to prescribe certain minimal standards to which all would have to conform. The workers would bear two-thirds of the costs of the premiums, the employers one-third. Eligibility would begin the fourth day of illness, and benefits would last twenty weeks. These payments would equal 60 per cent of the average local daily wage of insured persons. Maternity cases would receive four weeks of payments. Persons made ill by drunkenness, brawling, or sexual excess would not draw benefits. If the worker died, the burial allowance would be twenty times the average local daily wage. Agricultural and forestry workers generally did not come under the protection of the new program.

The government had the right to dissolve any fund which did not meet the proper actuarial standards, and it likewise could approve new funds. Existing company funds, funds which were "free" in the sense of being controlled by labor associations, and funds which certain construction workers had established would continue as long as they met minimal requirements. All other workers who came under the law's compass would join territorial funds, based on the Bezirk (district). Labor's suspicion of company funds was reflected in the strict rules which thereafter would control such funds. First, both employers and employees would share in the administration of such funds. Second, no employer could create a fund if he employed more than 100 workers unless he could prove to the political officials of his crownland that he did not thereby endanger the existing territorial fund. If he employed fewer than 100, he had to prove to the same officials that the survival of his company fund was guaranteed.

The Liberals were fearful that company funds and "free" or workers' funds would decline in competition with territorial funds. The very promising Josef Maria Baernreither hoped that the bureaucrats would understand that company funds covered men with higher wages and greater skills. It would be most unjust to subject a projected company fund to the standards obtaining in a territorial fund.[36] With a *sang-froid* reminiscent of Liberalism's more doctrinaire days, Julius Gomperz, who represented the chamber of commerce in Brünn, asserted that company funds were the most natural and the most appropriate forms of protection against illness. The intimate contact between employers and hundreds or thousands of their workers had a moral effect on both.[37]

The Right never admitted that company funds deserved special treatment. Professor Josef Kaizl, a Czech who often led the parade against mobile capital, was sure that the new bill still left the employer very much in control. Company funds and "free" funds were class institutions, the one dominated by the factory owners, the other by labor. Territorial funds on the other hand were neutral, and here employer and employee should work in concord. If not, he did not know where harmony could reign.[38] His countryman Adámek declared that he preferred territorial funds, for who would believe that the law would fulfill its promise of labor's right to help administer a company fund? An employer would discharge those who resisted his desires, and he would not hire a man who might be a health risk. Company funds increased class tensions. They were the operational bases for those who did not want to settle the labor question legally.[39]

In the final consideration of the territorial funds, Steinbach stressed their future role in providing an insurance system for agricultural and forestry workers. The cabinet did anticipate competition between the two types, but it rejected the idea of repressing one for the sake of the other.[40] And so, in the end, the Lower House accepted the paragraph as proposed. Political officials might indeed hamper the creation of new company funds. The territorial funds would obviously encompass the greater number of workers. But employees who remained on a

[36] *SPA,* pp. 4555, 4558, March 18, 1887.
[37] *Ibid.,* p. 4560, March 18, 1887.
[38] *Ibid.,* pp. 4135, 4138–39, Feb. 11, 1887.
[39] *Ibid.,* pp. 4570–74, March 21, 1887.
[40] *Ibid.,* pp. 4611–12, March 21, 1887.

company's payroll could resign from the company fund only to join in "free," labor-directed funds. They were not free to move into the territorial fund as long as their employer offered his own system of benefits.

Neuwirth's complaint over industry's double liability—to pay taxes for the relief of sick agrarian workers and to share in the costs of insuring their own labor force against illness—was a reminder that agricultural and forestry workers did not come under the provisions of the new sickness insurance. Friedrich Suess demonstrated the Liberal distaste for landlords whose influence had excluded such workers by moving the coverage of all persons who worked only for wages, but his amendment lost.[41] Baernreither tried to comfort his Liberal friends by enumerating the difficulties involved in insuring such types of labor. Wages in the country were too low, one small farmer often worked part-time for another, while the inclusion of farm and forest labor in territorial funds would make supervision and prevention of embezzling impossible.[42]

Unexpectedly, Kaizl cut off the Liberal objections with a proposal on February 21 to allow the diets to regulate sickness insurance for agricultural and forestry workers. A diet, he said, always would know rural conditions better than the Reichsrat would. A diet could individualize, whereas an imperial law would be a curiosity if it tried to take note of all the differences existing in Austria.[43] Steinbach used Kaizl's motion for his most illuminating discourse of the debate. He chided the committee for removing a phrase which would have allowed the Ministry of Interior to prescribe the insuring of certain individuals in farm or forest work *in parts of crownlands* as well as in crownlands. Why not recognize the great differences between conditions in North and South Tirol? At the moment he saw no chance to insure agricultural workers even in a single crownland. When the time did come, the inauguration of such an insurance pro-

[41] *Ibid.*, p. 4155, Feb. 11, 1887.
[42] *Ibid.*, pp. 4191–93, Feb. 15, 1887.
[43] *Ibid.*, pp. 4236–38, Feb. 21, 1887.

gram would reduce local and crownland tax burdens. Why then did the big landlords resist? The bright but untactful civil servant made no bones of his own sympathies. Insurance for peasant and lumberman would be far better than poor relief, for it would avert the sale of tools and clothes and the exhaustion of all savings when a crippling malady first struck. Thanking Kaizl for his defense of the proposed territorial funds, he resolutely declared that these funds would realize their full significance only when they included agricultural and forestry workers among their insured.[44] Although Baernreither protested that the Reichsrat could not leave to the decision of the individual crownlands those social reforms which might condition the entire structure of the state, the same Reichsrat accepted Kaizl's autonomist motion.

Moral issues inspired a plethora of rhetoric, as they had in the case of accident insurance. Johann Rogl of the Centrums Club, an agriculturist representing rural communes in Upper Austria, provocatively asked why a fine young male worker should help take care of maternity cases for which he had no responsibility, particularly in view of the likelihood that he would not need sick benefits himself for years. He wanted to excise all maternity payments from the program, but he would try only to deprive unmarried mothers of subsidies. Giving them protection was creating a privileged position for immorality. What would a decent female worker think when one of her delinquent sisters drew money from the fund?[45]

Although extreme German Nationalists had not yet proclaimed their schism from Rome, Karl Türk gleefully turned on the ultraclerical Rogl with sarcasm and some unconscious humor. If religion and the fear of Hell's tortures had not deterred the unwed, the loss of four weeks' insurance would scarcely constrain them. In spite of the fact that he represented rural communes also, he was of the opinion that city workers were less responsible for illegitimate offspring than farm workers.

[44] *Ibid.*, pp. 4239–43, Feb. 21, 1887.
[45] *Ibid.*, pp. 4276–77, Feb. 24, 1887.

Because of crowded living conditions, they were more easily tempted.[46] Karl Lueger and Eduard Suess joined Türk in blasting away at Rogl's motion to exclude unblessed events from coverage, and Biliński added rather quizzically that misery and hard luck were for the most part to blame for illegitimacy. In a cool academic vein he noted that the problem also involved the increase of the working population, which was "important." Whether moved by compunction or by visions of a decreasing labor force, a majority of the deputies voted to continue maternity benefits for all working women.[47]

The ravages of syphilis and an individual's responsibility for contracting the dread infection also stirred up a small tempest. Franz Roser, a practicing physician from Braunau who represented rural districts around Trautenau (Trutnov) in Bohemia, protested against the right of a sickness fund to deny all or partial benefits to a worker who suffered from "sexual excesses." The paragraph in point also would have allowed individual funds to disqualify persons who were hurt through deliberate participation in brawling or as a result of intoxication. Dr. Roser alleged that persons could develop syphilis through other infections or inoculations or by heredity. If a fund refused to help victims of syphilis, the latter would try to hide their predicament and resort to quacks to stay on the job.[48]

The Liberal physician prompted Rogl to protest subventions to rowdy and "sinful" people, and he again tried to penalize unwed mothers by proposing to put them with the brawlers, drunkards, and syphilitics on the "excluded" list.[49] Pernerstorfer, for the moment a left-wing German Nationalist, pounced upon Rogl's suggestion. He quoted "a well-known and respected Vienna dermatologist" to the effect that 60 per cent of the Austrian aristocracy was undergoing mercury treatments. In his opinion, Christ would last only twenty-four hours with "His party" in the Lower House, who would not tolerate His lax

[46] *Ibid.,* p. 4280, Feb. 24, 1887.
[47] *Ibid.,* pp. 4303–4, 4308, Feb. 25, 1887.
[48] *Ibid.,* p. 4347, March 9, 1887.
[49] *Ibid.,* pp. 4348–49, March 9, 1887.

views. What a shame that Rogl pretended that his opinions were a Christian way of looking at things![50] Türk, the country doctor, testified that in all of his years of practice he had treated only one worker with a primary syphilitic infection. A doctor should minister to the sick, not deliver them over to public disdain. Under the disputed phrasing, a doctor would have to "tell," and he joined with his colleague Roser in deploring the discrimination against syphilitics.[51] The canny Biliński ended the warm exchange by declaring that he also would like to strike out the denial of benefits for "sexual excesses," though he was duty-bound to recommend the opposite, in line with the committee's wishes. The hint was sufficient, for the Lower House followed Roser's recommendation. If the good doctor's theories of infection were somewhat too charitable, his accent on proper and timely treatment of a scourge that cost thousands of man-hours made sense to nearly all members. Significantly, no other Clerical Conservative had verbally supported Rogl.[52]

With the third reading of the bill on March 29, the Lower House sent to the peers a draft which had caused less difference of opinion than had accident legislation. The gentlemen in the Upper House, however, balked. They refused to accept Kaizl's formula for a regulation by the diets of coverage for agricultural and forestry workers. They followed the Liberals of the lower branch in an attempt to give company funds a stronger position, but the result of their action was postponement, not revision, of the deputies' verdicts.[53] Not unwisely Pražak advised the Emperor the day after Christmas in 1887 to sanction without further delay the law on accident coverage as a means of breaking the impasse between the two houses. When the public took notice of the publication and operation of the law which had passed, it would then put inexorable pressure upon parliament.[54]

[50] *Ibid.*, pp. 4352–53, March 9, 1887.
[51] *Ibid.*, pp. 4353–54, March 9, 1887.
[52] *Ibid.*, p. 4355, March 9, 1887.
[53] Gustav Kolmer, *Parlament und Verfassung in Oesterreich* (Vienna and Leipzig, 1902–14), IV, 349–50.
[54] Kabinetts-Kanzlei, Vortrag 4725, Dec. 26, 1887.

In February, 1888, Count Belcredi tried to comfort his fellow peers, when it became clear that the Lower House would not budge, with the statement that many agricultural and forestry workers would still come under the imperial insurance law. All who were contributors to accident funds would be in this category.[55] Some unconvinced Liberals supported a last-ditch motion by Baron Hye, a member of the Reichsgericht, which somewhat unclearly excluded from the diets' jurisdiction over sickness insurance any matter which properly fell within the sphere of imperial legislation. Probably because the motion meant next to nothing, the Upper House on February 14 turned it down and accepted the version which the obdurate Lower House had insisted upon.[56]

In 1889 both houses agreed in answer to numerous petitions to protect the rights of insured workers who could not keep up their contributions because of unemployment. Jobless members of funds would not forfeit their right to benefits for at least six weeks after losing their positions.[57]

From the beginning more workers enjoyed protection from sickness than from accidents. In 1890 a total of 1,548,825 had membership in 2,470 funds. Premiums collected amounted to 11,085,818 gulden, payments to beneficiaries, 9,073,300 gulden. By 1900 the number insured had grown to 2,538,896 in 2,942 funds. The program took in 30,125,144 gulden in that year and disbursed 27,730,706 gulden to ailing members.[58]

In the Austria of the 1880s the growth of occasionally terroristic radicalism among urban laborers, the government's consequent worry over such subversive activity, the conscience and political ambitions of the "Social Catholics," and a degree of self-interest on the part of the Liberal business community thus coalesced into a respectable system of social security. No one can doubt that effectiveness of the drive and energy which Egbert Belcredi and Alois Liechtenstein brought to their tasks as parlia-

[55] SPH, X Session, p. 567, Feb. 11, 1888.
[56] Ibid., pp. 586–87, Feb. 14, 1888.
[57] Kolmer, Parlament, IV, 350.
[58] Knarr, "Das Ministerium des Grafen Taaffe," p. 72.

mentary whips. The blood shed by the anarchists and extreme socialists did much to frighten the possessing classes into a program of positive relief. Within the bureaucracy, the gifted if undiplomatic Steinbach played ministry against ministry and, in the Reichsrat, fraction against fraction to secure the reforms that placed Austria on a par with other European industrial powers. If old-time Liberals grumbled over excessive governmental intervention, a younger star like Baernreither pointed the way toward an accommodation with the facts of life.

Assuredly there were overtones of pure politics in the constructive labors of parliamentarians and the regime. Czechs still had reason to link their struggle for power in Bohemia with their conationals' fight for decent conditions in German-owned factories. Clerical Conservatives hoped to win and to keep for an indeterminate period the artisans they had "rescued," and they were far from being pessimistic over their chances with factory operatives. Taaffe and his associates were as sure as Bismarck was that repression of socialism had as its corollary a more decent treatment of the labor force. If employers paid most of the costs of the new insurance plans, the government had double reason to congratulate itself. Businessmen were honestly frightened by the glimpses of savagery which isolated crimes revealed in the 1880s, and their instinctual desire to preserve their position in society meshed admirably with the government's resolve and the more theoretical philosophy advanced by the "Social Catholic" press and salons.

Ideologically, the Social Democratic Party that was founded in Austria in 1889 had reason to score the "palliatives" enacted by the parliaments of the decade. Yet these same plans, if by no means ideal for the workers, helped to turn their attention from violence to organization and well-planned strikes, from wild desperation to a growing consciousness of the latent power which labor possessed on the Austrian scene. Taaffe's era never can enjoy high marks in Social Democratic annals, thanks to the imposition of the Ausnahmszustand. Without the Taaffe legislation, nevertheless, it is hard to believe that Social Democracy as it existed in Austria in 1914 would have been possible. In the

end the proletariat did not refuse Social Democratic blandish-
ments, but at least the Social Democracy which emerged was a
prize example of evolutionary thought and tactics, not revolutionary. Though it scorned accident and sickness insurance as
the rich man's blinders for the poor, it lived to learn that me-
chanic, tram conductor, and factory operative cherished his
Kassen, his funds against adversity, and the limited security they
afforded him.

12 Shadows from Berlin and Mayerling

Taaffe's continuing alliance with Poles, Czechs, Slovenes, and devout Roman Catholic German Austrians never added to Bismarck's sense of security in international affairs. Prussia was actively engaged in an effort to cut Polish influence in Posen to a minimum, while the informal suspension of the Kulturkampf was indicative of Catholic vitality rather than of Bismarckian complaisance. Czechs and Slovenes were living memorials of periodic attempts to "civilize and conquer" the Slavs, and the presence of an unpredictable Alexander III at the head of the greatest Slav state intensified German worries over the "little brothers" to the west of St. Petersburg.

Bismarck had been less than sanguine in the spring and summer of 1887 with the rise of Boulanger in France and the spread of inevitable rumors of an alliance between France and Russia. Russian anger over the emergence of a united Bulgaria and over Austrian encouragement of the resentful Serbs meant the end of the Three Emperors' League in 1887. To minimize the chances of involvement on two fronts, the German Chancellor shrewdly made his "Reinsurance Treaty" with Russia in June, 1887, which he always regarded as a leash upon Austrian forays into the Balkans. Signing a pact of sorts with the chief Slavic power did not lessen his distaste for Taaffe's dependence on the Slavs of Austria (the Ruthenes always excepted). Such a policy threatened the basic German culture of the ally's realm and the order that the German language had long ensured its military and administrative forces.

A minor act of politeness on the part of William II's grandfather in 1887 threw into relief Bismarck's suspicion and rancor. While passing through Innsbruck, William I, in casual conversation with the *Statthalter* who welcomed him, recalled that Taaffe had "done the honors" when he journeyed to Milan in 1875. It seemed proper to the venerable gentleman to send a polite greeting to his former host, now Minister-President of Austria. In view of the chilly winds that ordinarily blew from Berlin, Taaffe was understandably pleased and called upon Reuss to express his thanks. The Minister-President had long retained a letter from a Berlin journalist of February, 1879, which assured Austrian press sources that William I gave Taaffe credit for securing the final approval of a Protestant church in Innsbruck.[1] This letter appears in the collection of papers which Taaffe left behind at his death, and there can be little doubt that he eagerly sought for a renewed sign of Hohenzollern friendship in 1887.

The German envoy immediately wired Bismarck that Taaffe obviously would make the most of the message, particularly to discredit the "German Austrian Party." Messages soon came from Berlin to Reuss in Vienna and to Otto von Bülow, close to the German Kaiser in Gastein. Reuss should see Kálnoky to deplore any such interpretation and request him to relay the "correction" directly to Franz Joseph. The Austro-Hungarian minister politely agreed to take the firm but tactless remonstrance to his sovereign and expressed his own surprise over Taaffe's indiscreet exploitation of the incident. William I was the least concerned of all the actors. Admitting that he shared his Chancellor's astonishment over Taaffe's attempt to exaggerate a mere pleasantry, he nevertheless by his manner made it clear to Bülow that the incident was closed. Bismarck, one infers, wanted a direct discussion between the two rulers to

---

[1] *Politischer Nachlass,* pp. 250–52.

destroy Taaffe's maneuver completely, but Bülow saw no chance of talking William I into such a step.[2]

Monts, the military expert at the embassy in Vienna, who yielded to no one in his disgust with Taaffe's stratagems to stay in power, eagerly reported to Bismarck late in the same year that their sly irritant was planting articles most favorable in his regime in the *Norddeutsche Allgemeine Zeitung.* German newspaper articles which blasted away at the Austrian coalition rarely escaped the vigilant censors when Austrian provincial papers tried to reprint them. The kind columns in the *Norddeutsche Allgemeine Zeitung* had a wide circulation in Austrian journals, however, and the German Liberals were protesting directly to the embassy. Though Kálnoky deplored Taaffe's "Slavophile" bent more often than ever, he lacked the energy to do more than express regrets. Could Bismarck do something?

The answer was emphatically affirmative. The chief editor of the offending journal received what amounted to orders to attack *Das Vaterland,* the only German Austrian paper which in Bismarck's opinion gave his citizens cause to worry over the state of the Alliance. If the Austrians did not quit laying their cuckoo's eggs in the German paper, there would be a big scandal, promised the affronted Chancellor. Reuss dutifully complained to Kálnoky, but he had no hope that the latter could take up the matter with Franz Joseph, with whom he was on rather ticklish terms.[3]

The Austrian monarch probably was too deeply enmeshed in preparations for a new army bill and the money it would require to worry overmuch about Taaffe's use of discretionary press funds. The tension with Russia did not appreciably relax, and Franz Joseph had every reason to give the man who had accom-

[2] See Reuss's dispatch No. 335, A 9269, July 25, 1887, UC-1, reel 223, frames 123–24, and draft of dispatch of Aug. 2, 1887 (Berlin), UC-1, reel 223, frames 127–32; Reuss's dispatch No. 348, A 9672, Aug. 5, 1887, reel 223, frames 133–34; Bülow's dispatch No. 20, A 9772, Aug. 8, 1887 (Gastein), reel 223, frames 135–36.

[3] Eduard von Wertheimer, *Bismarck im politischen Kampf* (Berlin, 1930), pp. 502–5.

plished the task of getting what was needed ten years before his total support. The monarchy was always pressed by the cost of equipping its soldiers and sailors, and Dunajewski, who had finally brought the deficit under control, was in earnest search of new revenues. No doubt reluctantly, he finally agreed with the Hungarian cabinet that both governments would increase the tax on spirituous liquors. Of all the crownlands, Galicia was especially noted for distilleries that operated on private estates. Revenue agents who visited these rural establishments had estimated the tax in accord with presumed yield, an action that encouraged the titled entrepreneurs to stuff their vats with mash as often as possible. The new regulations called for assessments on actual production, and thus there would be no point to stealthy overproduction.[4]

Galicia seethed with anger, expressed in telegrams to its deputies and in meetings which reiterated endlessly the "special treatment" meted out to the Emperor's most loyal national group. No one would believe that the distillers could pass the tax on to the consumers, for Galicia was one of the great areas for the sale of spirits, and the impecuniousness of the average customer was well known. From Abbazia (Opatija) the very sick leader of the Polish Club, Grocholski, tried to quell the rebellion among his deputies with appeals to their patriotism and self-interest. The German Liberals, whose voters owned many of the distilleries outside Galicia, prepared to make a common front with the disaffected Poles and even dreamed of breaking the Iron Ring and of toppling the cabinet.

On April 14, 1888, the Emperor received Apollinar Jaworski of the Polish Club in audience. The situation was desperate, for the ruler never before had worked on deputies when a mere tax was at stake. He asked the Poles not to leave the ministry in the lurch, and at once the politically wise prophesied speedy capitulation by Jaworski's colleagues. *Reforma* blustered that Galicia would never forgive Dunajewski for burdening his homeland with 15,000,000 gulden of increased taxes every year, but *Czas* was delighted over the august use of pressure. Had it not revealed a special sympathy for the Poles? The Emperor would turn to no others in such a patriarchal way, and so the Left had suffered another great defeat, the paper assumed.[5] Austrian public opinion in turn assumed, correctly, that the Poles had surrendered.

In the German Empire the *Norddeutsche Allgemeine Zeitung* echoed *Czas*'s story of an Austrian Liberal defeat. By opposing the increase in the tax on spirits, they were threatening the new defense measures. They warmly supported the German alliance, but it was the Poles who honored their Emperor and sacrificed their interests to his request. Reuss sent a long and vigorous note to Bismarck after reading the article. As before, he automatically assumed that Taaffe's press bureau had planted the résumé, primarily to blind German readers to recent Young Czech pleas for an Austro-Russian alliance. With some asperity, the German diplomat readily admitted that Taaffe had again fooled the German Liberals with his nimbleness. While the latter rather laboriously prepared to make an entente with the angry Poles against the cabinet, Taaffe and Dunajewski rushed to Franz Joseph and secured his consent to the unparalleled audience with Jaworski. Reuss assumed that Taaffe feared he would no longer be the commanding executive if the Liberals effected a front with the Poles. A few sensible Liberals had foreseen what did happen, but they did not expect to see their humiliation spread across a German newspaper as a means of glamorizing Taaffe's system. Could something be done to get the right story before the citizens of the German Empire? It was disgraceful that German journalists so treated "our only friends in the Austrian parliament."[6]

Bismarck saw to it that the editor was rebuked. If he published anything else favorable to Taaffe, the Chancellor reported,

[5] Cited in *Neue Freie Presse,* April 13 (*Morgen- und Abendblatt*), 15, and 17, 1888.

[6] See Reuss's dispatch No. 210, A 4483, April 20, 1888, UC-1, reel 215, frames 595–99.

he would lose the relations he had been enjoying "with us." But was the article so faulty in its interpretation of the Austrian Liberals? asked the Chancellor. It was clumsy of them to think that they could unseat the Polish Minister of Finance by such an involved intrigue. They had simply added to their ruler's resentments, already provoked by previous acts of negation. What a shame that these doctrinaires, cast by history as the adjuncts of the Habsburg throne, put their trust in useless oppositional bickering![7]

Some days later Bismarck was dictating a tense note to Reuss concerning Czech and Magyar participation in the Paris Exhibition. It was to be regretted that the Taaffe regime tolerated, not to say encouraged, decentralizing tendencies of dubious worth in the so-called Czechish lands. Worse yet, this regime permitted a systematic Czech flirtation with France to develop, to the consternation of the calmest German observers. "If anything can cripple our relations with Austria, it is coquetting with France," wrote the Chancellor.[8]

Early in October, 1888, the relatively untried William II made a state visit to Vienna. The Austrian government was readying the new defense bill for parliamentary treatment, and Bismarck had made up his mind to reprove Taaffe as blatantly as possible for his "ruinous" policies. The German Emperor ostentatiously conferred a decoration upon Tisza of Hungary during his stay but left Taaffe empty-chested. From Friedrichsruh, Bismarck wrote to his ambassador in Budapest, with an informational copy to Reuss, that the German Emperor could not bring himself to decorate Taaffe. It would have been politically unwise. "If your feet are stepped on, you have to yell. If you put too much importance on what happened, you will be stepped on again," was the Chancellor's veiled warning, which by devious channels might get to the snubbed Austrian.[9]

[7] See dispatch No. 331 (Berlin), April 24, 1888, UC-1, reel 215, frames 601–3.

[8] See dispatch No. 335 (Berlin), May 6, 1888, UC-1, reel 215, frames 619–21.

[9] See dispatch of Oct. 24, 1888 (Friedrichsruh), A 13663, UC-1, reel 223, frames 168–70.

The full extent of Bismarck's contempt for Taaffe's way of governing and of his anxiety over Austria's reliability comes out in a note to Reuss dispatched a week after the young Kaiser honored Tisza. Franz Joseph's only way out was a coup d'état, thought the Chancellor. Delaying the inevitable move was most dangerous, for the dynasty's reputation was not growing in the army or among the agrarian classes. Every nationality, the German included, had developed such a well-defined parliamentary and publicistic "image" that the concept of a "pure Austrian" had evaporated. Possibly Franz Joseph's character did not allow the operation Bismarck hoped for. Possibly Austria lacked the men to provoke the serious conflicts which would permit the necessary military intervention. Bismarck specifically excluded Hungary from these most confidential opinions. Presumably he saw no reason to cavil at Magyar treatment of their nationality problems.[10]

While the irascible German statesman dreamed of bayonet and artillery as the necessary cures for the Austrian sickness, his bête noire in Vienna was reshuffling cabinet posts. Since the imperial notices were dated a day after William II said farewell, the public looked for signs of Taaffe's revenge upon his master's ungenerous visitor. Reuss first analyzed the changes as proof that the ministry had become "clerical, federalist, and anti-German." Pražak surrendered the Ministry of Justice to Count Friedrich Schönborn, remaining simply as a minister without portfolio. Ziemialkowski, the loser to Dunajewski in the dispute over the new spirits tax, stepped down after almost fifteen years of tenure in favor of Philipp von Zaleski. The veteran Polish representative had at least understood the need for an Austria and never had been the blindly obedient agent of the szlachta or of the Polish clergy, declared Reuss. Zaleski, the governor of Galicia, was the szlachta's man, who had helped to reduce the Ruthenes to complete helotry. The Czechs had squeezed all they could from Pražak's tenure at the Justice Ministry. Now they wanted him to devote all his time to the "real interests" of

[10] Wertheimer, *Bismarck,* pp. 507–8.

the Bohemian crown. Schönborn excited the German diplomat's worst suspicions. Rarely had the German nobility of
Bohemia produced such a fanatical clerical, such a violent Czech
nationalist. By accepting Schönborn, Taaffe had indicated he
had to buy the entire Right to stay in office.[11] As the weeks
passed, Reuss and Monts decided that Taaffe had not recon-
structed his ministry out of pique against Germany.
Schönborn's appointment was secretly decided upon as early as
September 10, to keep some wavering Old Czechs from going
over to the Young Czech firebrands. Both of the reporters in the
German Embassy moderated their severe opinions of Taaffe a
bit when a Pole of Jewish ancestry became governor of Moravia
in the teeth of Czech demands for a man who was a federalist, a
member of one of the great families of the province, and fully
conversant with the Czech language.[12]

Before Taaffe could properly recover from the humiliation
administered by Bismarck through William II, his long-time
antagonist, Crown Prince Rudolf, exacted another kind of revenge by committing suicide at Mayerling on January 30, 1889.
The distrust between Minister-President and the heir to the
throne was an open secret, and Taaffe's utterly loyal behavior as
the Emperor's chief confidant during the first numbed weeks of
mourning merely added to the gossip which pitted the "sly
politician" against the "progressive" young prince.

The romantic Rudolf will always outglitter his prosy father in
the Sunday supplements and with all who bewail the frustration
of youth's fair dreams by older parties. Often mercurial, he was
faithful at least to two phobias: the aristocracy and the Roman
Catholic Church. To stem the growth of socialism, he favored
the division of the great latifundia, though it was not in the
country districts that socialism and anarchism were making in-

[11] See Reuss's dispatch No. 429, A 13041, Oct. 13, 1888, UC-1, reel
229, frames 216–21.
[12] See Reuss's dispatch No. 439, A 13430, Oct. 19, 1888, UC-1, reel
229, frames 231–33; Monts's dispatch No. 479, A 15287, Nov. 18, 1888,
UC-1, reel 215, frames 646–49; Monts's dispatch, A 15718, Nov. 26,
1888, UC-1, reel 223, frames 182–83.

roads in the 1880s. As for religion, he felt that Austria had always been the breeding grounds of ultramontanism and "Jesuitry."

If Rudolf manifested consistently one grand enthusiasm, it was for the army. He publicly praised the armed forces as the first and most distinguished profession of the empire. He believed in duels, he smothered his usual adoration of the Liberals when they threatened army expenditures, and he positively exhorted these same Liberals to make the army their very own. Its officer corps, he noted quite properly, was overwhelmingly middle class, Liberal, devoted to Emperor and state. Most of the time Rudolf preferred a Hungary dominated by Liberals to Taaffe's Austria, but the slightest sign of Magyar desire for a change in the army's language of command or of Magyar disrespect for the Austrians who died in Hungary in 1848–49 cooled his pro-Budapest sympathies immediately.

These upsets were rare, for ordinarily he doted on the Liberals of Hungary: they had beautified Budapest while Vienna languished, they had Magyarized the talented Germans and Jews of their land, and, since they really had no other state to gravitate to, one could smile at the antics of the worst of their nationalistic extremists. Budapest had life, swing, self-confidence, a special tone of its own—traits which every Liberal era produced. Hungary had been the bastion against complete reaction, and, though he noted electoral corruption, humbug and swindle in Magyar academic circles, and a Turklike contempt for the subject nationalities of Hungary, it is clear that he expected the Magyar Liberals to join with the German Liberals of Austria to frustrate the forces of black obscurantism.

Rudolf lived long enough to test some of his pet ideas. He wrote in time of the suicidal chauvinism of the Magyars. He turned eagerly to his German Liberal friends, begging them to effect a reconciliation with the Czechs and then jointly to overthrow Taaffe. They replied they could not undertake such a mission unless they, the Germans, were granted the decisive voice in negotiations. *They* would be the guarantors, not the

Czechs.[13] As the disappointments multiplied, what consolations occupied Rudolf's mind?

Why did not "this ragoût of nationalities" collapse? he asked. Because it still had to play a great role in the Near East. When Rudolf wrote of Austria's mission to the East, it was clear that he meant the march of German Kultur. To Europeanize and cultivate the Balkans, the Habsburg Monarchy had to retain one language for its army. German had to be an obligatory subject in all superior schools. Before the great duel with Russia there should be a decisive blow against Italy, which would then pay a big indemnity, surrender her fleet, and virtually demobilize her army. Meanwhile, there was to be cold-blooded Germanization of the South Tirol and Trieste. If the war with Russia turned out well, Germany and Austria would have to divide "Congress Poland," for the Poles were eternally unreliable and hopeless in statecraft. The rest of Austrian Slavdom had no yearning for Pan-Slav solutions, he was sure, and recognition of some kind of union of Bohemia, Moravia, and Silesia would satisfy the Czechs. Indeed, he feared Pan-Germanism much more than Czech nationalism. *Anschluss* was the terrifying word, not talk of the ancient Bohemian crown.[14]

Rudolf was far more his father's son than the playwrights and novelists would like to admit. He cheered the advance into Bosnia-Herzegovina, and he counted on establishing Habsburg overlordship in the Balkans. The army was his trusted medium, and it was Germanism which would embody European civilization for the Near East. He had a profound suspicion of the Austrian Germans who loved the Hohenzollerns, as did Franz Joseph, but both well understood the value of the German alliance against the most likely foe of the future, Russia. Each realized there had to be changes to placate the nationalities of the empire, though here Rudolf counted on Liberal cosmopolitanism, his father on aristocratic *noblesse oblige* and a gradual shift to reform of social and economic problems. But it was the son

---

[13] Oskar von Mitis, *Das Leben des Kronprinzen Rudolf* (Leipzig, 1928), pp. 104–5.

[14] *Ibid.*, pp. 319–52.

who despaired, and one recalls what he wrote as early as 1882: "We face very gloomy and odious times. One would almost think the old Europe has outlived itself and now goes to its dissolution. A powerfully great reaction must come, social upheavals, from which, after long sickness, a completely new Europe will flourish once again."[15]

Neither Rudolf nor Bismarck had understood Franz Joseph. Taaffe's position remained secure, despite the shocking event at Mayerling and the studied disrespect which the Chancellor had shown his Austrian counterpart. The King-Emperor's loyalty to his chief Austrian adviser was somewhat involved, to be sure, but, far more important, Taaffe was handling internal politics with greater skill than ever before.

The Poles had given way to imperial pressure on the new spirits tax, but they naturally had expected compensation. If the new schedules were to bring in the sums Dunajewski counted on, they would have to apply to all producers. In Galicia, the scene of the greatest uproar, more than 50 cities and about 100 landowners enjoyed the *Propinationsrecht,* the right to brew or distill alcoholic beverages without hindrance from state inspectors or licensers. If the state redeemed the *Propinationsrecht,* it would indemnify many who were hard hit by the new taxes and at the same time simplify the collectors' tasks. Taaffe and Dunajewski proposed the payment of 1,000,000 gulden a year through 1910 to buy out the privileged in Galicia, 100,000 gulden annually through 1911 for those in the Bukowina. Despite loud Liberal complaints, the bill passed both houses in June, 1888.[16] In each of the first two years that followed, the state collected about 21,000,000 more than before.[17]

The Emperor was gratified to have such sums for the military, but his and Taaffe's earlier worries over the introduction of a new defense bill in 1888 evaporated in the face of international

[15] Letter of Nov. 24, 1882, in *Kronprinz Rudolf: Politische Briefe an einen Freund, 1882–1889,* ed. Julius Szeps (Vienna, Munich, and Leipzig, 1922), p. 21.

[16] Kolmer, *Parlament,* IV, 270.

[17] Schenk, *Dr. Julian Ritter von Dunajewski,* p. 83.

tensions that the Liberals abundantly recognized. As Plener put the matter bluntly, the Russian troop concentrations in the vicinity of the Austro-Hungarian frontier intensified the importance of the alliance with Germany and eliminated previous Liberal anxiety over constantly increasing defense expenditures. One part of the bill called for the Lower House's surrender of its right of initiative in changing the size of the annual contingent, and there was some slight concern that it would be difficult to obtain the necessary two-thirds majority for this amendment of the Fundamental Laws.

Monts, the Liberals' confidant and most compassionate friend in the German Embassy, decided to help them avoid the debacle of 1879. Why not prove that the men he deemed to be the very foundations of the empire would live up to his verdict by overwhelming support of the new defense program? In the Grand Hotel in Vienna he met with Baernreither, Julius Derschatta, Otto Steinwender, and Moritz Weitlof. None was a nationalist of Schönerer's type, of course, and Monts's well-publicized intervention aided the regime in carrying the bill.[18]

The German Clerical Conservatives also had voted for the new defense arrangements, for the spirits tax, and for the redemption of the *Propinationsrecht*. In the half-decade that had followed the token victory they won in educational affairs in 1883, there was some notable governmental response to their plea for social legislation. But the episcopacy and the more conservative aristocrats who preferred country life to Vienna derived scant pleasure from a system which would give hedonists and anarchists better insurance coverage. The nurturing of a lasting reverence for Christian truths was more vital than even the succoring of the injured and of the bereft.

At the beginning of 1888 Alois Liechtenstein had proclaimed a second crusade to secure the "proper principles" in the Austrian school system. Conrad had resigned three years before, but his young and tough successor, Paul Gautsch, had given the proponents of confessional schooling no cause for jubilation.

[18] Kolmer, *Parlament,* IV, 68–69; Ernst Plener, *Erinnerungen* (Stuttgart and Leipzig, 1911–21), II, 366.

The latter finally erupted with such vehemence against his "sabotage" in the budget debate of April, 1888, that he decided that his position was shattered and requested the Emperor on May 8 for permission to step down.[19] The Emperor first declined his suit and then appealed directly and successfully to the Liechtenstein partisans to postpone their demands for action until the autumn.[20]

Thanks to the parliamentary consideration of the new defense bill, Liechtenstein's bill to revamp the school system did not come up until the spring of 1889. It was clear that he aimed at attracting as many "autonomist" votes as possible. In addition to the anticipated emphasis upon religion as the first subject of instruction and upon the right of the Church or of corresponding non-Catholic religious agencies to exercise joint supervisory power with the state in public schools, his bill assigned to the diets general control over physical facilities and teacher training. Just as controversial were provisions which limited compulsory full-time education to six years and which required a religious qualification for teaching. A teacher's denomination had to match that of his pupils, and Catholic pedagogues would need a specific *Missio canonica* before they could meet their classes. Private schools and private instruction were valid when they conformed to the pattern followed by public schools. Finally, the politic Prince exempted Galicia from the bill's prescriptions.[21]

Gautsch put down his reactions to Liechtenstein's bill in a *mémoire* for Franz Joseph. As Minister of Education, he wanted a confessional school in the sense that religious instruction should come first. Imperial law already guaranteed this, and the state had intervened to give necessary courses in religion when the clergy failed to do so. To emphasize religion's role in the

[19] Maria Magdalena Weyrich, "Paul Gautsch, Freiherr von Frankenthurn, Jugend, Unterrichtsminister, Ministerpräsident 1897–98" (unpubl. diss., Vienna, 1956), p. 24 (based on letter in possession of Baron Oskar Gautsch).

[20] See Reuss's dispatch No. 239, A 5514, May 12, 1888, UC-1, reel 215, frames 623–24.

[21] *SPA*, X Session, Beilagen 490.

schools, however, he recommended state salaries for the teachers of religion and a legislative recognition of the Church's influence over religious instruction. Liechtenstein's bill called for constitutional change, for it modified the state's superior control and direction of the general educational program. There was a political danger involved as well if Ruthene priests in Galicia, the South Slav clergy, and the Italians in the South Tirol got control of the schools. Increasing the competence of the diets over public schools was equally risky, for every expansion of a diet's legislative power increased the threat to national minorities and to the cultivation of the German language.[22]

The pressure from Clerical Conservatives had its effect in early May, 1889. The government finally abandoned its sphinx-like silence and submitted a school bill—to the Upper House. Gautsch retained the rule for eight years of compulsory schooling, unless parents could adduce excellent reasons why their children should stop after six years. Even so, there would be further part-time instruction. Whole districts, if rural or semi-rural, might escape the full force of eight years of compulsory schooling if the district officials proved the necessity of such a step and if the children received some kind of supplementary education until they reached the age of fourteen. Church officials were to care for religious classes. The actual number of hours devoted to such instruction was to be determined by provincial educational officials in cooperation with Church officials. If a lay teacher had to substitute for clerical teachers in courses in religion, such a layman could deal only with children of the same confession as his own. Provincial law generally would operate to discipline teachers who were disobedient or guilty of bad conduct. The state generally would supervise the activities of private schools, while provincial law would decide when the supporters of such schools should be dispensed from paying taxes for public schools.[23]

Contemporaries who knew Gautsch were sure that he never

[22] Verwaltungsarchiv, Vienna, Präsidialakt, 1966 (C.U.M. 1888), cited in Weyrich, "Paul Gautsch," pp. 25–26.
[23] SPH, X Session, Beilagen, 378.

intended his bill to pass. It invited ambiguous interpretations, and, if the Upper House did pass it, the chances of defeat' in the Lower House were overwhelming.[24] The peers were always more deliberate than the deputies, and, before their commission began hearings on the bill, Alois Liechtenstein resigned as chairman of the Centrums Club. The *Neue Freie Presse* spread the rumor that Cardinal Schönborn in Prague detected no loss in the Prince's action. Was not the aristocratic leader more intent upon flirting with demagogues like Lueger and Schneider than he was in obtaining the confessional school? The *Vorarlberger Volksblatt* simply said that the Prince had not fulfilled the party's confidence after years of trying. The *Katholische Kirchen-Zeitung* of Salzburg assumed that Liechtenstein had given up hope of getting anything for the Church from the Taaffe cabinet.[25] *Das Vaterland* cautiously reprinted the *Grazer Volksblatt*'s call to keep up the fight.[26]

Gautsch ran one considerable risk in sending his bill to the Upper House first. In that house the great princes of the Church had seats, and three of them served on the commission which had the task of evaluating his substitute for Liechtenstein's program. Cardinal Schönborn and his associates soon penned a report in which they rejected the idea of compulsory schooling if Catholic consciences suffered thereby. Catholic children should be separate from non-Catholics, the Church should have wide powers over teachers in Catholic public schools, and Church officials should have the determining voice on textbooks and program of study in the teaching of religion. Gautsch asked for a postponement of the commission's labors until he could reply for the government, and soon it was rumored that the princes of the Church had chosen this way to absolve the Clerical Conservatives from further responsibility for securing truly confessional schools. Why would they take such a step? To keep their followers in the governing coalition, to foil the designs of the Liberals, so long starved for a share in executive affairs, was the answer. There was muttering among the more devout Catholic

---

[24] Weyrich, "Paul Gautsch," p. 27.
[25] *Neue Freie Presse,* Oct. 1 and 4, 1889.   [26] Oct. 16, 1889.

peers, who never had the long-term view their bishops could afford, but also there was grudging admission that protests would do little to hasten a confessional system. Alfred Ebenhoch, a comparatively young deputy in 1890, earnestly revived the issue in the budget debate of that year. Catholic deputies would not heed Gautsch's moderatist siren song, valorously declaimed this passionately Catholic lawyer, destined one day to unite his conservative farm following with Lueger's ardent Viennese.[27] The Polish Club's Bobrzyński more realistically predicted what the majority would do. Carefully disclaiming authority to speak for the coalition, he nevertheless spelled out what all but the most diehard already knew. The governing parties planned no basic change in the constitutional regulations on education, for that would create a serious political crisis. They wanted the diets to carry out the general principles enunciated by the central parliament, and they hoped for an arrangement of curriculum and schedule that would allow the clergy adequate time to train the children. As for the opposition's steady dislike of greater decentralization in school affairs, the recent compromise in Bohemia was a welcome sign of relaxation.[28]

The Polish professor here touched upon the tense bargaining that had engaged the Germans of Bohemia with the Feudalists and Old Czechs since January, 1890. The eyes of the empire were riveted upon the faint signs of a durable armistice in the embattled crownland of Bohemia, and Taaffe's success in dealing with defense and the demands of his coalition undoubtedly created the atmosphere for the great discussion of 1890. If the German Liberals who assented to negotiations continued to resent his failure to court them, at least they admired the way in which he weathered the German Empire's snub. Not long before their own Herbst had experienced Bismarck's anger, despite their close ties with the personnel of the German Embassy in Vienna. If the Old Czechs realized they had achieved less than they wanted from the Ministries of Justice and Education for ambitious younger Czechs, at least they appreciated Taaffe's

[27] *SPA*, p. 14695, April 28, 1890.
[28] *Ibid.*, pp. 14725–26, April 28, 1890.

Fabian tactics against the confessional school. Had they been forced to accept some form of increased Church control of education, they would have fared even worse at the hands of those fierce advocates of religious neutrality, the Young Czechs. Polish Galicia might indeed suffer in the first years of the new impost on spirits, but the interests who ran the parliamentary club had indemnities and subventions to soften the blow. And Taaffe did nothing to threaten Galicia as a Polish dominion.

The observer who automatically dismisses adroitness and bargaining in politics will continue to agree with the German Liberal publicists and historians who dilated upon Taaffe's "muddling through" by means of well-timed concessions to his majority parties. Between 1887 and 1890 Taaffe and his associates paid necessary tributes for support, but they also won major victories in stalling Liechtenstein's school bill and in securing the increase in the spirits tax. Here they had the Emperor's direct aid, which in turn was predicated upon Franz Joseph's conviction that Taaffe and the Taaffe system were his best props in Austria. Without the bond between master and first minister, Bismarck's feint might have ended the experiment in conciliating the major nationalities. Distrust in Berlin, unending pressure from Budapest, and the exhausting task of keeping a disgruntled coalition together undoubtedly affected Taaffe's energies and morale. Thanks to his able exploitation of imperial influence and of the fear within his coalition of a Liberal return to high councils, he had won enough prestige to sponsor a German-Czech rapprochement. A decade of relentless bickering made him dubious of a complete settlement, and he was careful to stay in the background.

The Taaffe system had proved its efficiency between 1887 and 1890 as pure administration. Earlier it had demonstrated its concern for a healthier society by a realistic appraisal of the growth of nationalism and of the social challenges of industrialism. Its achievements were piecemeal, and often it deserved a reputation for temporizing and trimming. Yet fundamental changes were wrought, and by the beginning of the last decade of the nineteenth century the greatest of the problems, the German-

Czech rivalry, again had a chance of adjustment and compromise. The Germans had learned that the Czech nationality had rights which Taaffe would uphold and encourage. The Czechs had learned that Taaffe respected the essential German cast of the empire's vital parts. Having learned such lessons, they tried again to compose their differences.

13 The Bohemian Compromise of 1890

No serious student of the Habsburg sickness of the 1880s looked beyond Bohemia for signs either of possible improvement or of the telltale agonies of dissolution. If Austria's fate lay in Radetzky's camp in the middle of the nineteenth century, its locus had moved to Bohemia's fields and mountains thirty years later. The lands west of the Leitha River could endure territorial emendations that would pacify their Rumanian and Italian allies and could recognize what was essentially a personal union with Galicia. But an unresolved war between Germans and Czechs in Bohemia was a malignancy that threatened the very essence of the Austrian state. Taaffe's government came close to securing an armistice in 1890. It would be unhistorical to call the *Ausgleich* of 1890 by any other name. It never was realized, and government, Czechs, and Germans helped destroy its chances by false assumptions, poor timing, and, worst of all, by the fatal tendency of each nationality to gloat over seeming victories and to rage over presumed rebuffs. If Taaffe personally had been in better health, if Franz Joseph had been a little less outraged by Young Czech fervor, if Plener had been a little less bumptious in proving he was an effective champion of German culture—but the personal equations pale before the bare fact that Austrian Germans, however loyal to *their* Kaiser, knew that the mightier Hohenzollerns saw no sense in satisfying

Czechs. And the Czechs, reawakened to a sense of medieval greatness and Hussite combativeness and aware of the wealth and power their land could give their children, wanted more than placative gestures.

The repulse of the German Liberal attempt to fix German as Austria's official language evidently prodded Taaffe five years before the negotiations of 1890 into earnest discussions with his majority leaders concerning some kind of law on languages. Would it not be wise to insert a significant passage on this subject in the speech from the throne when the newly elected Lower House met in 1885? Heinrich Clam Martinič listened, reflected, and decided that such a statement would be quite dangerous. It would make the political world believe that the government was deferring to ultranationalists among the German Bohemians. It would be premature, for the majority needed to unite first on the "how" and "when" and the "how far." The House should first meet and arrange its internal organization. Then there could be time for measured appraisals of a law.[1]

When the Emperor opened the new parliament in November, 1885, he said nothing of a fundamental reappraisal. The moderate Liberal Scharschmid, however, did propose in February, 1886, a more restricted definition of German as the state's language. It would be the universal medium of communication for all of the government's inner services, for parliamentary business, for the text of the laws and public records. Other languages would be valid for the government's external service and for public schools if a certain percentage of the population or of children liable to attend school spoke such languages in a Gemeinde (commune). Excluded from the bill's jurisdiction were Galicia, the Trentino, Dalmatia, and the Littoral.[2]

While a committee rather hopelessly retraced thrice-familiar ground in weighing Scharschmid's motion, Taaffe tried to dampen a Czech campaign to commemorate the 800th anniversary of the founding of a Czech kingdom and the 50th jubilee of

---

[1] Letter of June 18, 1885, in *Politischer Nachlass,* p. 261.

[2] Gustav Kolmer, *Parlament und Verfassung in Oesterreich* (Vienna and Leipzig, 1902–14), IV, 203.

Ferdinand I's coronation as king of that kingdom. Rieger bluntly wrote him that the Young Czechs had already exploited the issue to such an extent that no one who was Czech would dare oppose the celebration. Indeed, Rieger fully supported the idea of the remembrance of the kingdom's establishment, and he declared that the *Oberstlandmarschall* and the Archbishop of Prague should attend the ceremonies as a sign of full governmental cooperation. Otherwise the Czechs would have every right to demonstrate against an unfair and shortsighted treatment of their due claims. If Taaffe expected him to interfere in this project, he should not anticipate effective aid when more important military bills came before the Lower House.

Taaffe tried to temporize with Rieger, for he already had secured disapproving statements from Prince Karl Schwarzenberg, a commanding figure among the Czech Feudalists, and from Archbishop Schönborn. These men of influence agreed with the Minister-President that the issue was very ticklish, even though Rieger hinted that the Czechs would not demand an immediate reply to their request for Franz Joseph's coronation.[3] The touchy question remained in abeyance, and in the autumn the regime repaid Rieger and the Old Czechs for their relative patience by publishing through the Ministry of Justice a highly controversial Instruction to the Superior Provincial Courts in Prague and Brünn. Because of the enormous amount of translation incurred in handing down decisions in these courts, verdicts and the legal reasoning justifying them in the future would be in the language used by the parties involved in the case. For the moment, existing practice would continue to obtain where the litigants' original pleas or petitions were in both of the languages current in Bohemia and Moravia. Signed by Pražak, the acknowledged Czech spokesman in the cabinet, the Instruction immediately impressed Germans as a blow against their language's position as the medium of internal governmental communication.[4]

The tension aroused by Pražak's Instruction and the inability

---

[3] *Politischer Nachlass*, pp. 404–5, 437–42.
[4] Kolmer, *Parlament*, IV, 208–9.

of the Germans of Bohemia to secure from the Diet there a
national demarcation of the crownland's Bezirke led to a painful
climax. In the last days of 1886 practically all of the German
members of the Diet quit its sessions and consequently were
formally expelled when they ignored directions to return.
Plener wrote his father that the Liberals planned their secession
as a deliberate blow against Taaffe. It was the only way to force
a new political configuration, for speeches had done nothing to
shake the cabinet. The boycott was a risk, but losing more seats
through electoral reform was a probability even if the Germans
remained in the Diet. They had weighed all of the factors, but
the fact that the Czech aristocrats rivaled the Young Czechs in
their diehard attitudes was decisive. Rieger's understanding of
the German position was not enough.[5]

Taaffe begged his colleagues to think of ways to placate the
German dissidents. Would the Czech majority issue a statement
which might mollify the absent deputies? Dunajewski sternly
advised against any moves to appease the Germans. If the latter
learned that noncooperation in the Diet could bring concessions,
they would use the same weapon against the government in the
Reichsrat. The cabinet should exert its influence for reconciliation only after the Germans indicated a willingness to resume
their places in the Diet. Gautsch was even more rigorous in his
recommendations. The cabinet should tell the Czechs that it
had no confidence for the moment in talks with the Germans. It
should even warn the Czechs that it would not appreciate any
stiffening of the German parliamentary opposition that might
result from Czech gestures of appeasement. The Minister-
President took no comfort from these flinty suggestions. German absence from the Diet was intolerable. If the regime could
not approach the Germans (and he admitted the moment was
inopportune), at least the Czech party, which was close to the
government, should try to end the deadlock.[6]

[5] Nachlass Plener, Karton 17, Nos. 1–2, letter of Dec. 21, 1886.
[6] Moses Mehring, "Die deutsch-böhmische Sprachenfrage während des
Ministeriums Taaffe (1879–1893)" (unpubl. diss., Vienna, 1924), pp.
91ff.

Late in 1889 Prince Georg Lobkowitz tried to renew negotiations between Czechs and Germans in regard to linguistic and educational problems, but in the end Schmeykal, to whom he addressed his propositions, insisted on a national demarcation of the Bezirke in Bohemia and upon the suspension of Stremayr's Ordinances in certain selected areas which the Germans deemed their very own.[7] The result was the continuing boycott of the Bohemian Diet by the Germans, a maneuver which annoyed and disturbed the Czechs quite effectively. Trained in secession and abstinence in the 1870s, they were painfully aware of the insecurity of any measure they might adopt in the absence of the Germans.

Taaffe, too, was as worried as before over the German recalcitrance. Actually he had inspired Rieger to give Lobkowitz some direction in formulating the projected compromise, and the quiet collapse of the scheme no doubt contributed to his growing discouragement over the Bohemian crisis. He felt that he had pushed the Czech leaders as far as he dared, and in his eyes the Lobkowitz formulas should have been enough to lure the Germans back to the Diet.[8] Reversing an earlier stand, he let it be known that he would accede to a new composition of curias for elections, one for Germans, one for Czechs, and one for the great landowners. He and the cabinet hoped that the last-named curia would serve as a buffer and mediator between the warring nationalities.[9]

Almost two years later there was a break in the gloom. The German Liberals of the crownland privately debated a return to the Diet before there was a settlement of the language problem. Seemingly Scharschmid wanted his people to make the first gesture toward reconciliation, at least if the Czechs would give some sign they would reciprocate. The Czech Feudalists dashed his hopes with their cool reserve, and Plener argued that future developments lay with the Young Czechs anyway. Their antics

[7] *Das Nationalitätenrecht des alten Österreich,* ed. Karl Gottfried Hugelmann (Vienna and Leipzig, 1934), pp. 159–60.

[8] Mehring, "Die deutsch-böhmische Sprachenfrage," pp. 92, 94.

[9] Paul Molisch, *Geschichte der deutschnationalen Bewegung in Oesterreich* (Jena, 1926), pp. 132–33.

would make Taaffe take some action, and it would pay the
Liberals to await the government's call for help. The Czechs
would end up bearing the odium of pure negation, he was sure, if
only the Germans would be patient.[10] Plener was absolutely
certain that a governmentally sponsored conference of Germans
and Czechs would arrive at nothing if the cabinet failed to invite
a Young Czech leader to attend. The Young Czech triumph in
the Diet elections of July, however, meant that no compromise
would emerge. The Emperor, Taaffe, and the Old Czechs were
determined to overawe the turbulent new element, which was no
way to hasten a settlement, in Plener's opinion. The Emperor
had entered the Bohemian arena with vehemence, but harrying
the Young Czechs would only stiffen their resistance to a reconciliation of the nationalities.[11]

The Old Czechs in the Diet, unofficially in touch with the
absentee Germans, put through regulations on the use of languages by autonomous governing bodies. The local officials in
Gemeinde and Bezirk would decide what language they would
use in their conduct of affairs. But in certain cases they had to
employ the language of the citizen who required their attention
or decision. This was true in any city which had its own charter
or in Gemeinden in which the linguistic minority amounted to 25
per cent of the population. A committee of a Bezirk also had to
use the minority's language if at least one of its Gemeinden was
predominantly inhabited by the minority and when a citizen of
such a Gemeinde applied for official attention.[12]

The Emperor withheld his approval, possibly because the
Germans had no taste for parity of languages in Reichenberg,
which did possess its own charter.[13] Certainly it was not because
the Young Czechs were opposed, for their impressive victories in
the Diet elections of the summer of 1889 had genuinely alarmed
Franz Joseph.[14] Indeed, Prince Schönburg since the Diet elec-

[10] Nachlass Plener, Karton 18, No. 322, letter of June 20, 1889.

[11] *Ibid.*, Karton 18, No. 320, letter of July 17, 1889.

[12] *Das Nationalitätenrecht,* ed. Hugelmann, pp. 160–61; Kolmer, *Parlament,* IV, 389–91.

[13] *Das Nationalitätenrecht,* ed. Hugelmann, p. 351.

[14] Ernst Plener, *Erinnerungen* (Stuttgart and Leipzig, 1921), II, 382.

tions had been quite busy sounding out moderate Germans and Czechs as to the chance of a grand conference to resolve their chronic differences. Statthalter Kraus, who had lost the Emperor's confidence because of his "slack" response to the Young Czech upsurge, received a polite letter from Taaffe giving him the chance to renew previous offers to resign because of ill health.[15] Since his replacement, Count Franz Thun, passed as a defender of the basic Czech constitutional ideas and had declared himself a proponent of a royal coronation in Prague, the Czechs overconfidently called him their "Coronation Governor."

In reality, Thun had already planned to punish *Národní Listy* once the Diet had ended its deliberations by suspending the paper's license to sell its editions retail. Editorials which skimmed close to the edges of imperial foreign policy had angered him, and Taaffe agreed that the Young Czechs needed a lesson that would hurt. The Minister-President warned the new *Statthalter* to wait for a flagrant incursion upon foreign policy matters, however. It would not be wise to punish the journal when it discussed internal affairs, the behavior of the Old Czechs, or the activity of either Thun or himself.[16] The revival of "coronation fever" and the Diet's passage of the new regulations on the use of languages by autonomous governing bodies thoroughly alarmed the Germans of Bohemia, for they admitted to themselves that Taaffe might well plump for the public enthronement of Franz Joseph as king of Bohemia as a means of refurbishing the Old Czechs' reputation.[17]

Taaffe's basic preoccupation with the waxing Czech desire to get maximum recognition of their interpretation of the historical past revealed itself in striking fashion in the autumn of 1889. Under strong pressure from Magyar nationalists, Tisza came to Vienna in October, 1889, to secure a change in the army's title and in the flags and emblems appertaining to Hungarian regiments. In a council of ministers representing both realms, Tisza failed to get the desired national insignia, but he did persuade the

[15] *Politischer Nachlass,* pp. 414–15.   [16] *Ibid.,* pp. 450–52.
[17] Plener, *Erinnerungen,* II, 385, 389–90.

Emperor to change the title of the army from "k.k. Armee" to "k.u.k. Armee," from "Imperial-Royal Army" to "Imperial and Royal Army." This famous "und" question had been prominent for years. By adding the conjunction, the Emperor either prepared the way for total division of imperial forces (the Austrian argument) or recognized what was already implicit and just in the agreement of 1867 (the Hungarian argument).

A strong element in the Czech insistence on their *Staatsrecht* and on the unity of the lands of Wenceslas' crown was this same precedent of 1867. The battle of Mohács symbolized the common fate of Habsburgs with Bohemia (and her dependent lands of Moravia and Silesia) and Hungary. If Taaffe, as Austrian Minister-President, yielded further to Hungarian pretensions, he would be in worse position than ever to fend off a coronation or a similar manifestation of the "correctness" of Czech historicism. On October 18, in the decisive council, Austria's spokesmen pressed for elimination of a phrase in the imperial proclamation which changed the army's title. The words in question indicated that the change took place after the Emperor listened to the depositions offered by his ministers for joint affairs and by both ministers-president.

Surely His Majesty realized from the unanimous opinion of the Austrian cabinet that the change in title would have the most serious consequences upon Austrian public opinion, especially in Bohemia, where the Diet would probably utter loud protests, said Taaffe. When Tisza asserted that he absolutely had to have some concession, the Austrian ministry acquiesced most reluctantly and only with the provisos that the Emperor would issue the portentous document as "Highest War-Lord" and with the absence of any implication of direct Austrian approval of the change. If the Emperor did not strike out the reference to "ministers-president" and if he did not order the change as the dynastic commander-in-chief, Taaffe announced he would hand in his resignation. No doubt, he added, his colleagues would join him.

Although Tisza agreed to the dropping of the phrase which Taaffe found unacceptable, the Emperor was not convinced that the troublesome words meant "agreement." Rather, they indicated simply that the ministers gave their views and the Emperor then made his decision. If both governments would strive resolutely to defend the change, however, he would allow the modification Taaffe wanted. And, like vassals of old, the two leaders gave binding promises to their lord to battle honorably for the new designation.

Taaffe also strongly recommended adding to the proclamation a precise guarantee of the existing emblems and oath. To avoid the slightest misunderstanding and to calm the growing unrest of more and more circles, he likewise wanted a statement of unity and indivisibility of the armed forces *for all times.* Tisza then replied that these additions would very much complicate matters in Hungary and courteously asked his Austrian counterpart to give up his requests. When the proclamation did appear, there was no mention of emblems and oath. The Austrian and Hungarian citizenry also read that the change in nomenclature did not disturb or infringe upon the unity and indivisibility of army or navy. The question of an eternal disposition was obviously side-stepped.

Taaffe was more successful in securing the modification of the phrase, "in accord with historical custom," which had been proposed as the justification for the Emperor's action. "Custom" and "customary" were words that stirred up historical reminiscences, argued the statesman for whom history was often a poison. In Maria Theresa's day a customary phrase was "Hungarian and Bohemian Army." If historical references were made, if there were appeals to custom, agitators in Bohemia could make capital of them. Thanks to the Austrian minister's trepidation, the Emperor declared in his proclamation that he was following the custom of his ancestors.[18]

Taaffe was not the only public figure anxious to keep the Czech marriage of nationality and history under some control. Plener, the best known of the Germans who defended German history in Bohemia, moved to counterattack the rising Czech anticipations by the usual formula of an interpellation in the

[18] Kolmer, *Parlament,* IV, 81; RMRZ 361, Oct. 18, 1889.

Reichsrat. Repeating the usual strictures against Czech inroads upon the unity of the state and its constitution, he asked the cabinet what it intended to do to allay the German anxieties over the recent decisions of the Diet. He insisted that a reasonable protection of the German nationality did not conflict with the national development of the Czechs or the needs of the state. When he added to this slippery cliché an appeal to Taaffe's regime to do something about the festering antagonism, he raised the hopes of all moderates.[19] In the cabinet session which considered a reply to the interpellation, Franz Joseph made it clear that he wanted an understanding with the Germans. Very much aroused by Young Czech successes, he had no real hope of relief through the Old Czechs. In rather brutal fashion he said Rieger's followers deserved no great attention, since politically they were already almost dead.[20] Presumably the ruler felt that the Czech-oriented aristocracy could arrange affairs with the German Liberals in a manner that would confound the radical nationalists in each camp without recourse to the increasingly discredited Old Czechs.

Before Taaffe and the cabinet could decide on a proper response to the Plener complaints, which seemed to be a bid for negotiations, the Liberal leader arose again to express German exasperation. Denying that the state had needed to promise the Czechs any concessions in 1879, he asserted that the cabinet had to take a stand concerning the latest Czech claims. And, giving another opportunity to those who loved to find burning personal ambition in all of his moves, Plener pontificated that the Austrian constitution was too precious a possession to endure violations which kept Taaffe and Company in their ministerial chairs. Did the government want to drive the outraged Germans to actions beyond mere abstinence from Diet proceedings?[21]

Rieger undertook a refutation of Plener's arguments, but he interspersed his lively defense of Czech rights with a reminder that he and Prince Lobkowitz had not been too proud to ap-

---

[19] *SPA*, X Session, pp. 12944–45, Dec. 3, 1889.

[20] Mehring, "Die deutsch-böhmische Sprachenfrage," p. 97.

[21] *SPA*, pp. 13044–45, 13049, Dec. 12, 1889.

THE COMPROMISE OF 1890

proach Schmeykal in search of a *modus vivendi*. If there was to be a compromise, he noted significantly, both sides would have to yield some points. If Rieger hinted that he was willing to chance a far-reaching discussion, Taaffe demonstrated considerable snappishness in replying to Plener's interpretation of the Austrian constitution. It would seem that the deputy from the Eger Chamber of Commerce demanded an answer not only in the name of his associates but of all of Austria and of the lands beyond, expostulated Taaffe. He could only regret that an Austrian would so speak of Austria's internal affairs in parliamentary sessions. If the cabinet truly bartered the constitution to stay in power, it would have no more public support than a party which concentrated its entire effort upon destroying and then replacing a ministry.[22] Plener was indeed ready to lead the German deputies from the Reichsrat if Taaffe did not make a full statement on the proposed coronation and the Czech constitutional claims, and he deliberately sharpened his attack by accusing Taaffe of thinking only of his exalted post, which he had managed to retain by making unending concessions for a decade.[23]

Years later Gautsch told Plener that Taaffe fashioned his reply to the interpellation proper to accord with Kálnoky's views on foreign policy. Dunajewski had suggested a ministerial statement to the effect that the matter of coronation was the Emperor's prerogative and so above discussion. There was a possibility it would take place, the Minister-President should inform the parliament. Gautsch then advised a conference with the Minister of Foreign Affairs, who violently opposed the idea of a coronation. A cabinet meeting over which the Emperor presided then decided that it could not agree to the desired ceremony in Prague.[24] The considerations which ran through Kálnoky's mind are suggested by a German Embassy report on what its experts anticipated from the recently reassembled Austrian Lower House. Monts, who signed the scornful predictions,

---

[22] *Ibid.*, p. 13059, Dec. 13, 1889.
[23] *Ibid.*, pp. 13060–62, Dec. 13, 1889; Plener, *Erinnerungen,* II, 391.
[24] Plener, *Erinnerungen,* II, 391–92.

spoke of "smuggling" Czech as an official language into the purely German districts of Bohemia, thanks to the recent action by the Diet, which he expected Taaffe to approve. While admitting that Taaffe did not honestly want the Czechs to get control of the Moravian Diet, he dismissed the Austrian minister's policy as "hand to mouth." The Young Czechs were clearly opposed to Taaffe, while the Old Czechs were more peremptory than ever in their demands.[25] One can well imagine what Monts would have written if Franz Joseph's advisers had decided upon the royal ceremony in the Bohemian capital.

Taaffe's reply to the German Liberal interpellation was distinctly reassuring to the minority in Bohemia. While he reserved every regime's right to initiate proper constitutional change when state interest so demanded, he informed the Lower House that the present moment called for peaceful and progressive development. For that reason he and his colleagues would plan no principal changes in the constitution or in the related matter of crowning the Emperor as king of Bohemia. Naturally his government would continue to respect and advance the proper claims of each nationality in the crownland.[26] Schönburg was soon busy arranging a conference, dry and businesslike, between Taaffe and Plener. During the course of talks with the Czechs, Plener requested the government not to approve the Diet's bill on languages used in autonomous governing bodies or its bill on provincial schools. Taaffe agreed, but he firmly declined to invite Young Czechs to the discussions and evaded commenting on Plener's statement that the regime should honestly try to conform to the German point of view. In later years Plener recalled that the Minister-President did not have high hopes for success. It seemed rather that a higher will had insisted on another round between the feuding parties.[27] In the last days of 1889 the German Diet deputies and representatives of the Old Czechs consented to meet in Vienna under the government's auspices.

[25] See Monts's dispatch No. 384, A 16369, Dec. 3, 1889, UC-1, reel 215, frames 676–80.
[26] *SPA*, p. 13139, Dec. 17, 1889.
[27] Plener, *Erinnerungen,* II, 393–94.

Chlumecky wrote Plener from Meran that a successful compromise would put the Liberals in a difficult spot, but he predicted that Taaffe would face even more serious problems, whether the discussions succeeded or came to naught. If the opposition would use cleverness and foresight, it might eliminate him. Should the talks fail, he could scarcely recover from the blow. If they succeeded, then the Old Czechs were lost and Taaffe's days were numbered. Clearly, even to a moderate of Chlumecky's type, Taaffe's downfall meant more than peace in Bohemia.[28]

The leaders of the Young Czechs issued a declaration on the day of the formal convoking of the conference in which they declared that the satisfaction of the Germans was the sole purpose of the negotiations. They absolutely rejected any agreement that would impair the special constitutional status of the kingdom of Bohemia, its indivisibility, and its administrative unity. Plener and Rieger exchanged their respective statements of aims in the first days of the meeting. Very roughly, the Germans sought partition of the crownland, while the Old Czechs feared such a remedy. The Germans wanted to split along national lines also the Senate of the Superior Court of Bohemia, the Bohemian School Board, and the Bohemian Agricultural Board. Here Rieger indicated there could be some modifications, though probably not for the last-named agency. Plener was willing to accept the idea of national curias for Diet elections, for the Germans never again could hope to be in the majority, while Rieger emphasized the need for Czech as the internal language of business in Czech districts. In addition, the Old Czech leader wanted the appointment of a Czech official in German districts to handle Czech documents, the crownland's financial support of minority schools, a larger number of Czech judicial circuits, and the creation of a Czech chamber of commerce in the Königgrätz (Hradec Králové) area. As for the controversial Diet law on autonomous governing bodies and the

[28] Letter of Dec. 30, 1889, in *Briefe zur deutschen Politik in Österreich von 1848 bis 1918* ed. Paul Molisch (Vienna and Leipzig, 1934), p. 316.

languages they could employ, he declared the Germans could not expect to continue their monopoly in Reichenberg.[29]

Taaffe had heard such debates throughout his decade of service. He told his fellow ministers that he anticipated no lasting reconciliation and that therefore there was no need to be too yielding. The state required some kind of armistice which would give neither antagonist a full victory. The cabinet had to keep the residue of power in its own hands, and he especially disliked the idea of a Czech senate in the Bohemian Superior Court, since such a change would incite the other nationalities of Austria to demand the same.[30] The Emperor at a court dinner for the conferees told Plener that he still wanted German as the language for internal services, though he did not support the idea of a completely "scientific" separation of the two peoples of Bohemia.[31]

Meanwhile Gautsch produced a plan for the organization of the School Board and Schönborn did the same for the Superior Court. As expected, the hottest fights centered about the processing of legal cases insofar as language was concerned. To avoid the pressure which Taaffe envisaged in case Czechs and Germans had fully equal and separate senates in the Superior Court, the cabinet declared it would entrust three of the eight already existing senates of this court with cases exclusively involving German-speaking citizens. To appease the Czechs somewhat, Schönborn agreed that even in German district and circle courts there should be one official who knew both languages. In a district court he would not have to be a certified magistrate. In general the cabinet ruled out any modification of the rule that German had to remain the language of internal business. To balance the score, it had no intention of withdrawing the Language Ordinances of April 19, 1880.[32]

The German conferees accepted the idea of having an official act as translator in German courts, but the Czechs rejected this

29 Plener, *Erinnerungen*, II, 397–98.
30 Mehring, "Die deutsch-böhmische Sprachenfrage," p. 100.
31 Plener, *Erinnerungen*, II, 398.
32 Mehring, "Die deutsch-böhmische Sprachenfrage," p. 100.

as an insult. While the latter assented to Schönborn's plan for the Superior Court, the Germans found it unsatisfactory. For several days the opposing sides wrestled with the crucial issue of languages to be employed in the administration of justice. Rieger vowed that the Old Czechs would not retreat from their principle that a Czech deserved treatment in his own idiom wherever he lived in the crownland, while the Germans felt no compromise was worth while as long as Stremayr's Ordinances affected the core localities of German Bohemia. In the end, basic decisions on languages were postponed. The conferees admitted they could not unite on the linguistic requirements for personnel to man the courts of first instance. The Stremayr Ordinances would undergo revision only after the court districts were redrawn. In the next session of the Diet, there would be a complete review of the bill affecting the languages used by autonomous organs of government. With the exception of Prague, however, all cities with charters would receive the same treatment as the nonchartered municipalities. Plener was sure that the Germans had made no real headway on the language issue, but a later critic aptly points out that the proposals offered by cabinet members, though not accepted, all pointed to some revision of the Ordinances of 1880. And the politically embarrassed Old Czechs also must have realized that an acceptance of nationally demarcated districts inevitably would have modified Stremayr's prescriptions.[33]

The protocol published after fourteen sittings revealed a greater accommodation of views on other issues, and, according to Plener and the Young Czechs, sizable victories for the Germans. In the Superior Court, twenty-six of the councilors had to know both languages, i.e., would be Czech, while the remaining fifteen were dispensed from knowledge of Czech, i.e., would be German. Each group of councilors would form a disciplinary senate to overlook the procedures and activities of juristic personnel in areas predominantly Czech or German. The Minister of Justice was to choose men for the posts on the Superior Court in terms of their earlier careers in areas inhabited

[33] *Ibid.,* p. 105.

by persons of their own nationality. These regulations clearly
enhanced the principle of partition.

School affairs likewise took on an air of separateness. The
future provincial School Board would hold plenary sessions on
common Bohemian questions, including the erection of minority
schools, but ordinarily it would function in two sections, one for
the German community, one for the Czech. In membership, the
Germans continued to have a representation out of proportion to
population. A highly involved statement on reorganization of
the provincial Agricultural Council repeated the pattern of a
high degree of independence for each nationality. The Czech
and German sections would receive imperial and provincial
subventions in proportion to population and the incidence of
taxes on property. Here, too, Germans who were not completely irreconcilable might well see an advantage, for they knew
that their tax contributions were relatively higher than those of
the Czechs.

Other decisions concerned minority schools, a chamber of
commerce for eastern Bohemia, the national demarcation of
court districts, and the preparation of plans for electoral reform. In the future, mixed school districts would have to erect
minority schools in any subdistrict in which there were more
than forty school-age children belonging to the minority if their
parents had resided in the subdistrict for at least five years. If
there were more than eighty of such children, their parents
needed only to reside three years in the subdistrict. School
districts could apply for provincial funds to defray the costs of
such minority schools. The new chamber of commerce would
relieve the pressures on the Prague and Reichenberg chambers
without depriving either of these strongholds of German mercantile spirit of their parliamentary representation.

The proposed delimitation of judicial units involved communications and traffic considerations as well as the national allegiance of the citizens of Bohemia. To secure a maximum of
justice in drawing the new boundaries, the state promised to
increase the number of courts insofar as its financial resources
permitted. The Diet would pass on the new delimitation of the

THE COMPROMISE OF 1890

court districts, which a special commission of jurists and party leaders would work out. To match the partition in the judicial sphere, both nationalities would form two curias for representation in the Diet. Joined with the curia of the great landowners, these bodies would pass on future provincial laws. Each would have the right to veto a bill which changed the constitution and electoral laws of the crownland or which modified the rules on languages in autonomous governing bodies or in educational institutions not specifically assigned to one ethnic group.[34]

Franz Joseph could not restrain his glee when he boasted of the happy conclusion of the conferences to Major von Deines, the German empire's military plenipotentiary. With a touch of condescension, the monarch praised both nationalities for their show of good will and Taaffe for his astuteness. With a smile he admitted that his Minister-President did not enjoy much sympathy in Berlin, but he was the only man who could build from existing conditions. The compromise could not have come earlier, opined the happy ruler, for the Young Czechs first had to humble the Old Czechs. Kálnoky also was full of praise for Taaffe, admitting to Reuss that the Austrian statesman was indeed a Viennese, with all of the good and bad that the capital's sons possessed, but also a good Austrian completely loyal to the idea of fighting for the alliance.[35]

What was the public reaction to this mixed bag, which the signatories solemnly declared to be a unit and which the Czechs accepted with the understanding that their German colleagues would then press for an end to the German secession from the Diet? The *Neue Freie Presse* in wonderment admitted that the conference's decision had outstripped all expectations. Best of all, the Czechs had accepted almost entirely the German position on public schools and the provincial School Board.[36] Grimly echoing the German paper's conclusions, *Národní Listy* ex-

[34] For the full text of the protocol, see Kolmer, *Parlament*, IV, 399–406.
[35] Eduard von Wertheimer, *Bismarck im politischen Kampf* (Berlin, 1930), pp. 518–20.
[36] Jan. 18, 1890.

claimed, "The operation was a brilliant success, the patient is dead!"[37] After some further reflection, the *Neue Freie Presse,* still a bit bewildered that the cabinet had done so much to fulfill the German Liberal propositions, decided that Taaffe would have to give further token of his intentions before there could be confidence in the permanence of the compromise.[38]

The *Neue Freie Presse* and Plener went too far in their enthusiasm, which looked like exultation to the Young Czechs. When Plener reported on the protocols at the German-Bohemian Party Day in Teplitz (Teplice), he failed to temper his understandable desire to accent the successes achieved with some phrases that might indicate some willingness to live with the Czechs. Coexistence was implied, and the speech was generally moderate. But boasting that the Liberals had compelled the regime and the Czechs to acquiesce in the concept of a divided Bohemia gave the Young Czechs the proper weapon to berate their aristocratic and upper middle-class opponents among the Czechs. Furthermore, Plener paraded before the public eye his conviction that the Germans would reverse the Stremayr Ordinance of 1880 in their cherished Bohemian strongholds. Germans no longer would have to worry over preparation for subordinate or major posts in administration or judiciary, for dual proficiency in languages would undergo progressive de-emphasis in German Bohemia.[39]

All elements of political power, save for the Young Czechs, ratified the protocols of Vienna. While the same Young Czechs debated their ultimate stand, the *Statthalter* of Moravia asked Taaffe if he might dissolve a tendentious society in that land which was attempting to undermine the Czech conservative fractions in favor of the more radical party. The Minister-President sent word that he had no objections if legal niceties were observed and if the dissolution antedated the Young Czech decision on the Vienna protocols. If they accepted the compromise, he did not want to seem ungrateful. If they rejected it, he wanted

[37] Quoted, *ibid.,* Jan. 18, 1890, *Abendblatt.*   [38] Jan. 19, 1890.
[39] Ernst von Plener, *Reden* (Stuttgart and Leipzig, 1911), pp. 509–17.

no talk of complaints that the regime was taking vengeance upon them.[40]

On February 3 Schönborn directed an ordinance to the Superior Court in Prague which in fact suspended the full operation of the rules which Stremayr had issued almost ten years before. Ordering the selection of a commission to redraw the boundaries of certain judicial districts, the Minister of Justice also decreed the new distribution of personnel in the Superior Court according to the formula adopted in the conferences. Unfortunately he ended his otherwise proper directives with the tactless statement that knowledge of Czech obviously would not disadvantage a person who applied for posts that did not require such a competence.[41]

German Liberal self-confidence was so apparent that Reuss felt compelled to write Berlin that it would be premature to think of Plener's joining Taaffe's cabinet. Dunajewski, despite strong opposition from Bacquehem and Gautsch, was still Taaffe's indispensable mouthpiece, and Reuss also felt that Taaffe would avoid as long as possible a disruption of his admittedly slim majority.[42] That majority suffered an obvious shock when the Young Czechs published a manifesto on February 26, denouncing the *Ausgleich* as an actual partition of Bohemia. In their opinion, German would still have a privileged position in the internal administration in Czech areas while Czech officials would have to leave German areas. To ascertain the true popular reaction to the Vienna protocols, they suggested that they and the Old Czechs resign their seats and run on the issue of these agreements.[43]

As if to provoke the Young Czechs further, Taaffe recommended a definite imperial rejection of the Diet's bill to regulate the languages used by autonomous officials. Though he ad-

[40] *Politischer Nachlass,* pp. 665–66.
[41] For the text of the ordinances, see Kolmer, *Parlament,* IV, 409–11.
[42] See Reuss's dispatch No. 61, A 2734, Feb. 21, 1890, UC-1, reel 215, frames 681–85.
[43] Mehring, "Die deutsch-böhmische Sprachenfrage," p. 112.

mitted the fairness of most of the proposal's clauses, he emphatically defended the right of a chartered city like Reichenberg to exercise self-determination in regard to the medium of communication it would employ.[44] When the Old Czechs signed the Vienna protocols, they had prepared the way for such a *mémoire* from Taaffe to the Emperor, of course, and for the inevitable exploitation of the bill's rejection by their vigorous antagonists.

Added incitement to Young Czech recklessness came with the regime's confiscation of their manifesto of February 26. Though Taaffe had kept the rather puzzled and finally resentful *Statthalter*, Count Thun, from the *Ausgleich* conferences and had also supplied him with 10,000 gulden in discretionary funds to "work on" the Young Czech press, such discreet measures meant little when Thun's police seized the party's manifesto.[45] As the Young Czech pressure on Rieger and his colleagues continued to grow, the latter frantically sought a few changes that would offset obvious and general dissatisfaction among their voters. In a supplementary conference in Vienna on April 14, their pleas for modification of Taaffe's steady claim that the executive alone had control over the inner service's language went for nought.[46] Two days later Grégr recapitulated on the floor of the Lower House his party's complete disdain for the compromise and the "traitors" who had signed it. He did not deny that the Diet would ratify the protocol's changes, but he asserted that new elections would then repudiate the compromise. In a particularly venomous passage he declared that the Germans had always wanted to exile from their strongholds the Czechs who had witnessed the ovations which Bohemian Germans had given Bismarck, Moltke, and valiant William in 1866. Once the North Bohemian area became a pure German island, it would one day disappear from the eyes of Austrian statesmen in a mighty show of thunder and lightning, to pursue its destiny with the rest of the Elbian Germans. Meanwhile the rest of German

[44] Kabinetts-Kanzlei, Vortrag 361, Jan. 24, 1890.
[45] *Politischer Nachlass,* pp. 474–78.
[46] Mehring, "Die deutsch-böhmische Sprachenfrage," pp. 113–14.

Austria would try to denationalize the Slavs as preparation for Austria's absorption by the German Empire. Taaffe had sent Thun, a modern Duke of Alba, to Prague to stifle liberal-minded men and then he had coerced some Czechs and Germans into agreeing to proposals hatched in Prince Reuss's palace, to credit the conclusions the public had reached.[47]

Rieger valiantly countered with a series of questions. Was it helpful to continue the German bitterness to the extent that they would look more and more beyond the frontiers for salvation? Did Grégr really believe the Czechs could win acceptance of their constitutional ideas against the will of the German population? Was it the Vienna conferences which gave German status as the language for the inner services? As long as you face overpowering factors, why try to charm them away with big words or provoke them? It was no patriotic service to whip up chauvinism and to demand what could not be had. His party hoped that someday the internal and external hindrances to the recognition of the Czech *Staatsrecht* would disappear, for it believed that full acceptance of the Czech position was in the dynasty's interest. The *Ausgleich* was not a completed action. Certain principles were agreed to, but the total question of Czech-German relations in Bohemia was still open to discussion.[48]

Slovene spokesmen praised Rieger, for the pattern arrived at in Bohemia could serve their aspirations in Styria, Carinthia, Carniola, and the Littoral. Leopold Gregorec somewhat hollowly assured the House and presumably himself that the expulsion of Austria from the German scene deprived the policy of Germanization of every excuse, but he added that the more people tried to Germanize the Slavs, the more the entire empire ran the danger of being devoured by "Prussian Pan-Germany."[49] Franc Šuklje reproved Grégr for his attack. If he really thought that the Germans won all the points, would he say that they would have signed these agreements twelve or fifteen

---

[47] *SPA*, pp. 14201, 14203–05, April 16, 1890.
[48] *Ibid.*, pp. 14256–57, 14261–63, April 17, 1890.
[49] *Ibid.*, pp. 14245–46, April 17, 1890.

years before? Perhaps the compromise did keep the Czechs from
gaining new ground, but it definitely guaranteed them a sure
position in return. But no one should think that peace would
last in Bohemia if agreement was limited to that crownland. The
Slovenes expected Taaffe and the moderate Germans to honor
the long-standing Slovene demands.[50]

The disgruntled German Nationalists had already anticipated
the Slovene reaction. Türk saw in the *Ausgleich* a surrender of
the common German interest in Austria. How could the state
deny the Czechs of Silesia what the Germans of Bohemia received? Partition would bring a merciless denationalization of
Germans wherever they were in a minority in Bohemia. Germans actually needed to imitate the energy implicit in the Czech
national revival if they were to survive.[51] Steinwender, much
exercised by the proposed grant of a veto to the landed curia in
future Bohemian diets, bluntly admitted that Germans would
regard attempts at an *Ausgleich* in Carinthia as a breach of the
peace. "Where we have the power, we will certainly not misuse
it. But neither will we yield it up or share it."[52]

In line with Taaffe's studied reserve, the government deputized Dunajewski to reply to critics. The fluent Pole took pains
to repeat Taaffe's comment on the proposed coronation and
emphasized the cabinet's unity of opinion in the matter. But he
said little else, save for a witticism directed at Grégr. If that
gentleman believed that the Germans had secured everything
they desired, he should rejoice, for a great political force which
had all it wanted was dead.[53]

Since financial expertise was Plener's forte, he was quick to
express regret that the Minister of Finance had substituted for
Taaffe in defending the protocols. Perhaps Dunajewski was not
really warm in his admiration for the settlement, jeered Plener,
who was hardly unaware of the rumors which placed him in the
shrewd Pole's office. Actually, the German Liberal leader was
at his best in answering the silly and the probing objections.

[50] *Ibid.*, pp. 14312, 14317, April 19, 1890.
[51] *Ibid.*, pp. 14233–35, 14238, April 17, 1890.
[52] *Ibid.*, p. 14282, April 18, 1890.   [53] *Ibid.*, p. 14278, April 18, 1890.

Why worry over the veto power of the landed curia when it was restricted to nationality problems? Was it possible that the two nationally organized curias would agree in such a sphere, only to be frustrated by the aristocrats? Less happy were his words to the Slovenes of Styria and Carinthia, who were not to think that they could ask at the moment for the same position which the *Ausgleich* guaranteed the Germans of Bohemia. Times could change, of course, he comforted them.

Plener also chose to discover Taaffe's old malice and anti-Liberal bent in the continuing activity of the old coalition and in the injudicious muzzling of Young Czech meetings and journals. It was a shame that the lift in spirits which all of Austria experienced right after the signing of the protocols had evaporated. The general change in internal policy which all had hoped for did not come. Rather, the regime tried to limit and isolate the compromise to Bohemia.[54] Obviously Plener did not see an inconsistency between such a criticism and his own remarks on preserving the *status quo* in Styria and Carinthia.

On May 19 the *Ausgleich* Diet assembled to consider governmental bills on the provincial School Board, the provincial Agricultural Board, on minority schools, the creation of national curias, and changes in the Bohemian Diet's electoral system. Thun glumly reported that the special commission of twenty-seven which would report on the bills included four Young Czechs and two unreliable Old Czechs. From the beginning he worried over the constancy of Rieger's men, particularly when Jacob Škarda declared he was not bound by his party's acceptance of the protocols. Yet Thun had to admit to Taaffe that the Old Czechs were hard pressed. Even the most intelligent of their people were increasingly opposed to the agreements made in Vienna.[55]

If Taaffe could keep a discreet distance from the conferences of January, 1890, he enjoyed no such privilege once the Diet's commission fell to wrangling over the bargains reached. Monts

[54] *Ibid.*, pp. 14293, 14295, 14297, 14300, April 18, 1890.
[55] Telegrams of May 20, 22, and 23, 1890, in *Politischer Nachlass*, pp. 478–80.

wrote Berlin that Taaffe's passivity since January had destroyed the chances of a German Liberal–Old Czech coalition which alone could function as a truly enduring Austrian majority. Dunajewski was the culprit, wrote the excited counselor, and Germany could expect continuing Polish intrigues and a growth of German and Czech radicalism as a result.[56] When the Diet actually met, the German Embassy momentarily discerned some improvement, for Dunajewski had adopted some of Plener's ideas and indirectly was undermining Falkenhayn and his "Jesuit friend," Vogelsang.[57]

A very obvious Young Czech move in the commission to make a dent in the government's traditional right to determine the language of internal business forced Taaffe and his associates to move directly into the arena. Jan Kvíčala introduced a motion to regulate by law of the Diet the media of communication employed by the provincial School Board. The terms he specified were *Verhandlungssprache* and *Geschäftssprache,* which meant the media used in dealing with the public face-to-face and in the written implementation of the public's petitions, complaints, and the like. His bill recognized absolute equality of Czech and German in the School Board's operations, and so acceptance of his proposal would violate Taaffe's constant assertion that the executive power alone could decide on the language of inner business. Gautsch, during the January negotiations, had absolutely refused to allow a breach in the principle of an executive control of the medium used in inner services, and he informed the Emperor that it would not be wise or possible to allow the future School Board to regulate anything other than the medium which each section would employ.[58]

Absolute refusal to consider any part of Kvíčala's bill would have increased Old Czech embarrassment. On the other hand, acceptance of a legislative control over *Geschäftssprache* was

[56] See Monts's dispatch No. 116, A 4846, April 10, 1890, *German Foreign Ministry Archives,* microfilm copy at the National Archives, Washington, D.C., ser. K719–K724, frames 192431–38.

[57] See Reuss's dispatch No. 170, A 6371, May 18, 1890, UC-1, reel 215, frames 699–704.

[58] Kabinetts-Kanzlei, Vortrag 1786, April 27, 1890.

unthinkable. The cabinet tried to wiggle out of the dilemma by promising future administrative regulation of the *Verhandlungssprache* to accord with the fact that the new School Board would operate through sections distinguished from one another by language.[59] Gautsch implored Thun to work on the aristocratic members of the commission to drop the word *Geschäftssprache* from the bill. Otherwise the government would have to declare that the bill ran counter to the right of the executive and so was invalid. If the Germans would agree to a change that did not abridge executive prerogative, the government would concur. Otherwise the government would reaffirm its full freedom to act to protect its powers.[60]

When Richard Clam Martinič reported that he and Count Friedrich Karl Kinsky probably could not keep a majority of their aristocratic colleagues from supporting Kvíčala's bill when it went before the Diet, Thun regretfully informed Taaffe that this analysis was no doubt correct. Clam Martinič actually had pleaded for the cabinet's acceptance of a legislative normalization of the language question within the School Board, but Taaffe saw no way to release the Czech conferees from the letter of the pact they had already made with the Germans.[61]

Prince Alfred Windischgrätz, working with Thun and Plener to give the Old Czechs an admittedly minor concession in the matter of languages within the School Board, proposed a continuation of administrative control as long as each section could use its own tongue for its separate deliberations and expediting of business. Moreover, every member of the Board could use the language he preferred in plenary sessions.[62] Gautsch assured the Emperor that the language used between the School Board and other offices of the bureaucracy in Bohemia was still determined by decree of the central government. When the Czech section of the Board dealt with Czech district school councils or with Czech schools, of course, the *Geschäftssprache* would be Czech. The

---

[59] Mehring, "Die deutsch-böhmische Sprachenfrage," p. 114.

[60] Telegram and draft of second telegram, Gautsch to Thun, May 30, 1890, in *Politischer Nachlass,* p. 483.

[61] *Ibid.,* pp. 484–86.   [62] *Ibid.,* p. 487.

same would be true of relations between the German section and its subordinate organs and institutions.[63]

Meanwhile Taaffe tried to persuade the Young Czechs to end their policy of "negation." Refusing to call off their successful campaign against the Old Czechs, the party leaders directed the Minister-President to seek constructive proposals from the club's membership in Prague itself. Though a telegram went from Vienna to *Národní Listy* in line with such advice, its contents, thanks to Taaffe's wish, went unpublished.[64] The Old Czechs were on the run, and their rivals had no reason to relax the pursuit. Kvíčala's proposition indeed fell before Windischgrätz' compromise when the Diet voted on June 1, but the regime still faced an unpleasant legacy in a bill actually proposed by an Old Czech, Škarda. Most Czechs had resented Schönborn's partial suspension of the Language Ordinances of 1880, and it was easy to get a majority for a resolution asking the cabinet to formulate for the Diet laws relating to the organization of courts and regulating the use of languages by imperial officials in Bohemia.[65] Taaffe and his colleagues ignored Škarda's invitation until autumn. The fact that the Diet had no stomach for further debate on the other major portions of the *Ausgleich* explained the meaningful silence in Vienna. On June 3 the bill to reorganize the School Board passed the Diet, and the hard-worked Thun sent the deputies home for the summer.

Franz Joseph acted as his own advocate when the Delegations met in Budapest right after the close of the Bohemian Diet. Tackling both Rieger and Plener, he rather petulantly demanded the speedy legislative approval of the Vienna protocols and denied that the Czechs were justified in their excitement and perturbation. Rieger plainly said that there had to be some change in regard to the use of Czech in internal services, and the Emperor replied generally that he had to keep in mind the best interests of the state's bureaucracy. When Rieger reminded the ruler of the linguistic regulations in Galicia, South Tirol, and

[63] Telegram from Thun, June 1, 1890, *ibid.*, p. 487; Kabinetts-Kanzlei, Vortrag 2692, June 21, 1890.

[64] Plener, *Erinnerungen,* II, 427.   [65] *Politischer Nachlass,* p. 482.

Dalmatia which did not seem to pose threats or problems for
state officials there, Franz Joseph testily retorted that Austria
could not permit the time to come when imperial officials would
no longer understand German. Plener concluded that the monarch simply was poorly informed and excessively self-willed in
these direct incursions in behalf of the *Ausgleich*.[66] *Politik*
defiantly commented, after the exchange between Rieger and the
Emperor, that there would be no completion of the compromise
unless the Czechs received satisfaction in the matter of the
language for internal service. The rest of the Old Czech press
echoed this warning, and during the summer additional evidence
of insurmountable Czech resistance piled up.[67]

In misery over the insults which Young Czech orators had
flung at him, Rieger turned to Pražak for help. If the government did not persuade the Germans to accept the introduction of
Czech as a language for internal services, the Old Czech Club
would fall to pieces. Its deputies were laying down their mandates in steady succession, and Rieger hinted desperately that the
unpublicized way in which Polish became the official tongue in
Galicia might be a pattern for Czech in Bohemia. Pražak turned
over the letter to Taaffe with the rather cool remark that the
Czechs had scarcely bettered their chances for German compliance with their wishes when they contrived the election of a
German whom the Bohemian Germans distrusted and disliked as
the representative of the Germans of Prague on the provincial
School Board. With an equally chilly reply, Taaffe confined
himself to the opinion that changes in external or internal languages of service would help the Old Czechs very little if their
internal party relationships did not take a turn for the
better.[68]

By the time Taaffe had dispatched his note, Rieger had published a letter in which he foretold his approaching retirement
from the political world. At the age of 72, he hoped for a fair

---

[66] Plener, *Erinnerungen,* II, 428; Kolmer, *Parlament,* IV, 423–24.
[67] Erich Leichtenmüller, "Die Wiener Zeitungen und der böhmische
Ausgleich" (unpubl. diss., Vienna, 1952), p. 88.
[68] *Politischer Nachlass,* pp. 489–91.

appraisal of his work after his death. Soon thereafter Heinrich
Clam Martinič and Prince Karl Schwarzenberg likewise an-
nounced their farewells to politics. When the Germans showed
their pique over the slow progress of the *Ausgleich* by advising
German businessmen in Bohemia to support the province's ex-
position only if the Czechs were more reasonable, the Old
Czechs publicly declared there would be no *Ausgleich* unless
Czech became a language of internal service.[69]

The government cautiously attempted to keep the chasm between Germans and Old Czechs from widening. The president
of the Superior Court in Bohemia warned court officials against
keeping records of court actions which concerned Czechs in the
German language, and his orders specifically cited the Stremayr
Ordinances of 1880.[70] The Emperor and Taaffe on the other
hand arranged for the resignation of Heinrich, the man whom
the city fathers of Prague had mischievously elected to the
School Board despite his bad reputation among the Germans
whom he was to represent.[71]

The one concession which the Old Czechs believed would save
their skins and forward the *Ausgleich* was not in Taaffe's power
to grant. Rieger journeyed to Vienna early in August and
renewed his advocacy of an ordinance which would allow Czech
full status as a medium for internal communications in Czech
districts. If the government would agree, he promised to secure
a written pledge from his party to support the rest of the *Ausgleich*. In a franker mood Richard Clam Martinič told
Bacquehem that the only way to arrest the breakup of the Old
Czech Party was to grant Rieger's request.[72] Taaffe said his
cabinet could not budge from the position that relief should
come only through joint German–Old Czech agreement. The
Germans were most eager to secure passage of the *Ausgleich,*
and the Old Czechs might well profit from the German mood in
direct negotiations. The Minister-President warned that Rieger
and his party would get nowhere, however, as long as they

---

[69] Kolmer, *Parlament,* IV, 424–26.   [70] *Ibid.,* IV, 426–27.
[71] *Politischer Nachlass,* pp. 492–93.
[72] Mehring, "Die deutsch-böhmische Sprachenfrage," p. 120.

insisted upon an understanding with the Young Czechs. The present ministry or even one that might take its place could not bargain with the latter fraction before it purged itself.[73] Since Taaffe's earlier overtures to some leaders of the Young Czechs were known, his dictum aroused no enthusiastic response among the harried moderates.

The Diet met again in the autumn, preceded by fruitless attempts of both Czech parties to concoct a common strategy. In the commission which discussed anew the pledges made in Vienna, the Germans pushed hard and successfully for the full Diet's consideration of the plan to revamp the provincial Agricultural Board. Since it was imperative from the German point of view to partition Bohemia according to nationality before hearing Czech arguments on the eternal issue of languages, Herbst tried to hurry the commission which was at work on the project. Thun declined to promise results before the early months of 1891, and his reply to Herbst spurred Young Czechs to greater attempts to obstruct and the Old Czechs and Feudalists to make a variety of interpellations which, they insisted, would merely clarify the formulas sketched at Vienna.

The formal debate on the provincial Agricultural Board repeated the tedious claims that both nationalities had made for decades. The Germans swore they would not capitulate to "tricky" Czech modifications, while the Young Czechs continued to wave the flag of indivisible *Staatsrecht*. When Karel Mattuš, one of the Old Czechs most respected by the Germans, moved the disqualification of men who were not bilingual for the presidency and the governmental representative's post on the Agricultural Board, he provoked the Germans into a formal boycott of the Provincial Exposition. Pettiness among middle-class deputies had an echo in the deliberations of the aristocrats of the province, who failed absolutely to agree on the distribution of seats in the future curia planned for them. The regime sent the unyielding deputies home late in November but promised a new session early in 1891.[74]

As late as November 13, Taaffe was hoping for passage of the

[73] *Ibid.*   [74] Kolmer, *Parlament,* IV, 428–35.

bill on the Agricultural Board and German cooperation with the Provincial Exposition.[75] Thun had warned him, however, that the Old Czechs would cast their votes in harmony with the answer they received on Škarda's far-from-forgotten interpellation.[76] And it was Thun who vainly sought to persuade Rieger on November 17 not to interpellate the government anew in regard to a reorganization of Bohemian courts and the linguistic regulations for provincial officials. Rieger phrased the interpellations in such a restrained fashion that the Old Czechs became panicky. Wounded by their obvious lack of confidence, he prepared to resign from the Reichsrat, and Prince Lobkowitz, the *Oberstlandmarschall,* anxiously sought an audience with Taaffe to give his opinions on the way in which the cabinet should handle both interpellations. The Minister-President cordially invited the Prince to come to Vienna, particularly since the latter had been able to stave off further Czech pressure for an answer during the last days of the Diet's stormy discussions.[77]

While dealing with the Czechs through Lobkowitz, Taaffe simultaneously outlined to Baernreither what he would like to settle with the German Liberals. First, he had virtually ordered the government to work for Liberal victories in two rural constituencies, and he had no doubt the *Statthalter* of Bohemia would "deliver" the mandates. The Minister-President thought it would be improper to link this sign of graciousness with his hope that German Liberals would rejoin the Provincial Exposition Committee, but it would be a courtesy if the Germans did drop their opposition to the Exposition by sitting with the committeemen. Indeed, he hoped Plener and Schmeykal would assure the *Statthalter* of an eventual German collaboration.

Baernreither wrote Plener of his interview and hinted that it was time to take advantage of the government's displeasure with the old coalition. A lot could be accomplished by sending a few men to the Exposition Committee, and it would not do to be petty. Would Plener use his influence upon the *Neue Freie Presse* to subdue its volcanic utterances? Baernreither was al-

[75] *Politischer Nachlass,* pp. 493–95.   [76] *Ibid.,* p. 496.
[77] *Ibid.,* pp. 500–3.

ready telegraphing Chlumecky for the same kind of representations to the editors. In short, whether there was further
compromise or not in Bohemia, Baernreither wanted some
agreement with Taaffe, who had encouraged him in such
hopes.[78]

Lobkowitz meanwhile asked the cabinet to cite (*aufzählen*)
and quote verbatim (*anführen*) all ordinances on the language
question in its reply so that the Diet could properly embark upon
a discussion of all of them. The cabinet countered with an offer
merely to cite, a procedural move which would effectively limit
the Diet's freedom to treat a matter previously reserved to the
executive branch. The ministers also declined to go into the
question of the proper bases for the organization of the Bohemian courts, pleading that the existing state of affairs did not
permit such action. Any revision of rules on languages in the
province's offices would have to await the drawing of frontiers
for court districts. The cabinet did promise it would then obey
the wishes of the Diet as closely as possible in this troublesome
issue and would strive to meet the justified interests of litigants
insofar as the crownland's unitary status, the equality of nationalities, and the claims of the bureaucracy allowed.[79]

Christmas festivities permitted a limited mingling of cabinet,
Czechs, Plener, and the necessary intermediaries, but Plener did
not succeed in effecting Dunajewski's dismissal and Lobkowitz
had precious little to take home to the Czechs.[80] It is true that
the cabinet addressed its comments on the Škarda interpellation
to Prince Lobkowitz and merely instructed Thun, far less palata-
ble to the Czechs, to declare that the statement also applied to
and answered Rieger's later interpellation. Such tortuous procedure emphasized the unreality that had completely enveloped the
struggling factions a year after they met in Vienna. The Germans were displeased because the bare listing of all language
ordinances failed to establish clearly a German monopoly over
internal communications. The Czechs were furious that they

[78] Nachlass Plener, Karton 18, Nos. 663–65.
[79] Mehring, "Die deutsch-böhmische Sprachenfrage," pp. 118–19.
[80] Plener, *Erinnerungen,* II, 438–39.

received, "like school children," a book of ordinances for their edification.[81]

In January the Diet finally approved the bill to reorganize the Agricultural Board. Despite student threats and steady insults from the Young Czechs, twenty-six of the Old Czechs joined with Germans and men of the aristocracy to complete the second great step toward peace in Bohemia. More than a few Old Czechs abstained or joined Škarda in voting against the proposal. Rieger had already informed Lobkowitz that the Old Czechs who did vote favorably would proceed no further unless the Diet considered simultaneously with the question of setting up national curias some explicit changes in the crownland's electoral system. The Germans then protested that the Czechs violated the order of business agreed to in Vienna. Passage of the proposals of January, 1890, should precede settlement of electoral reform, or else the Germans could not hope for their "proper" place in the crownland's administration.[82]

The deliberations of the Diet in January, 1891, marked the final bankruptcy of the attempt to settle the "Bohemian question." The word *Ausgleich* would reappear quite frequently to the end of Taaffe's stewardship, but the sudden and severe reversal which had overtaken Rieger and his moderates ended the promising atmosphere of late 1889. Plener put much of the blame on Taaffe, whom he found listless and discouraged throughout the period of limited gains. Mehring, probably the only student who read the cabinet's discussions of the problems of these years before they were burned, felt there never was a chance in 1890, after the Young Czechs had proved their capacity to outplay the Old Czechs. In his opinion the more promising year was 1887, when Lobkowitz approached the Germans without success.[83]

The documentary evidence which remains indicates that Taaffe was very much his old self as the contending nationalities fought for advantage rather than for armistice. Very much like

[81] *Ibid.*, II, 442; Kolmer, *Parlament*, V, 2.
[82] Plener, *Erinnerungen*, II, 444; Kolmer, *Parlament*, IV, 436.
[83] Mehring, "Die deutsch-böhmische Sprachenfrage," p. 98 n. 2.

diplomatic representatives of the mid-twentieth century, his chief hope was to keep the antagonists talking to each other. Hence he delayed an answer to Škarda and to Rieger and quickly warned Thun through Schönborn in January, 1891, to postpone without fail a bill on the introduction of general electoral reform in Bohemia. The *Statthalter* obviously was following Taaffe's instructions in his attempts to lure the Germans back to the Exposition by giving them two seats on the Landesausschuss, for the Czech anger over the boycott was profound. It was Taaffe, however, who had to write to the protesting Plener that the Germans should show a spirit of accommodation in the question of cooperating with the Exposition *before* they could expect definite promise of two seats. His emphasis on a prior German capitulation reflected his feeling that he had gone far enough in testing the patience of those aristocrats and Old Czechs who still might deliberate with the Germans.

Taaffe had developed a good sense of timing in a decade of political extemporization. When the still reasonably cooperative Czech factions announced they would agree to no national curias without a simultaneous electoral reform, he wired Thun to get the budget confirmed and then adjourn the Diet. If there was to be further advance along the road of compromise, it would need a more private preparation. Before the Diet did go home, however, the industrious Thun secured the approval of the Old Czechs and Czech Feudalists for the two German seats on the Landesausschuss. Taaffe most generously thanked his *Statthalter*, who politely gave all of the credit to the Old Czechs. The Prague governor was one of the best of Taaffe's executives, primarily because he shared the Minister-President's disposition to assign a large authority to those who by birth or personality were good at intricate negotiations. Since the Germans had more to gain from the Vienna protocols than the Czechs, Thun was one of the few who could procure minimal Czech acquiescence. Taaffe and the strong Germans in his ministry, Gautsch and Schönborn, had the task of persuading the Germans to relinquish a detail here and there to give the Old Czechs and their aristocratic allies a chance to survive the Young Czech onslaught. In the end, the grand design was no more than a rickety scaffolding, but the blame was of the times as well as of the men.[84]

All discussions of the nationalities problem in Austria in the pre-World War I days inevitably dragged in the Compromise of 1890. For one thing, many of the perturbed analysts were German Austrians, and the "might have been" enhanced their feelings of desperation. The generation of 1914 either had too much humanity or too little imagination to project the exchanges of population that came after both World Wars, but their sons and grandsons could and did admit finally that partition of Bohemia was the only possible solution short of population transfers.

Since the German element had surrendered its political predominance in Bohemia and had embraced the idea of an ethnically demarcated crownland, why did the Czechs resist? The Slovenes, who were positive that they would benefit from similar dispensations in Carniola and Carinthia, wondered at their cousins' stubborn resistance. Did not demarcation connote, at long last, a recognition of the equality of Slavs with Germans? The Poles, the monopolists of Galicia, had secured such status thanks to the fact that "their" Germans were a scattering of bourgeois tradesmen in the larger towns, often Jewish by faith or extraction. The implications of the protocols signed in 1890 were quite different, the Slovenes obviously had decided.

The Young Czechs successfully resisted the Germans of Bohemia, the Old Czechs, and Taaffe's cabinet because they had no trouble proving that Czech was still a secondary language. As long as the internal services did not utilize Czech on exactly the same basis that it used German, the Young Czechs had a cause that inflamed all but the most reticent of their countrymen. The riots of 1897 proved that the Germans would not have accepted honest equality, of course, and these later events absolve the Young Czechs of much of the blame for the fiasco of 1890.

The Poles who feared Russia and the Slovenes who detested

[84] For a taste of Taaffe's and Thun's activity and relationships, see *Politischer Nachlass*, pp. 509, 511, 512, 537–48.

Italians had a vested interest in the success of the German-Czech talks of 1890, but neither intervened actively. When Rieger and the Czech-oriented aristocracy felt the full blast of the Young Czech propaganda, they ran to Taaffe or retired precipitately from politics. A Plener could not resist a costly bit of crowing over German "victories," though he was aware of the Viennese Liberal press's tendency to push the German advantage to the uttermost. The Emperor's disgust with the Young Czechs was a reality which Taaffe and Thun could not ignore. Given the political climate of 1890, it is surprising that the protocols were signed in the first place.

Was the failure of the rapprochement an important link in the chain that led to the dissolution of 1918? If the Bohemian Diet had accepted the major premises of the protocols, would the Czechs have wiped from their minds those second thoughts that took them by the thousands into collaboration with the Russians during World War I? Were the Slovenes realists in assuming that division, partition, segregation, were the keys to a decent survival in the ancient empire?

In 1890 the Germans of Bohemia were protecting the essentials of their economic and social position in that crownland, though certainly they persuaded themselves (and honestly) that partition meant parity and that the privileges left to their language were an imperial necessity. The Emperor shared their feelings, and Taaffe's interesting exchanges with Pražak indicated that these two officials saw no reason for Young Czech discontent.

A new generation of articulate Czechs was not willing to accept the gradualism that Palacký and Rieger had represented. An older generation of German Liberals dared not surrender the core of power which German businessmen, teachers, and bureaucrats symbolized in Bohemia, for, on the German Left, irredentism flaunted its attractions. The Compromise of 1890 might have served as a pattern for the areas jointly inhabited by Germans and Slovenes, but elsewhere its value was dubious. The gulf between Pole and Ruthene in Galicia and between Italian and Slovene in Istria was culturally and psychically unbridgeable. In Bohemia, where the two cultures were amazingly approximate by 1890, it was the poison distilled by history and literature that killed the compromise. The idea of segregation was endurable only when it guaranteed absolute parity. Otherwise, the struggle for the indivisible kingdom of Bohemia, Moravia, and Silesia had to go on.

14

The Last Years, 1890–1893

Taaffe's deft balancing of the forces at his disposal between 1887 and 1890 depended upon a modicum of restraint among his Czech and Polish supporters. If the Old Czechs or the dominant aristocrats in the Polish Club lost control of their voters, the Taaffe system was in trouble. From the summer of 1889 on, the former party was increasingly embarrassed in Bohemia. The elections of that period for the Diet returned fifty-five Old Czechs and forty-two Young Czechs, a very unsettling proportion when one remembers the suffrage qualifications in town and country. In time the Young Czechs would be ineffably bourgeois and respectable. In 1889 their victories among the well-to-do farmers and businessmen raised serious doubts as to the future of the coalition which dominated the central parliament. Could such firebrands consort with German Clerical Conservatives and Slovenes, even if the Poles did agree to the new alignment? The ministry did not need to worry until the next general elections. Because of the unpromising course of the Czech-German compromise by late 1890, however, the cabinet decided to dissolve the Reichsrat a bit before the end of its appointed time. Newspapers had for some time gossiped over a rivalry between Gautsch and Dunajewski, and the question of new elections did at first split the cabinet. After the struggle was at an end, *Czas,* presumably at Dunajewski's direction, republished a Viennese account of the maneuvering within the ministry. Essentially, the Minister of Finance wanted no change in the composition of the majority. Certainly he had no desire for German Liberal participation. When Zaleski wavered, Dunajewski remained obdurate and offered his resignation. Another story told of a later conference with the Emperor, in which the man who had been Taaffe's strongest aide demanded the removal of Gautsch and Bacquehem as the price of his staying on.[1] Reuss reported that the strong-willed Pole had fought hard against "dismissal," but it is better to say that the situation had become impossible for the man whom the German Embassy and the German Liberal press blamed for most of Taaffe's sins.[2]

Emil Steinbach, known for his assiduous work in the preparation of the social legislation of the 1880s and for meliorative doctrines which fitted loosely under the rubric of "Catholic Socialism," became the new Minister of Finance. Plener disliked him for his impudence and possibly because he, not Plener, joined the cabinet. Of Jewish ancestry, Steinbach exhibited the energy and originality that Taaffe increasingly depended upon.[3] In no time the café wits smiled over the inevitable "Steinbach cabinet, called Taaffe's." The Liberals, on the eve of elections, cautiously admitted they might later collaborate with a regime that had seen the errors of its first decade. Steinbach's appointment did not seem to affect the professionals in the party one way or another. With the great battle for partition of Bohemia still raging, they had little time for canvassing Steinbach's socioeconomic plans. Chlumecky publicly declared a truce in nationalistic, constitutional, and religious conflicts, and he secretly besought Taaffe's aid in securing from other major parties a similar suspension of debate. Taaffe promised to do what he could, while Reuss, informed of the overtures, lectured Chlumecky on

[1] Josef Schenk, *Dr. Julian Ritter von Dunajewski* (Vienna and Leipzig, 1934), pp. 95–96.

[2] See Reuss's dispatch No. 34, A 954, Feb. 4, 1891, UC-1, reel 229, frames 247–48.

[3] Ernst Plener, *Erinnerungen* (Stuttgart and Leipzig, 1921), II, 448–49; Alexander Spitzmüller, "Emil Steinbach," in *Neue österreichische Biographie, 1815–1918* (Vienna, 1923–35), II, 48–62.

the Liberal need to show moderation and constant cooperation if they were to win the Minister-President's confidence.[4]

The obvious flirtation between Taaffe and the Liberals plus the encroachment of the new Christian Social organization upon districts which previously had strong Democratic tendencies compelled Ferdinand Kronawetter, a long-time Democrat, to pen a rather amazing appeal to Plener. When Alois Liechtenstein defeated the veteran "radical" in Hernals, the disappointed parliamentarian received a note of sympathy from Plener. In reply, the Democrat begged the Liberal leader to bring his following into the Democratic fold, to become truly "progressive." How else could the people get a decent political education? How else could honest Liberals end the "poisonous" radicalism and nationalism which professors were purveying to university students? Kronawetter quickly admitted that "Democrat" was a word which was suspect, though he knew not why. Would the name, "Young Liberal Party," serve as an umbrella for a union of Liberals and Democrats? Would Plener and Chlumecky seriously discuss his proposition, which he would keep totally under wraps?[5] The letter was of course a manifestation of Kronawetter's deep concern over Christian Social anti-Semitism and the inroads it was making in the Vienna area. For the broader picture of Austrian politics, however, it was a most revealing indication of the restored prestige of the Liberals. After years in the wilderness, they again had a chance to enter into fruitful combinations and possibly to influence Taaffe's future course. It would be superfluous to search for Plener's serious acceptance of the Democrat's bid. There were richer veins to mine.

The German Liberals and the Poles came to the new Reichsrat of 1891 with roughly the same number of mandates as before. The shifts in power concerned the Old Czechs and the German Clerical Conservatives. The former returned as a small handful of 12, while the Young Czechs numbered 37. Of the remainder of the Czech deputies, 18 were Feudalist landlords

[4] See Reuss's dispatch No. 38, A 1153, Feb. 10, 1891, UC-1, reel 215, frames 718–20.
[5] Nachlass Plener, Karton 18, Nos. 674–75.

and 8 belonged to moderate fractions. The history of the first year of the tug of war over the Bohemian *Ausgleich* indicated only too well what could happen to such gentlemen's resolves once the Young Czechs sponsored public meetings and gathered petitions. A new radicalism jostled the Catholic German Right. If Hohenwart soon refashioned his conservative club of German Conservatives, Rumanians, Slovenes, and Italians—all of pious bent—Liechtenstein and Lueger were the heroes of the "mass" Christian Social movement. Some 27 who once followed the dashing Prince now joined Hohenwart, for the bishops of Austria had warned the voters against revolutionary race baiters. But on the fringe of the respectably devout were 14 of the men whose antics gave the hierarchy such pain. Forerunners of the great Christian Social phalanxes of the future, they could as yet expect no wooing by the Minister-President unless he found himself in a most parlous situation. If the Emperor and Taaffe were more concerned over Schönerer's following, they were relieved to note that only two secured seats. At the same time, 17 German deputies were strongly Nationalist in the Reichsrat of 1891, and they did not hide their contempt for Liberals who might consort with Taaffe.[6]

In March the Minister-President tried to construct a coalition. He had already told Reuss in January, before the elections, that he did not expect to have a clear and reliable majority. It would change from time to time, and for educational affairs the regime might even depend on Young Czech support.[7] Such a hint, which Taaffe realized would soon reach German Liberal ears, was a tacit promise to save the essential framework of the Liberal school system. Bringing the Polish Club and the German Liberals together was a very difficult maneuver, however. Jaworski in Galicia had openly declared his hesitation over a rapprochement, but he toned down his remarks somewhat

[6] Gustav Kolmer, *Parlament und Verfassung in Oesterreich* (Vienna and Leipzig, 1902–14), V, 6–12. For figures for the earlier Reichsrat, see *Neue Freie Presse,* March 6, 1888.

[7] See Reuss's dispatch No. 65, A 2031, March 6, 1891, UC-1, reel 215, frame 724.

in interviews in Vienna.[8] After a meeting between Jaworski and
Liberal leaders on March 25, *Das Vaterland* and "official" papers reported that the uncomfortable conferees did no more than
make arrangements for the expeditious conduct of the session.[9]

Richard Clam Martinič talked at length with Taaffe and
Hohenwart in early March, and he wrote to Franz Thun in
Prague that there was no real plan to move to the Left. At most,
the cabinet wanted to concoct a colorless speech from the throne
which would enable the Left to vote for the budget and other
nonpolitical measures. Talk of a Liberal-Polish coalition
against Taaffe was ill founded, for the Poles knew the Emperor
did not want it. Rumors of adding the Young Czechs to the
majority were similarly unjustified, for only the most radical
Slovenes and Dalmatians would favor such an alignment. As a
Czech, Clam Martinič was sure that the Magyars were trying to
influence the Emperor to sanction a German Liberal return to
power in Austria, but he predicted that Taaffe would move quite
gingerly in his relations with the Liberals until the Young Czechs
had lost sufficient face and nuisance value to chance another
general election.[10]

The speech from the throne of April 11 appealed directly for
patriotic self-denial in place of partisan demands. The parties
should tone down their existing differences and try to find a
common ground for healthy action. The Liberals listened politely and replied that they would be happy to follow the imperial
call if the school system remained as it was and if the arrangements made for the compromise in Bohemia became laws.[11]
Several influential Poles in turn announced that they opposed the
confessional school, though they did not surrender the principle
of a decentralization of the school system.[12] In place of chilly
formalities, a situation dangerously close to flirtation had devel-

[8] *Neue Freie Presse,* March 25, 1891.   [9] *Ibid.,* March 31, 1891.
[10] Letter of March 15, 1891, in *Briefe zur deutschen Politik in Österreich von 1848 bis 1918,* ed. Paul Molisch (Vienna and Leipzig, 1934), pp. 281–83.   [11] Kolmer, *Parlament,* V, 19–21, 34–38.
[12] Plener, *Erinnerungen,* III, 7.

oped. Would the allies of the 1870s unite to save the Emperor's trusted first minister?

In June, 1891, a spokesman for the United German Left announced that this large segment would vote for Taaffe's discretionary funds, something the Liberals had not done since 1879. In return, they expected the government to forward progress of the compromise in Bohemia. Taaffe cordially expressed his special satisfaction that a party representing numerous German voters and filled with so many talented men was responding to the Emperor's call for productive parliamentary labors.[13] Reuss heard from good sources that ministry and party already had precisely worked out the polite interplay. Taaffe was still very much worried over the way in which the parliamentary process could unfold, but he also seemed happy in a conversation with Reuss that he no longer was subject to the impulses of an executive committee of party leaders. The German envoy declared that the Austrian monarch reposed more confidence in his long-time Minister-President than ever before, for the new constellation of powers was much more pleasing in the highest quarters.[14] As the speeches on budgetary affairs continued to exude goodwill of a sort almost forgotten, Taaffe's optimism markedly rose. *Das Vaterland,* some Polish Clericals, Young Czechs, and every deputy who disliked the German Liberal point of view exhibited alarm and desperation over the new course, while an amazed German attaché reported that a Carinthian Hofrat, under obvious government orders, warmly welcomed a meeting of the Deutsche Schulverein in Klagenfurt.[15]

Meanwhile Taaffe replied to the unceasing Young Czech demonstrations for *Staatsrecht* by reaffirming the government's hope to complete the Bohemian *Ausgleich.* Moreover, the ministry would continue to insist on German as the language for internal business. A unitary administration was a necessity,

[13] Kolmer, *Parlament,* V, 40–43.

[14] See Reuss's dispatch No. 183, A 5506, June 18, 1891, UC-1, reel 215, frames 726–32.

[15] See Ratibor's dispatch No. 192, A 5667, June 23, 1891, UC-1, reel 215, frames 733–37; Ratibor's dispatch No. 195, A 5902, June 30, 1891, UC-1, reel 215, frames 738–40.

apart from the impossible monetary costs which a change in policy would entail.[16] No wonder Vienna buzzed with rumors that Falkenhayn and Pražak would step down in the autumn, that the Ministry of Commerce would have two branches, one of them filled by Biliński, a Pole who was notably positive in his support of the Triple Alliance and Taaffe's experimental course.[17]

Events in Bohemia during the summer reinforced the chances of a Liberal participation in the ministry. The great Bohemian Exhibition, at which a few German Bohemian businessmen did have booths after all, attracted Slavs from the Balkans, French gymnasts, and a crew of anti-Semites from Vienna. The Emperor had also promised his presence, and, just before he arrived, the Czechs celebrated the hundredth anniversary of Leopold II's coronation as king of Bohemia. To show their fealty without joining in the general festivities, picked Germans greeted the Emperor in their capacities as mayors of towns and as representatives of local administrative boards. Franz Joseph pointedly made a special trip to the German bastion of Reichenberg, and if he did not mention the word *Ausgleich* in his stilted public replies to addresses of welcome, his generalities left no doubt of his desire for legal accords between the warring nationalities. The trip was a rather sad and sour experience for a man who already knew defeats better than victories. At least he escaped injury from a bomb which presumably had been planted by an anarchist on a bridge he was to traverse.[18]

The correspondence which traveled between Vienna and Prague before the Emperor's trip was underway also reveals Taaffe's great desire to avoid hurting German feelings. He wanted the title, "King's Pavilion," changed on entrance cards lest Germans misconstrue it. Thun told him the cards were already so styled and could not be changed. The *Statthalter* advised against the trip to Reichenberg because the German industrialists there

---

[16] Kolmer, *Parlament,* V, 50.

[17] See Ratibor's dispatch No. 195, A 5902, June 30, 1891, UC-1, reel 215, frames 738–40.

[18] Kolmer, *Parlament,* V, 52–54; Plener, *Erinnerungen,* III, 10–12.

had been so prominent in boycotting the Exhibition. He also mentioned the extensive class antagonisms latent in the town and recommended Karlsbad as a substitute. The Emperor went to Reichenberg, anyway.[19] When Lobkowitz suggested an imperial audience for mayors and district officials, Taaffe warned him to have equal representation from the two nationalities.[20] Thun's illness and the press of business upon the Emperor raised the issue of a postponement of the imperial visit. Count Zedtwitz, president of the committee in charge of the Exhibition, energetically urged Taaffe to drop any thought of postponement, for he feared that the "party" which had generally snubbed the Exhibition would then boast of its decisive influence over the government. Taaffe firmly rejected such comments, with a stiff request that Zedtwitz's committee do everything in its power to assure the Emperor a decent reception when he did come at a later date.[21]

The Austrian Minister-President was somewhat more understanding of the Czech motives when his own government ordered the police and *Statthalter* in Prague to keep a much closer check on Pan-Slav outbursts which occurred when official committees at train stations met and welcomed Polish and Czech-American delegations. Thun rather vigorously explained away some of the "exaggerations" which had prompted the orders from Vienna, noting that the Czechs and other Slavs of the empire had no other way to counter the "unpatriotic and petty" German attempts to turn the Exhibition into a fiasco. Franz Joseph obviously had been much perturbed by the speeches and singing in Prague, while Kálnoky was sarcasm incarnate in his references to the jubilation in the Russian press. Taaffe, a bit stricken by the Foreign Minister's reproof, continued to insist on a restoration of order, but his tone indicated sympathy for Thun's estimate of the situation.[22] When the visit was at an end, Thun tried to prevent the government's decorating the mayor of Reichenberg, since such an honor would detract from the order destined for the mayor of Prague. Taaffe diplomatically replied that the reward

[19] *Politischer Nachlass*, pp. 578–80.   [20] *Ibid.*, pp. 585–88.
[21] *Ibid.*, pp. 591–94.   [22] *Ibid.*, pp. 595–603.

was for the town's hearty welcome, not for the person of an acknowledged German nationalist. Since Prague was the larger city, however, its mayor would receive an order of higher rank.[23]

Throughout the summer of 1891 the Emperor evidenced great resentment over the demonstrations of Slavic brotherhood at the Exposition. He rarely believed Thun's asseverations that the authorities were doing all possible to keep the agitation under control, and he thought more than once of canceling his trip. Taaffe had a prickly task in mediating between the aroused monarch and Thun, who could not resist blaming the Bohemian Germans for almost everything that happened. Obviously Franz Joseph and Kálnoky were most concerned over the effect of the scenes upon foreign opinion, particularly in the German Empire, and Taaffe could not avoid seeing that the Foreign Minister's barbed remarks were implicit criticisms of the government's coalition between 1879 and 1889. Kálnoky's jibes, Plener's pronunciamentos, and the editorial page of the *Neue Freie Presse* began to sound very much alike. Taaffe would have been a most insensitive politician if he had approached the bargaining sessions of the autumn of 1891 with a sincere hope for Liberal collaboration. Ten years of estrangement, the Emperor's distaste for Plener as a man, and Taaffe's own poor state of health were factors which prejudiced the renewed search for a coalition from the start.

Mutually painful conversations between Taaffe for the government and Plener and Chlumecky for the Liberals eventuated in December with the appointment of a Liberal, Count Gandolf Kuenburg, to the cabinet. He was Plener's nominee, and Taaffe took him over August Weeber, whom Chlumecky had suggested. The Liberals steadfastly maintained their freedom of action as long as Taaffe did not create an honest cartel of parties as his majority. They assented to Kuenburg's appointment as a token of their expectation that the government would be more attentive to German interest.[24] When Taaffe replaced the old-

[23] *Ibid.*, pp. 650–51.
[24] Plener, *Erinnerungen*, III, 24–29.

time Liberal Czedik with the Polish Biliński as general director
of the state railway system, Plener suspected anew that the
Minister-President had not lost his basic sympathy for the parties
which had been anti-Liberal. Yet the Liberal leader later admitted that the Poles needed some unguent after the Emperor
personally decided against their request for a decentralization of
the railway system. In time of war there had to be an efficient
military control of the life lines to Galicia, and it would not do to
confuse the vital communications through employment of the
Polish language by the engineers, brakemen, and other operatives.[25]

Despite some signs of Liberal weariness over the Bohemian
quarrels, the likelihood of a sincere and fruitful partnership
between Taaffe and the party depended upon the fate of the
Vienna agreements of 1890. As Armand Dumreicher, deputy of
the Klagenfurt chamber of commerce, wrote to a hometown
editor, the appointment of Kuenburg guaranteed the Liberals
that the cabinet would not initiate policies inimical to Liberal
interests any more, though the party would stay on guard and
avoid surrendering its freedom of action until Taaffe gave further
proof of his sincerity.[26] The spring session of the Bohemian Diet
of 1892 torpedoed all chances of further action which might
appease the Germans. The Feudalists and the Old Czechs
plainly declared there was no sense continuing the study of the
Ausgleich. *Politik* saw no virtue in keeping promises which
totally gainsaid the popular will, while the aristocrats argued it
would actually be dangerous and unpatriotic to keep up the
hopeless bargaining. *Národní Listy* was delighted that the
nobles had finally realized the Czech people would not swallow
the Vienna protocols, though the Young Czech daily regretted
what it called the continuing failure of the great landowners to
identify themselves with the Czech people.[27]

When Thun thanked the same aristocrats for their help in

[25] *Ibid.,* III, 26–28.
[26] Letter of Dec. 23, 1891, in *Briefe,* ed. Molisch, p. 269.
[27] Quoted in *Neue Freie Presse,* March 2, 7 (*Abendblatt*), and 8
(*Abendblatt*), 1892.

passing the new laws on the Bohemian School and Agricultural
Boards, he reiterated the cabinet's hope that the Diet would
complete all parts of the *Ausgleich*. Plener rejected this approach as unsatisfactory, and the *Neue Freie Presse* compared
Thun's action to the modest defenses employed by women who
are ready to be ravished.[28] Taaffe resignedly seconded Thun's
suggestion to avoid a full-scale discussion in the Diet of the
prorogation of the *Ausgleich,* but he and the cabinet did not
agree with Thun on closing the Diet as soon as it passed the
budget. If this happened, the Germans would reproach the
government for gagging them.[29]

Plener was already berating Taaffe through Kuenburg over
the refusal of the Czech aristocrats to continue discussion of the
original protocols. The Old and the Young Czech journals were
trumpeting their victory joyfully, complained Plener, who solemnly declared that his colleagues were not raging about a
passing injury. Calmly, but with a steady anger, they were
asking themselves why they had supported a government which
did not keep its pledges, even though the Emperor personally
underwrote such pledges.[30] In conversation about the same time
with Prince Georg Lobkowitz, the ruler listened equably to the
Czech aristocrat's excuses for failure to push the compromise
and to the statement that the government unfortunately would
have to reckon with the Young Czechs as a fact of life. He
insisted to Lobkowitz that the government nonetheless needed
the Germans in the Lower House, though he admitted that it
might take many more years to effect a reconciliation in Bohemia. The Prince left with the impression that Franz Joseph was
reconciled to the impasse, and he frankly considered such a
development a relative advantage in future attempts to scuttle
the protocols.[31]

Of all the suspended *Ausgleich* agreements, the Germans were
most eager to secure a virtual partition of Bohemia by means of

[28] March 25, 1892; Kolmer, *Parlament,* V, 70.
[29] Kabinetts-Kanzlei, Vortrag 1408, April 6, 1892.
[30] Nachlass Plener, Karton 18, No. 272, March 27, 1892.
[31] Letter of April 30, 1892, in *Briefe,* ed. Molisch, p. 325.

newly drawn judicial districts. To restore some degree of friendliness after the sterile session of the Diet, the Taaffe cabinet
issued a decree on April 27, 1892, signed by Schönborn, creating
a new court district centering on Weckelsdorf. The Young
Czechs cried out that the government was rending the crownland
and implied they would challenge the constitutionality of the
decree.[32] In fact, they arraigned Schönborn for exceeding his
powers, but the shakiness of their position was revealed in the
vote which exonerated him, 238 to 41.[33] *Hlas Naroda* sourly
declared that the hotheads had simply secured parliamentary
approval for further acts of partition, while the *Neue Freie
Presse* came to the unheard of conclusion that the ministry had
departed more than ever from the course it first followed in
1879.[34] In June, Czech athletes performed in Nancy, and a noted
Young Czech orator deplored the frontier that "a brutal power"
had dictated and pledged that nothing could separate the Czechs
and the French. "Our enemies are your enemies, your enemies
are ours."[35]

Such disloyal sentiments hardened the Austrian monarch's
mind against any degree of dependence upon the Young Czechs,
just as they raised hopes in Liberal circles of a return to imperial
favor. Taaffe had two long and exhaustive talks with Plener,
Chlumecky, and Josef Heilsberg in Kuenburg's presence, and he
reported to Franz Joseph some of the details. First, he rejected
the Liberal hope that their unofficial participation in the government would allow them to encroach upon the executive branch
in the appointment of officials. He did tell them that he would
accept their suggestions, ponder them, and then decide on personnel. When they asked if Kuenburg would have some appointive powers in the Ministry of Justice, he parried with the
assurance that all of the ministers exchanged friendly recommendations on posts to be filled. Quite stubbornly, however, he

[32] Kolmer, *Parlament*, V, 71; Plener, *Erinnerungen*, III, 33–36.
[33] Kolmer, *Parlament*, V, 73–74.
[34] *Neue Freie Presse*, April 27 and 28 (*Abendblatt*), 1892.
[35] Richard Charmatz, *Österreichs innere Geschichte von 1848 bis 1907*
(2d ed.; Leipzig, 1912), II, 74.

denied that Kuenburg should expect to have the jurisdiction that a minister with a specific portfolio enjoyed. The future of Falkenhayn and Schönborn he and his conferees did not touch upon, for the latter knew that he would tolerate no questioning of their tenure. As for Pražak, he guessed that the Liberals' chief target would soon ask for his pension. The Minister-President cautiously predicted to the Emperor that the Liberals would not cause trouble over the stabilization of the currency. Taaffe was rather ironic in tone in his deferential report to the monarch.[36] No doubt each man derived a glimmer of satisfaction from the Liberal advances.

An intermediary representing the highest German Liberal circles saw Prince Egon von Ratibor in the German Embassy. Would the German press which stood close to the German government support a Liberal bid for power in Austria? Not quite convinced that Plener, Chlumecky, and Heilsberg would rise to a position of decisive importance, the Prince preferred to suggest to Berlin that nothing be done to discourage the German Nationalists in Austria. They might not be Austrian patriots, but they were the German Empire's friends. When they came out in droves to see Bismarck, they cheered him as a great German. They were not demonstrating in favor of his campaign against the German government. The numbers in which they appeared proved that their strength in Austria was not measured by the small number of deputies who represented them in the Lower House. Not very logically, the enthusiastic Prince also argued that the anti-Semites who joined in the adulation were but a negligible quantity in any estimation of Austrian political parties.[37]

In August, 1892, German Liberal hopes rose again with Pražak's retirement from the cabinet. In a most courtly letter, Taaffe had reminded Pražak of his many earlier offers to resign in case of political necessity, and he adjured him to mention only

[36] Letter of July 6, 1892, in *Politischer Nachlass,* pp. 267–69.
[37] See Ratibor's dispatch No. 188, A 6227, July 15, 1892, UC-1, reel 216, frames 53–58.

conditions of health and age in the traditional letter of resignation. Allusions of a political nature would be embarrassing.
Pražak loyally complied at once, and another obstacle to the
rapprochement with the Liberals disappeared into the calmer
precincts of the Upper House.[38] He represented years of steady
Czech pressure upon the central government, and the fact that he
was an Old Czech and so politically almost valueless did not
dampen general Czech demonstrations against his resignation.
Ratibor sagely noted that the official press insisted that a German Liberal cabinet was an impossibility, and he predicted that
Taaffe's precarious health would be the decisive factor in any
full-scale reconstruction of the ministry.[39]

Kuenburg had functioned informally as a German *Landsmannminister,* and the Czechs were much aggrieved that Taaffe
did not immediately fill Pražak's place. A Young Czech appointee was beyond Franz Joseph's imagination, and a Feudalist
would have stimulated criticism on all sides. The hiatus momentarily disarmed the Liberals, who got nothing from a brief session of the Bohemian Diet in the autumn. Before each side
could return to the game of plaguing Taaffe in the Reichsrat until
he offered a "concession" to one or the other, the German
Empire made up for its snub of 1888. The reparation was indeed
handsome, for the harassed Austrian veteran received the highest Prussian order. Franz Joseph was especially pleased, and
leading German Liberals told Reuss that they appreciated the
courtesy shown their Emperor.[40]

Berlin's marked respect for Taaffe had no direct connection
with his failure to appoint a Czech to act in Pražak's place, but
uneasiness in Old Czech and Feudalist circles paralleled the
continuing violence of Young Czech utterances. The *Neue
Freie Presse* crowed over the steady decomposition of the old

[38] *Politischer Nachlass,* pp. 294–97.
[39] See Ratibor's dispatch No. 221, A 6965, Aug. 11, 1892, UC-1, reel
229, frames 254–56; Kolmer, *Parlament,* V, 75–77.
[40] See Reuss's dispatch No. 264, A 8614, Oct. 14, 1892, UC-1, reel 223,
frames 234–38.

majority. Croats and Slovenes had deserted Hohenwart, while the rift between the "Old Ultramontanes" and the activists under Liechtenstein and Schneider widened. When the government took a look at the progress of the Young Czechs in Bohemia and Moravia, it realized what a small choice it had in calling upon what was left in the Czech camp.[41]

Taaffe somehow did not concede the necessity of a reconstruction of the ministry favorable to the Left. In a famous reply to Prince Karl Schwarzenberg, who quite excitedly had blasted away at Hungary and at Kuenburg in a widely publicized defense of Young Czech constitutional theory, Taaffe allowed that he might soon propose a Czech *Landsmannminister*. The *Neue Freie Presse* sniffed at his elusive diction and rapid repartee. By offhandedly suggesting that a bill to settle the language question might come either from the House or from the cabinet, he deliberately insulted the Liberals and their agreement of 1890 with the Czechs.[42] Kálnoky told Reuss he was not happy over Taaffe's performance, which had roiled the United German Left. But he believed that the Germans would calm down and that there would be no real change in internal affairs.[43]

Kuenburg had maintained close relations with his Liberal confreres, and, not having been apprised of the content of Taaffe's statement, he submitted his resignation. There was another halfhearted attempt to assemble a cabinet that would please Poles, Liberals, and the deputies who followed Hohenwart and Coronini, but the mixture was too exotic. Hohenwart said he "knew what was up." No one should expect him to put his head on the block, a sentiment which found immediate sympathy with the Poles. The Liberals then resorted to the old maneuver of voting against the ministry's discretionary funds, which simultaneously failed to pass and failed to shake Taaffe's entrenched position. Reuss dejectedly told Caprivi that his

[41] *Neue Freie Presse,* Nov. 18, 1892.
[42] Nov. 24, 1892; Kolmer, *Parlament,* V, 84–85.
[43] See Reuss's dispatch No. 311, A 9958, Nov. 29, 1892, UC-1, reel 216, frames 63–71.

friends were on the wrong track again. Taaffe was never happy with the idea of a Liberal in the cabinet. Rather, the Emperor had wanted to give the party some satisfaction, but now it was not likely that Taaffe would appoint another.[44] Moreover, Prince Karl Schwarzenberg was convinced that Taaffe had no liking for the Liberals' plan to unroll the language question in the Reichsrat. With much relief, he comforted himself with the supposition that political circumstances had blunted another "Hungarian plot."[45] Dumreicher, of rather pronounced Nationalist views, blamed Steinbach, "that cosmopolitan converted Viennese Jew," for the failure to unite Poles and Liberals at the cost of Hohenwart and the Conservatives. He was sure that Franz Joseph wanted more Liberals in the cabinet but that the Poles were persuaded to make enough difficulties to frustrate the imperial wish "respectably."[46]

If the ministry in 1892 made no progress in Bohemia and actually retrogressed in its quest for a stable parliamentary coalition, it did accomplish a stabilization of the currency. To be sure, the initial impulse came from Hungary, whose great cattle and grain barons were fed up with the vagaries of international clearinghouse processes. The Austro-Hungarian paper currency was still popular with debtors and opponents of "big capital," and even a Liberal like the geologist Suess was fearful that gold sources were drying up. Echoes of the American debate on bimetallism invaded the Austrian discussions, but Steinbach swallowed his own personal theories to work for the devaluation of gold coins by 50 per cent. If Karl Lueger sounded like William Jennings Bryan in his denunciation of the "betrayal of the people," most of the literate class and the business world were reasonably pleased that Austria had joined the charmed circle of financially stable states. It was a degree of compensation for the recurring headlines on nationalistic em-

---

[44] *Neue Freie Presse,* Nov. 29, 1892; Plener, *Erinnerungen,* III, 62–64; see Reuss's dispatch No. 312, A 10088, Dec. 3, 1892, UC-1, reel 216, frames 78–82.

[45] Letter of Dec. 3, 1892, in *Briefe,* ed. Molisch, pp. 283–84.

[46] Letter of Nov. 29, 1892, *ibid.,* pp. 300–1.

broilments, and, like social legislation, it brought the realm on a level with the ally across the Inn River.[47]

Kálnoky's assumption that the internal situation would not change very much after Kuenburg's resignation was reinforced by the ministry's issuance of another invitation to coalition action on February 5, 1893. It contained the usual appeals to patriotism, but it also stated quite clearly what Left and Right could expect if they would agree to a working partnership. All clubs declined the bid, though the Liberals and the Poles were careful to emphasize their resolve to give every proposal that came to them a decent appraisal.

Budgets, extraordinary defense credits, the gold standard—such items the essentially patriotic Liberals and Poles would indeed approve. But the abscess that threatened the state's ultimate recovery was Bohemia, and the disorders which affected that land in the spring and summer of 1893 led directly to the collapse of Taaffe's system. The final act began with another session of the Diet, in which the cabinet manfully tried to secure approval of two new court districts for German-speaking Bohemians. The Young Czechs stormily protested, the Old Czechs swore they would go no further until linguistic equality was a reality, and the aristocrats relapsed into an embarrassed formalism that did nothing to advance the government's endeavor. The shouts and wild destructiveness indulged in by the Young Czechs on May 17 exceeded all past experiences, and Taaffe helplessly ordered a closing of the session. When talk did not conjure away the specter of purely German judicial districts, fists, flying inkwells, and smashed urns brought the regime to reason.[48] A memorialization in Prague in July of Hus's execution at Constance brought a demonstration against the aristocrats, too "lukewarm" in their fight for Czech rights. When T. G. Masaryk and Julius Grégr differed over future tactics, Masaryk was the one censured by the executive committee of the Czech

---

[47] Plener, *Erinnerungen*, III, 39–52; Alexander Spitzmüller, "Emil Steinbach," pp. 56–58; Shepard B. Clough and Charles W. Cole, *Economic History of Europe* (Boston, 1946), p. 624.

[48] Kolmer, *Parlament*, V, 94–108; *Politischer Nachlass*, pp. 569–78.

Club. The imperial insignia on official buildings and on lowly tobacco shops suffered mutilation and worse. While the police embarked upon a hunt for social and nationalist radicals, the obviously aroused Emperor pointedly thanked Galicia and the Poles for their constant patriotism and support during a reception of the province's nobles. That the monarch was on maneuvers heightened the appositeness of his remarks. A nationality which had full reason to resent what had gone on in Posen did not openly shout for an end to the alliance with Germany and the magnificent German army.

The "plot" which the police in Prague had discovered was largely the brain child of an agent provocateur. The unruly street scenes and the consequent tension which had overcome the German families of Prague, plus the mounting number of arrests, persuaded Taaffe and the Emperor that a suspension of civil rights and of trial by jury was the proper medicine.[49] When the Reichsrat reassembled in October, the government faced Germans who felt cheated over the impasse in Bohemia and Slavs who had a hard time reconciling their honest distaste for antidynastic rioting with their fear of losing their civil liberties when they protested the *status quo*.

It is small wonder that Taaffe and Steinbach resorted to a sensational resolution of their troubles in the autumn of 1893. The *enragé* Young Czechs had driven the Old Czechs into virtual retirement and had paralyzed the resistance which an anxious Emperor expected from the nobles of the crownland. In the German lands outside Bohemia, German Nationalists were preaching annihilation of the "do-nothing" Liberals, with their opulent Jewish friends and their insensitivity to the needs of farmers and small businessmen. What had once been a reliable German Clerical Conservative bloc was dissolving at the hands of the magnetic Lueger and of the Prince who saw more political gain in the streets of the capital than in the quiet and pious countryside. The Polish Club was intact, but it always had functioned as a guardian of Galician rights first, as a cooperating imperial factor, second.

[49] Kolmer, *Parlament,* V, 108–12.

No wonder Steinbach and Taaffe deemed the existing disposition of power insufficient to end the stalemate. Calling new elections would modify the basic picture very little. Though documentary proof does not exist, it was thought in 1893 and thereafter that Steinbach prevailed upon his desperate chief to embrace the idea of a sweeping electoral reform. The idea was hardly new. The Social Democrats pounded away incessantly for universal, secret, and direct elections, and the Young Czechs had decided early in 1893 to work for a democratic franchise. Representatives of big cities asked for more deputies, as did the Ruthenes, surely that most discriminated against of the Emperor's peoples. Plener continued to talk of his labor chambers, and, more realistically, nearly all of the German parties recommended direct elections in the curia of rural voters.[50] Baernreither wrote Plener in September, 1893, that the recent summer in Bohemia, when added to his three years of remaining in the background of Liberal deliberations, had convinced him that the party needed a new look. He wanted electoral reform, and he admitted that his particular version had some singular features. He dreaded his colleagues' pettiness and flabbiness when he broached his project. But the Liberals were lagging behind their constituents, he was sure, and he predicted the ruin of the party if it did not renounce outmoded men and ideas.[51] Baernreither did not have long to wait for proof of his fears, but his conviction that Liberalism had to get moving on the issue of a wider franchise was indicative of the political climate of the time.

On August 18, 1893, Taaffe reminded his associates in a cabinet session of the several bills for electoral reform and stated his determination to take hold of the situation by bringing in a government plan. It would be unwise to ask for universal suffrage, for that request would be interpreted as a political maneuver to scare together a majority for the budget and other essential laws. He had discarded the idea of a special curia for workers, since such a fifth curia would entail a constitutional change and require two-thirds approval. Worse, it would dis-

[50] *Ibid.,* V, 333–42.   [51] Nachlass Plener, Karton 18, No. 56.

criminate against agrarian laborers and would add a more or less impressive number of socialistic deputies to the existing party system. By modifying the tax qualification and adding a literacy test, the cabinet needed only a simple majority to push through a reform.

Three days later the ministers debated the necessity of electoral reform. Falkenhayn, convinced that the Social Democrats hoped to slay capitalism through universal suffrage, opposed the government's taking the initiative toward reform. It would be better to let something emerge from parliament. If the cabinet did assume leadership, it should propose vocational representation, the only sure way workers could count on having their interests protected. Welsersheimb warned against a halfhearted action. All citizens should enjoy the franchise, not just those who could read and write. Schönborn disagreed thoroughly with such an "extremely democratic principle," while Zaleski simply stated that Taaffe should introduce a reform bill. Steinbach stressed the need for inner cabinet unity on the question. If the parties seized the initiative, they might force through completely unacceptable provisions. Taaffe seemed satisfied that he had a majority of his colleagues favorable to a bill, and he turned aside the Defense Minister's interesting suggestion with the reminder that the Reichsrat was in a state of confusion. Proposing universal suffrage would seal the fate of the government's bill from the start. One had to remember what was possible. If the cabinet could not put through its plan, however, it would have to consider dissolving the Reichsrat.

Schönborn, Gautsch, Steinbach, and Zaleski proceeded to work out the plan of a reform, and August von Plappart, a *Sektionschef* in the Ministry of the Interior, completed a draft which the cabinet discussed in three sessions in September.[52] He estimated that 40 per cent of all Austrian males would be able to vote under the new regulations, whereas 15 per cent had voted in the general elections of 1891. The 1,780,000 who participated at that time would be increased by 3,440,000. What were the

---

[52] Eduard Heller, "Zum Sturz des Ministeriums Taaffe," *Historische Studien, A. F. Pribram dargebracht* (Vienna, 1929), pp. 216–19.

new prescriptions? Briefly, every male twenty-four years of age or more could vote in either rural or urban curia if he had fulfilled his military duty and if he could read and write one of the languages current in his province.

Schönborn prophesied that such a thoroughgoing revision of voting rights would never meet with the approval of the great parliamentary parties. They had too much to lose, and the peers would be even more unfavorable. Falkenhayn refused to believe that the draft maintained the curial principle, for the new rules would wreck the intelligentsia in the urban curia and the independent peasants in the rural. In reply, the shrewd Steinbach wondered why one should petrify the power of great parties when it was clear that monarchical prestige waned whenever great political factions alternated as ministries. Since his colleagues might be quick to note that Austria was not England, he used the phrase "standing majority" as synonym for "great party," and he expressed hope that the peers would overshadow the Lower House after passage of this reform. Throughout Steinbach glorified the lack of a strong majority in the Lower House, for this circumstance alone guaranteed the crown's full sovereignty. Gautsch felt that the existing balance of power in the Lower House lacked what was necessary to advance welfare legislation. The convulsions which might arise from such inaction would be more serious than those bound up with the electoral proposal. He also pointed to the workers' meeting, which avoided nationalistic recriminations. Reform would help banish the nationalities question in favor of humanitarian measures.

In the end, only Falkenhayn refused to go along with the program to enlarge the franchise, and on September 25 the Emperor passed judgment on its specific regulations. Ordinarily the text of the minutes of cabinet sessions was dry and unexciting. Somehow Taaffe's honest enthusiasm breaks through the usual pattern in the meeting with the Emperor. Anxiously he repeated what he must already have stressed with sovereign and fellow ministers—that labor could get to parliament only if it bested the incumbent deputies in fair fight. The reform did not create a special privilege for labor. The number of mandates in rural and urban curias remained as before, and a six-month residence requirement would prevent a flooding of strategic districts at election time by agitators. With an eye upon Schönborn and the conservative devout whom he represented, he noted that illiterates, usually sure pledges against radicalism, would be able to vote if they had fulfilled their military service or if they were of school age before attendance became compulsory. Moreover, Liberals and Social Democrats would have to cease their platitudes concerning citizens who were good enough to die for the fatherland but not good enough to enjoy the franchise. With special insistence, Taaffe argued that his bill was less radical than others before the Lower House. It would leave the landed curia and the curia of the chambers of commerce untouched and still prevent the emergence of a sole commanding party which would negate the monarch's influence. Franz Joseph was brief but laudatory in his comments. The reform was far-reaching, but that was no error. He wanted the ministers to initiate the reform, lest the parties push through their more extreme programs. The government had to move. Once the bill was public, the ministers would have to go to the uttermost limits to secure its passage.[53]

When Taaffe casually announced his reform on the first day of the new session, the surprise was complete. Plener by chance met Hohenwart at the end of the noisy and confused sitting, and both of them raged over the Minister-President's failure to acquaint them beforehand of his "fantastic project." In later years the Liberal leader frankly admitted that he saw at once in this bill a chance to rid Austria of Taaffe and his system. From the moment of his fortuitous conference with Hohenwart, he worked indefatigably to this end.[54] Reuss relayed the obvious to Berlin. Adding 3,500,000 voters to the lists would destroy the preponderance of the bourgeoisie in the Reichsrat. Socialists would

---

[53] Fortunately, the texts of the cabinet meetings between Aug. 18 and Sept. 25 were largely preserved by Ludwig Brügel in his *Geschichte der österreichischen Sozialdemokratie* (Vienna, 1922–25), IV, 198–208.

[54] Plener, *Erinnerungen*, IV, 86–87.

appear there, while Young Czechs and German Nationalist
ultras would profit in Bohemia. The German envoy ventured
the guess that Taaffe, galled most of all by dependence on the
Liberals and worried by the increasingly successful Social Democratic demonstrations, hoped that the situation would improve
after enlarging the electorate. In Berlin an unconvinced reader
put "Micawber" in the margin beside Reuss's guess. As for
Steinbach and the Emperor, Reuss felt that the former wanted to
destroy the Liberals, even at the cost of yielding to Social Democratic clamor. The monarch, swayed by a sense of justice,
wanted to do something for the unrepresented.[55]

The press was almost unanimous in its reprehension. Leading the pack, the *Neue Freie Presse* ridiculed the obscure plottings of the Social Democrats, so easily outtrumped by a smiling
Taaffe, with electoral reform in one hand and a bill to keep
Prague in leash in another. What did he plan? Nothing less than
the drowning of the middle classes and of the independent
peasantry with a flood of have-nots. What a sight—Taaffe with
a Phrygian cap pulled over his graying hair, dancing the carmag-
nole before the astounded citizenry.[56] *Bohemia* simply stated
that no deputy on the Left could talk any longer of an unclarified
situation. Nothing now could be clearer than the ministry's
purpose. *Das Vaterland* at first expressed concern over the
revolutionary impact which the bill would have on party relationships to the government and to each other. On second
thought, it worried over what would happen to the small amount
of stability which did exist. Society was now reckoning with
undreamed of possibilities on all sides. *Politik* had doubts that
the bill would forward federalistic purposes. Rather, the regime
seemed to want to push the nationalities question to another
sphere. *Hlas Naroda* smelled nothing but centralism in the
proposals, while *Národní Listy* likened them to a whip which
Taaffe would use to hurry along the Liberals. In Lemberg the

[55] See Reuss's dispatch No. 256, A 8321, Oct. 11, 1893, UC-1, reel
216, frames 107–14.
[56] Oct. 11 and 12, 1893.

Gazeta Narodowa resented the provocative secretiveness which the Minister-President had used, and it predicted a speedy union of usually disparate elements against him.[57]

Kálnoky complained testily to Taaffe in a missive of October 15 that he had to confess to foreign questioners that the Austrian government had yet to give him any information on the bill. How could one direct foreign policy without courteous treatment from each realm? Hungary had never so treated him, though he did not want to convey an impression of personal humiliation. Although his post limited him to the most general comments on Austrian internal affairs, he had to say that the ministers common to both realms would be affected if the reform passed and opened the Reichsrat to the Social Democrats.[58] When Taaffe tried to beg off on grounds of a misunderstanding, Kálnoky promptly wrote the Emperor, repeating his displeasure and enclosing Taaffe's reply.[59] In a conversation with Reuss, the Foreign Minister was more composed. Though he did not like the bill's contents or the mode of its announcement, he did not think that an expansion of the electorate was unhealthy in itself. The present House was so riven by national hatreds that it could not function. But a change required the preparation of public opinion, press discussion, direct consultation with parliament. Kálnoky implied that he did not believe Taaffe's excuse that lack of time prevented their conferring before October 10. Rather, Taaffe knew that Kálnoky would have been in opposition.[60]

In Budapest, Franz Joseph began to realize that electoral reform would be a hazardous enterprise. Visits from Chlumecky, president of the Lower House, and from Kálnoky had not dissuaded him from holding out for Taaffe's project even if new elections were necessary. Indeed, the Emperor assured the veteran Liberal politician that he had been urging a wider franchise upon Taaffe for years, in view of the workers' movement.

[57] Cited, *ibid.,* Oct. 11 (*Abendblatt*) and 12 (*Morgen- und Abendblatt*), 1893.

[58] *Politischer Nachlass,* pp. 307–9.

[59] Heller, "Zum Sturz des Ministeriums Taaffe," p. 219.

[60] See Reuss's dispatch No. 262, A 8538, Oct. 17, 1893, UC-1, reel 216, frames 123–29.

Petty adjustments no longer would do, and the Germans should try to calm their exaggerated fears. That the other two great parliamentary parties were also upset by the bill should prove the ministry did not plan a destruction of the Germans, argued the monarch. When Kálnoky appeared, he received rather much the same lecture. If the cabinet had wanted to strike at the "German party," he as Emperor would have been the first to stop such a move. Withdrawal of the bill was an impossibility. The affair had to be handled without passion.[61]

While the ruler strove to strengthen Taaffe's position with such leaders, the three greatest concentrations of power in the Lower House stonily rejected what the Emperor had warmly approved. The United German Left bespoke its interest in an electoral reform that would give the laboring class some representation immediately and increase the number of deputies for the rural and urban curias. It had no intention of approving Taaffe's plan, which threatened to revolutionize all existing national and imperial factors. The Polish Club also endorsed the general idea of a broader franchise along autonomous lines, while rejecting the ministry's formula. The Conservative Club said almost the same thing as it turned its back on the cabinet.[62]

In the first reading Taaffe insisted that *raison d'état* compelled his government to seek a properly timed and sufficient widening of the franchise. Otherwise, politically restless elements would threaten civil society and the state itself. The "titans" of the oppositional parties repeated the objections which the caucuses had phrased. Deputies who wanted thoroughgoing change harped on Taaffe's retention of the curial arrangements. In the past such extremes had often guaranteed Taaffe a sensible compromise. In October, 1893, the vast majority of the deputies were frightened and outraged by the Minister-President's espousal of what was a tremendous modification of the political bal-

---

[61] Plener, *Erinnerungen*, III, 88–89; see Reuss's dispatch No. 263, A 8622, Oct. 20, 1893, UC-1, reel 216, frames 129–32; Reuss's dispatch No. 265, A 8658, Oct. 22, 1893, UC-1, reel 216, frames 137–40.

[62] Kolmer, *Parlament*, V, 346.

ance in the curias. Count Hohenwart left an unforgettable impression when he arose, shaken and aroused, to pass biting judgment on Taaffe's behavior. The *Neue Freie Presse* exulted that the unbroken parallel paths trod by both men now diverged sharply.[63]

Reuss nevertheless notified Caprivi that Taaffe let it be known to all who were interested that he would neither retire nor withdraw the bill.[64] As late as October 27 officials in the Ministry of the Interior were waiting for a signal to publish an imperial patent for new elections.[65] Two days before, Taaffe presided over a council of ministers and declared his intention of effecting agreement with the three great parties which had denounced his reform. Significantly his colleagues asked to accompany him as he talked with his opponents. Hohenwart was unmistakably hostile, though Jaworski went through the motions of seeing Chlumecky concerning a reconciliation of the Left with the government. On October 26 the old-time Conservative told Taaffe he should give way to Alfred Windischgrätz, indeed, even persuade the latter to take his post. With dignity Taaffe promised to report the recommendation to the Emperor, though he turned aside the frank reference to the trouble he might have finding a successor.

Kálnoky had relayed these particulars to the Emperor in Budapest on October 27. Moreover, he blamed Steinbach primarily for a situation which Kálnoky deemed absolutely impossible. The Minister of Finance had always intrigued to keep Taaffe and the Liberals at odds. Had not the sharp-tongued Bacquehem said that Taaffe always improved during a bout of sickness when Steinbach brought him some victuals in the form of Plener's and Chlumecky's bones? The wily gentleman was behind the disastrous promise of a new Czech *Landsmannminister* and he planned to fabricate an unblushing Slavic-Clerical machine to run Austria after obtaining electoral changes. Kál-

---

[63] Oct. 25 and 26, 1893.
[64] See Reuss's dispatch No. 268, A 8718, Oct. 25, 1893, UC-1, reel 216, frame 144.
[65] Heller, "Zum Sturz des Ministeriums Taaffe," p. 209.

noky also accused Steinbach of planning to break up the Triple Alliance. In view of the Emperor's extreme sensitivity on this issue, it is clear that Kálnoky was determined to drive Taaffe and his chief aide from power by this mishmash of gossip and guesswork.[66]

Unexpectedly the Emperor returned from Budapest on October 28, and Kálnoky postponed his leave. Next day Franz Joseph presided over a decisive council of ministers. Falkenhayn blustered that the Liberals were exploiting the situation to get back into power as part of a coalition. As a Conservative who had no control over his friends in the Lower House any longer, the less than impressive Minister of Agriculture could say little else. Welsersheimb, acutely unhappy over what might be a disastrous postponement of the new Landwehr bill, counseled dropping the controversial reform and capitalizing upon the willingness of the decisive parties to form a coalition. New elections would only intensify the conflict. Naturally, concluded the Minister of Defense, all portfolios should be at His Majesty's disposition. Gautsch agreed, with the frank admission that the cabinet as then constituted could get nothing done. Bacquehem, Schönborn, and Zaleski too saw no way out of bowing to the new coalition in the Lower House. Zaleski chivalrously noted that the Poles wanted Taaffe to stay as Minister-President after reconstruction of the cabinet. The "villain of the piece," Steinbach, agreed with Welsersheimb that passage of the bills which provided for the state's vital needs was worth the price of the coalition. Rather wistfully he ventured the opinion that new parliamentary combinations in the future would diminish the "nationalities question."

Franz Joseph grumbled over the way in which parliamentary personages had constituted themselves as a sort of committee to decide what would happen. He could envisage such a coalition, but he did not care for their providential manner, which went too far. Pessimistic over the life expectancy of the new grouping, he did not want to surrender electoral reform. Whether the present

[66] *Ibid.*, pp. 220–25.

bill went too far was another question. He, like the cabinet, had
not anticipated the storm it had aroused.

Taaffe's post mortem was brief. He had expected trouble
from the Left, but not from the Right. He could not imagine a
continuing Hohenwart-Plener alliance without a radical change
in party conditions. The Emperor then thanked his ministers
and regretted that for a while he would have to do without men
of their caliber. In a brief canvass of possible candidates to
succeed Taaffe, the council ruled out Badeni, the governor of
Galicia, because of intrigues in the Polish Club, and Thun, the
governor of Bohemia, who was much compromised by the unpleasantness in that crownland.[67]

Next day a gracious but impassive monarch met the gentlemen
who had dared to take the initiative for a new government.
Hohenwart, Jaworski, and Plener unanimously buried the cabinet and its electoral plan. They would entertain the idea of a
broader franchise, but not one which would alter their parties'
existing preserves (*Besitzstand*). They would definitely underwrite a new cabinet on the new Landwehr provisions and in
maintaining exceptional conditions in Prague. When they mentioned Windischgrätz as a possibility for the Minister-
Presidency, they received neither rebuff nor commitment.
Franz Joseph still smarted from the humiliating reverse his long-
time favorite had endured at the hands of party chieftains. As
Reuss soberly communicated to Berlin, parliament had forced
this change upon the Emperor—a new and hazardous phenomenon in Austria.[68]

On November 4 Windischgrätz began the work of rebuilding
the cabinet. A week later a note from the Emperor relieved
Taaffe of his posts as Minister-President and as Minister of the
Interior. With uncommon warmth the head of the dynasty
praised his long-suffering servant for his patriotism, his attention
to duty, and his self-sacrifice. Few of those who made a practice

[67] *Ibid.*, pp. 225–33.
[68] See Reuss's dispatch No. 274, A 8941, Oct. 31, 1893, UC-1, reel
216, frames 151–57. Plener obviously told Reuss the details of the meeting. See his *Erinnerungen,* III, 105.

of weighing the words of imperial farewells and citations doubted the sincerity of the traditionally brief message. Taaffe as a public figure and as a confidant was through, nonetheless. The lengthy tenure he had both enjoyed and borne guaranteed him a reputation and enemies. They would have sufficed to keep him in modest retirement. Death, more effective yet, came in November, 1895. Taaffe had survived his release from high responsibility only two years.

15 Conclusion

Taaffe's attempts to widen the bases for a viable society in Austria met with German Liberal and Social Democratic ridicule and denunciation in his lifetime and later, and the stereotype of a "sawdust Metternich" has only recently begun to give way to the image of a knowing politician who presided over significant changes in Austrian life. Much of this Minister-President's success depended upon his astute evaluations of Franz Joseph's plodding reactions, and it would be unhistorical to deny Taaffe's own reliance on the inert force which an army, a dutiful bureaucracy, and the aura of monarchy afforded. The Liberals and the Marxists alleged that what was done in his term of office was piecemeal, grudging, and smudged by the old practices of benevolent despotism and restricted parliamentarianism. The former were eager to pit Crown Prince Rudolf and "civilization" against weary routine, aristocratic wiliness, and strong-willed "fanaticism" that masqueraded as a popular front against free thought and free trade. The latter, however, were not unwilling to tolerate a creaking state structure if it provided a convenient point of departure for schemes of social redemption.

The final eclipse of 1893, in which Clerical Conservatives and Poles at last made common cause with the German Liberals, destroyed for some years the chance of a Conservative-Slavic defense of the Taaffe system. The disintegration of 1918 and the civil strife and genocide of the 1930s and 1940s forced reconsiderations of the complexities of the Habsburg state, quite beyond saccharine evocations of waltzes and military parades, and it has been the spiritual heirs of Social Catholicism who have suggested that Taaffe deserves another hearing. Down to 1914 his one-time collaborators evinced little gratitude. The Church had not reconquered the schools, and, for most Czechs, the Compromise of 1890 was weighted in favor of the Germans. The Poles owed as much to Liberals as they did to Taaffe, and his retirement scarcely ended their exploitation of Galicia and their command of strategic posts in the cabinet. Very few of the deputies who were members of the Iron Ring shook off a real fear of sudden leveling when confronted with the electoral reform of 1893, and the ghost of Taaffe's last stratagem deterred them from composing lauds to his memory. Dunajewski's economic liberalism smacked too much of the professor's unworldly study and militated against their dream of a renovation of lower middle-class and peasant society. Worse, he nullified with his economizing many of their eminently political schemes for canals, flood control, and agrarian credit. The logical consequence of his budget balancing was the imposition of the gold standard, which comported more with the desires of the capitalists of Vienna than with the Iron Ring's concept of a decent break for small-scale producers. Only the realization that the monarchy, with its fluctuating paper, yielded in prestige to the more advanced Western states, plus a hope that Steinbach could continue a program of social melioration, persuaded them to vote against their original convictions. For many, too, the inevitable compromising with Hungary was a wretched business that built up a regime in Budapest which flaunted its Liberalism and its Magyarization of "lesser breeds." Whether chagrined, bored, or frightened, the blocs which were Taaffe's mainstay wasted no time after 1893 in constructing an apology for his years of tenure.

Taaffe first deserves reappraisal because he maintained the wealthier half of his master's realm in reasonable order for fourteen years. If this is no striking advance over the years of

Liberal ascendancy after 1867, it unquestionably compares favorably with the chaos which disfigured parliamentary life from 1893 to 1900, ending when another career bureaucrat in the latter year took advantage of the parties' exhaustion to renew the quest for viability. The armed peace of 1871–1914 depended upon a balance of power in international affairs and upon opportunities for expansion beyond the confines of Europe. To keep the peace, the major powers required armed forces that could play a significant part in neutralizing an alignment of potential enemies. The military arm also guarded against internal disturbance, which would stimulate the ambitions of watchful neighbors. Taaffe's first great victory was in the domain of armament, and his insistence upon maximum linguistic unity within the Dual Monarchy's regiments kept those forces as a reasonably effective guarantee of international and internal stability.

The Minister-President likewise kept up the working relationship with Hungary, and in these endeavors he earned a minimum of criticism from his adversaries. If the distillers complained that Hungary came off better in regard to quotas, the general public was satisfied that the Emperor's army had been saved from Magyar nationalist intrigue. The dualistic system worked decently only when cool ministers-president in each capital ignored the opinions of their more volatile deputies. Taaffe earns no more credit than does Tisza, obviously, for his willingness to stand up to extreme Magyar chauvinism helped Tisza as much as the latter's stubbornness over the spirits levy reduced Polish intransigence in Austria. Co-ordinating the economic, military, and diplomatic policies of the two halves was a challenging *métier,* and Taaffe was second to none of the Emperor's ministers in meeting the challenge.

Again, he preserved Austria from the subversions of anarchism and irredentism with a maximum of discretion and a minimum of brute force. Modern democracies are very much aware of the perplexities involved when individuals who will the destruction of a state appeal to the civil liberties which the same state promises all citizens. The classic picture of repression of every kind of radicalism by ruthless nineteenth-century prime ministers has taken on softer contours thanks to the infiltration of democratic societies by democracy's enemies. The traditional Marxian condemnations of Taaffe's "police state," with their detailed accounts of banishments, confiscations, and occasional trials, are pale anticipations of the purges and legalized assassinations of a later era. If one believes that anarchy was preferable to a privileged society that was beginning to recognize individual rights, one should continue to file Taaffe among the despots. If one assumes that his chief duty was to prepare Italians for reunion with Italy and Rumanians for royal Rumanian citizenship, one can question his distaste for irredentism. Since he lived in a world that was not yet convinced that national self-determination would serve the best interests of all, he did his best to maintain the empire he was sworn to uphold, but far more by politic neglect than by positive repression. Oberdank had planned the death of the Emperor-King, and all the loyal protestations of the prosperous shippers of Trieste could not eliminate that fact.

It was equally a virtue in a generation of materialism and relative legitimacy to strive for financial stability. Strong states had fine armies and irreproachable currencies, and the bankers who floated the bonds for "preparedness" were always more complaisant when an empire had bills and coin that were easily converted. The folklore of capitalism during its European apogee was sure of this point, and the strength of the argument silenced many who initially and fundamentally preferred the freedoms of a standard that did not enthrone gold. In the race for prestige Austria could not be last. The fear of sinking to Russian and Turkish levels recurs monotonously in the parliamentary speeches of the 1880s. Taaffe, Dunajewski, and Steinbach saved the country from such humiliation, and the psychological profit may well have overbalanced the economic malaise which the less favored of Austria blamed upon a gold standard.

These same underprivileged, lower middle class and workers, received compensation in the form of social insurance. If lim-

ited by financial resources and by the imagination of the men
who voted its provisions, the new system of protecting labor and
handicrafts did alleviate the worst abuses of speedy industrialization. Syndicalism and anarchism did not develop in the
Austrian labor movement, and the revisionist tendency in Austrian Social Democracy was its noteworthy characteristic.
Despite the rigors of defeat, humiliation, and inflation that followed the collapse of 1918, Vienna did not succumb, as Munich
and Budapest temporarily did, to the Communist influences from
the east. The accent on gradualism and the relatively un-
troubled development of Austrian socialism and trade unions
owe much to the leadership which Taaffe and his associates
demonstrated in the field of social legislation. Sixty years later
historic Bohemia, Galicia, and Dalmatia were following the
Soviet example, while the German Austrian lands continued to
choose a "middle way." Western appeasement prior to 1939
and the might of the Red Army certainly erased most of the
factors which otherwise would have been determinant in the
struggle between limited socialism and Communism, but the
continuing positive rejection of the extreme solution by German
Austrians has its roots in Taaffe's program. Bismarck, Vogelsang, and even a chastened response from Austrian Liberalism
played their parts in the erection of a scheme of insurance for
workers, but it was Taaffe who inspired his cabinet and his
parliamentary allies to realize the social imperatives of the
1880s.

Achieving a true reconciliation of the nationalities of Austria
was Taaffe's proclaimed goal, but the degree of his failure should
not obscure his several solid accomplishments. Easing the way
for the Czechs to return to the Reichsrat, he gave them a
university in Prague, a definite chance at posts in the Bohemian
and Moravian bureaucracy, and political control of the Bohemian Diet. In view of the tremendous strides they had taken
culturally and economically, he would have been completely
negative if he had failed to sponsor such changes. Nonetheless,
the beginning of a true equality for these worthy citizens entailed
years of hard bargaining and endless abuse. Taaffe was the first

Minister-President to force the Germans to consider the Czechs as a vital element on the Austrian scene, and the final German insistence upon partition was testimony to his educative skills. In their hearts the minority in Bohemia knew that their years of predominance were over, and Taaffe served as a concrete and convenient villain during their decade of "national humiliation." By 1890, he seemed to be more pro-German, less pro-Czech. In reality, he was but continuing, though certainly with less spirit, the dialogue that he hoped would lead to mutual forbearance and respect. Young Czechs excoriated him and his aloofness, but many of them lived long enough to remember his gradualism with appreciation. With Taaffe, they secured the means to prove that they were entitled to sit with Germans and Magyars without apology. The Slovenes, still definitely junior partners, traversed the Czech route *in parvo,* though Taaffe did order the publication of regulations which established their claims to equal treatment under the law.

Admittedly Taaffe petted and abetted the Poles, as the Liberals had done before him. A man who knew of the strategic rail lines into Galicia and the inviting nature of the Carpathian passes had little chance to do otherwise. Austrian Poland was a sensitive and exposed salient, whose dominant nationality had to believe and trust in Vienna's protectorate. The fate of relatives in Prussian and Russian Poland catalyzed their reasoned enthusiasm for Habsburg direction, and it was good politics to assume that a resurrected Poland might well invite an archduke to mount its throne. In review of Taaffe's Polish policy, one can only ask if the free Poland of 1919–39 remedied the social disequilibrium which he and other ministers dared not tackle. Again, was it sensible Habsburg policy to lecture the Poles on their duties to the Ruthenes? In a province that lay open to Russian propaganda and troops, there was no wisdom in catechizing a historic Catholic nationality for its obvious exploitation of Little Russians. The policies of Russification had disaffected the Little Russians of the tsar's Ukraine, but their ultimate loyalty was scarcely in doubt when Vienna rather than Kiev was the alternative.

Taaffe's greatest failure was his inability to prepare the Germans of Austria for a less exalted role in the empire. In Bohemia, partition emerged as a solution which Germans could live with and which someday the Czechs might have acquiesced in. Despite the imperial family's ire over extreme German nationalism, the sovereign and his chief adviser moved warily to avert an intensification of such disloyalty. Schönerer fabricated his own downfall, and the government moved vigorously only when he had hopelessly compromised himself. To diminish the effectiveness of irredentist propaganda among the Germans, Taaffe did well to restrict his police to watchful waiting. It would have been suicidal to grant the Slavs some needed concessions and simultaneously inhibit effervescing demonstrations for friendly German heroes, for the Hohenzollerns were sincerely committed to the survival of Franz Joseph's Austria, with or without Taaffe. It is proper to ask what auspices would have assuaged German anxieties during a period of undeniable dispossession. Some years later mob action drove Kasimir Badeni from office when he underestimated the resentments bred of such dispossession, and Beck, the finest of the Ministers-President of the period just before World War I, had to rely on parties that were formally supranational (and which were only coalescing in Taaffe's time) to divide the German front.

The inordinate allusions to Austria-Hungary as the "ramshackle," "polyglot," and "feudally retarded" empire once subjected references to advances in political maturity there to disbelief. But it will not do to ignore the feminist and Fenian disturbances in Great Britain, the student riots in the Latin Quarter over rationalism and *élan vital,* and the Italian demonstrations against Adowa, monarchy, and sheer hunger while recalling the ugly manifestations that occurred in Vienna, Prague, and Laibach. All voting Europe saw periodic appeals to the streets and to direct action, and Taaffe's progress toward a larger electorate and his treatment of the problems of civil liberties hardly set him apart from the prime ministers of other parliamentary states. The reform of 1882 was a sensible recognition of relative advances in culture and of economic need.

Participation in political life dimmed the chances of agitation that would only have frustrated literate Slavs and the resentful small businessmen and artisans, and, though the new voters did not appreciably change the ratios of strength within the Lower House, the ratification of measures for social insurance was accelerated after they went to the polls in 1885. When Taaffe proceeded in a negative direction to throttle radicalism and vituperation in the press, he largely excused himself by the mildness of his methods. Anyone who really wanted to read the offending paragraphs in a confiscated journal could repair to a favorite café and a trusted waiter, and Marxian tradition avers that the Crown Prince's lackey rounded up forbidden weeklies for his master. Correspondents who covered workers' meetings consistently reported a degree of placidity on the part of police observers that surprises observers of more efficient authoritarian regimes. It is true that Taaffe publicly expressed more concern over radicalism than did many of the members of parliament, and he did request extensions of restrictions when all knew that he had no hope of getting them. It is also true that the composed behavior of the socialists on May Day of 1890 dissipated much of the bourgeoisie's alarm. Behind parliament's reluctance to approve further extraordinary measures and the careful maneuvering of the workers, however, was Taaffe's essentially moderate approach. If he was not careful to distinguish between socialism and anarchism in terminology, he made up for his uncertainty by circumspection in the quarantines his police enforced.

Bismarck's shadow indubitably fell upon Taaffe and his works, and the senior Chancellor's scorn helped deliver the Minister-President to relative oblivion. In retrospect, the Junker's attitude was essentially perverse, for he fumed over Taaffe's dealings with Austrian Slavs while he desperately kept open his own wire to St. Petersburg. The Young Czech flirtations with the French and the forthright denunciations of Prussia by Austrian Poles may well have alarmed him, but his irritability over Taaffe's encouragement of Slavic elements scarcely warranted the snub which he pointedly inflicted through the German

Emperor. The credit Bismarck received for restraining Austria-Hungary from blundering into a war with Russia over Serbia and Bulgaria requires proof that the Dual Monarchy was likely to chance such an adventure. Furthermore, Alsace and Lorraine were worth many grenadiers' bones, and Bismarck's exasperation over Near Eastern crises did not mask his more serious preoccupation with the *revanchards*. It was clear to all that Hungary was the favored ally in Berlin in Bismarck's time, and it was perhaps natural that the arbiters of the destinies of Posen and Alsace could converse more sympathetically with seigneurs who overrode the objections of mere Croats, Slovaks, and Rumanians. It took some time for romantic and horse-loving Englishmen to pierce the true nature of the hegemony exercised by the Magyar aristocracy and even longer for unconscious devotees of Social Darwinism in every land to question events in Strassburg and Bromberg. Taaffe fought his daily battles with grasping allies and mulish sovereign during Bismarck's last decade of glory. A dazzled world found it hard to believe that one was not a magician, the other anything but an inept time-server.

The Austrian's worst enemy was his geniality and his tendency to temporize. The facts of political life did not often give him much option, to be sure, but one cannot read the remnants of the cabinet minutes without sensing a disposition to drift, to await inspiration from more positive colleagues, to consult with authoritative factors in the Reichsrat. To criticize him for converting that body into a *luogo di traffico* is to impugn every canny politician who ever lived, but the phrase did hurt. Its currency pointed up what was Taaffe's worst luck, namely, the control of the great Viennese dailies which had international circulation by the German Liberals. The *Neue Freie Presse* was worth several divisions when realistic diplomats canvassed the monarchy's potential, and its inveterate philippics against Austria's chief minister convinced persons who otherwise might have found him "progressive" that he was an impediment to civilization's advance along the Danube.

Dramas in blank verse and the accretions of romantic legend

have cast Taaffe as Rudolf's dark foe. The mercurial heir apostrophized electricity and Hungary alike as evidences of true liberalism and progress, and there is no doubt that he despised and brooded over Taaffe's system and Taaffe's political confederates. Anticlericalism explains much of the tension between the two men, though Rudolf's inability to see the limits of Clerical Conservative influence upon Taaffe is as much of a riddle as his conviction that Hungary was the bright hope of all truly emancipated souls. In the sorry aftermath of Mayerling, the Minister-President loyally obeyed unspeakably petty commands that an outraged dynast uttered in an attempt to stifle all gossip. One cannot otherwise explain the spying upon Vetsera's mother when that lady went to visit the deceased's grave. But the contrast between Rudolf's excited notes to Szeps and Taaffe's appraisal of the possible and achievement of the possible is quite definite. A new Emperor-King who depended upon doctrinaire liberalism in both of his realms certainly would have been unfashionable and probably fatal, unless shored up for an indeterminate length of time by a most un-Liberal military regime.

The final judgment on Taaffe cannot ignore the checks which Franz Joseph must have imposed upon his minister's initiative and thought. The last notable Habsburg was single-minded in his insistence upon good order, moral, social, and financial, and the army was his chosen instrument. His patriarchal and unrealistic pronouncements sometimes alternated with brief glimpses of reality, but the complexity of dealing with a ruler who wanted a first-class army, an economical administration, and bureaucrats who would suspend their national allegiances in an age of unmanageable ethnocentrism goes far to explain the defensiveness which increased with Taaffe's tenure. The story of subterfuges and persuasions will never be known, for the proper Minister-President dictated no remembrances of pressures applied and resignations submitted. He stands on his public record and upon the comparatively few state papers that are left. An effective politician, a good president of a council of ministers which provided considerable excellence and some unmistakable mediocrity, and an aristocrat who realized that Austria had to respond to the social and national aspirations of its peoples, Taaffe was the ideal *Kaiserminister*. His compromises and his hesitations were many, and sometimes they derived from the enormity of his assignment. A century which has learned what perversions are subsumed in the phrases, "People's Minister" and "People's Democracy," is less intolerant of monarchical appointees who tried to come to terms with industrialism, nationalism, and social radicalism. In terms of the irreducible facts posed by the Austrian Empire and by the late nineteenth century, Taaffe did well. Since the ministrations of Bismarck, Witte, and the Young Turks also failed to save great empires from eventual collapse, Taaffe's era needs no excuses that the whole age should not make.

Bibliography

PRIMARY SOURCES

Haus-, Hof-, und Staatsarchiv, Vienna
    Kabinettsarchiv. Geheimakten, I. Ministerwechsel in Österreich
        1870 bis 1918.
    Kabinetts-Kanzlei. Vorträge, 1881, 1883–88, 1890, 1892.
    Ministerrath für gemeinsame Angelegenheiten, 1879, 1889.
    Nachlass des Ministers Julius von Horst.
    Nachlass Plener.
Verwaltungsarchiv, Vienna
    Innern-Präsidiale, 22, 1880, 1882.
    Nachlass Hohenwart.
    Österreichische Ministerratsprotokolle, 1882–85.
*Stenographische Protokolle über die Sitzungen des Hauses der
    Abgeordneten des Reichsrates,* Session IX, X, XI, 1879–93.
*Stenographische Protokolle über die Sitzungen des Herrenhauses des
    Reichsrates,* Session IX, X, XI, 1879–93.
German Foreign Ministry Archives 1867–1920, microfilmed at
    Haddon Hall for the General Library, Univ. of California,
    Berkeley, reels 214, 215, 216, 223, 229. Microfilm copy at the
    National Archives, Washington, D.C., ser. K719–K724.

MEMOIRS, LETTERS, AND COLLECTIONS OF PAPERS

Bloch, Joseph S. *Erinnerungen aus meinem Leben.* Vienna and
    Leipzig, 1922.
Funder, Friedrich. *Vom Gestern ins Heute.* 2d ed. Vienna, 1953.
Molisch, Paul, ed. *Briefe zur deutschen Politik in Österreich von
    1848 bis 1918.* Vienna and Leipzig, 1934.

Plener, Ernst. *Erinnerungen.* 3 vols. Stuttgart and Leipzig, 1911–21.

——. *Reden.* Stuttgart and Leipzig, 1911.

Pollak, Heinrich. *Dreissig Jahre aus dem Leben eines Journalisten.* Vol. III. Vienna, 1898.

Skedl, Arthur, ed. *Der politische Nachlass des Grafen Eduard Taaffe.* Vienna, Berlin, Leipzig, and Munich, 1923.

Steinitz, Eduard von, ed. *Erinnerungen an Franz Joseph I.* Berlin, 1931.

Stremayr, Carl von. *Erinnerungen aus dem Leben.* Vienna, 1899.

Suess, Eduard. *Erinnerungen.* Leipzig, 1916.

Szeps, Julius, ed. *Kronprinz Rudolf: Politische Briefe an einen Freund, 1882–1889.* Vienna, Munich, and Leipzig, 1922.

Wolfrum, Carl, Otto, Wilhelm, and Ludwig. *Erinnerungen an Carl Wolfrum.* Vol. II. Leipzig, n.d.

BIOGRAPHICAL MATERIALS

Allmayer-Beck, Johann Christoph. *Vogelsang: Vom Feudalismus zur Volksbewegung.* Vienna, 1952.

Beck, Georg. "Die Persoenlichkeit des Grafen Eduard Taaffe." Unpublished dissertation, Vienna, 1949.

Bibl, Victor. *Georg von Schönerer.* Leipzig, 1947.

Corti, Egon Caesar, and Hans Sokol. *Der alte Kaiser.* Graz, 1955.

Ermers, Max. *Victor Adler.* Vienna and Leipzig, 1932.

Friedjung, Heinrich. *Julius Freiherr von Horst.* Vienna, 1906.

Das hohe Haus: Parlamentsbilder aus Österreich. Vienna, 1896.

Kuppe, Rudolf. *Karl Lueger und seine Zeit.* Vienna, 1933.

Mitis, Oskar von. *Das Leben des Kronprinzen Rudolf.* Leipzig, 1928.

Neue österreichische Biographie. 14 vols. Vienna, 1923–   .

Österreichisches Biographisches Lexikon, 1815–1950. Graz and Cologne, 1954–   .

Pichl, Eduard. *Georg Schönerer.* Oldenburg and Berlin, 1938.

Redlich, Joseph. *Kaiser Franz Joseph von Österreich.* Berlin, 1929.

Schenk, Josef. *Dr. Julius Ritter von Dunajewski.* Vienna and Leipzig, 1934.

Skalnik, Kurt. *Dr. Karl Lueger: Der Mann zwischen den Zeiten.* Vienna, 1955.

Tschuppik, Karl. *Kaiser Franz Joseph I.* Hellerau bei Dresden, 1928.

Wertheimer, Eduard von. *Graf Julius Andrássy.* 3 vols. Stuttgart, 1910–13.

Weyrich, Maria Magdalena. "Paul Gautsch, Freiherr von Frankenthurn, Jugend, Unterrichtsminister, Ministerpräsident 1897/98." Unpublished dissertation, Vienna, 1956.

LARGER STUDIES

Albertini, Luigi. *The Origins of the War of 1914.* Vol. I. London and New York, 1952.

Andrássy, Julius. *Bismarck und Andrássy.* Leipzig, 1924.

Auerbach, Bertrand. *Les races et les nationalités en Autriche-Hongrie.* 2d ed. Paris, 1917.

Benedikt, Heinrich. *Die wirtschaftliche Entwicklung in der Franz-Joseph Zeit.* Vienna and Munich, 1958.

Brügel, Ludwig. *Geschichte der österreichischen Sozialdemokratie.* 5 vols. Vienna, 1922–25.

——. *Soziale Gesetzgebung in Oesterreich von 1848 bis 1918.* Vienna, 1919.

Charmatz, Richard. *Österreichs innere Geschichte von 1848 bis 1907.* Leipzig, 1909.

Clough, Shepard B., and Charles W. Cole. *Economic History of Europe.* Boston, 1946.

Cole, George D. H. *A History of Socialist Thought.* Vols. II and III. New York, 1953, 1956.

Czedik, Alois von. *Der Weg von und zu den Österreichischen Staatsbahnen.* Teschen, Vienna, and Leipzig, 1913.

——. *Zur Geschichte der k.k. österreichischen Ministerien, 1861–1916.* Teschen, Vienna, and Leipzig, 1917.

Denis, Ernest. *La Bohême depuis la montagne-blanche.* 2 vols. Paris, 1903.

Deutsch, Julius. *Geschichte der österreichischen Arbeiterbewegung.* 3d ed. Vienna, 1947.

Eisenmann, Louis. *Le compromis austro-hongrois de 1867.* Paris, 1904.

Engel-Janosi, Friedrich. *Österreich und der Vatikan.* 2 vols. Graz, Vienna, and Cologne, 1958, 1960.

Franz, Georg. *Liberalismus. Der deutschliberale Bewegung in der Habsburgermonarchie.* Munich, 1955.

Fuchs, Albert. *Geistige Strömungen in Österreich, 1867–1918.* Vienna, 1949.

Die Grossindustrie Österreichs. 6 vols. Vienna, 1898.

Hantsch, Hugo. *Die Geschichte Österreichs.* Vol. II. 2d ed. Graz, Vienna, and Cologne, 1953.

Hugelmann, Karl Gottfried, ed. *Das Nationalitätenrecht des alten Österreich.* Vienna and Leipzig, 1934.

Jászi, Oscar. *The Dissolution of the Habsburg Monarchy.* Chicago, 1929.

Kann, Robert A. *The Habsburg Empire.* New York, 1957.

——. *The Multinational Empire.* 2 vols. New York, 1950.

318   BIBLIOGRAPHY

Kohn, Hans. *Pan-Slavism, Its History and Ideology.* Notre Dame, 1953.

Kolmer, Gustav. *Parlament und Verfassung in Oesterreich.* 8 vols. Vienna and Leipzig, 1902–14.

Langer, William L. *European Alliances and Alignments, 1871–1890.* New York, 1931.

May, Arthur J. *The Hapsburg Monarchy, 1867–1914.* Cambridge, Mass., 1951.

Mecenseffy, Grete. *Geschichte des Protestantismus in Österreich.* Graz and Cologne, 1956.

Miskolczy, Julius. *Ungarn in der Habsburgermonarchie.* Vienna and Munich, 1959.

Münch, Heinrich. *Böhmische Tragödie.* Berlin, 1949.

Die österreichische-ungarische Monarchie in Wort und Bild. 24 vols. Vienna, 1886–1902.

Rauter, D. *Österreichisches Staats-Lexikon.* Vienna, 1885.

Reddaway, W. C., et al., eds., *Cambridge History of Poland, 1697–1935.* Cambridge, 1951.

Sandonà, Augusto. *L'irredentismo nelle lotte politiche e nelle contese diplomatiche italo-austriache.* 3 vols. Bologna, 1932–38.

Taylor, A. J. P. *The Habsburg Monarchy, 1809–1918.* 3d ed. London, 1960.

Tomek, Ernst. *Kirchengeschichte Österreichs.* 3 vols. Innsbruck, Vienna, and Munich, 1937–1959.

Wiskemann, Elizabeth. *Czechs and Germans.* London, New York, Toronto, 1938.

Wodka, Josef. *Kirche in Österreich.* Vienna, 1959.

Zöllner, Erich. *Geschichte Österreichs.* Vienna, 1961.

MONOGRAPHIC STUDIES AND PAMPHLETS

Adler, Victor. *Das allgemeine, gleiche und direkte Wahlrecht und das Wahlunrecht in Österreich.* Vienna, 1893.

Andrássy, Julius. *Ungarns Ausgleich mit Oesterreich.* Leipzig, 1897.

Baernreither, Josef M. *Zur böhmischen Frage.* Vienna, 1910.

Bauer, Otto. *Die Nationalitätenfrage und die Sozialdemokratie.* 2d ed. Vienna, 1924.

Boyce, Gray C., and William H. Dawson. *The University of Prague.* London, 1937.

Brachelli, H. F. von. *Statistische Skizze der Österreichisch-Ungarischen Monarchie.* 10th ed. Leipzig, 1885.

Brote, Eugen. *Die rumänische Frage in Siebenbürgen und Ungarn.* Berlin, 1895.

Čapek, Thomas. *The Slovaks of Hungary.* New York, 1906.

Charmatz, Richard. *Deutsch-österreichische Politik*. Leipzig, 1907.

Eder, Karl. *Der Liberalismus in Altösterreich*. Vienna and Munich, 1955.

Fellner, Fritz. *Der Dreibund*. Vienna, 1960.

——. "Kaiser Franz Joseph und das Parlament," *Mitteilungen des Österreichischen Staatsarchivs,* IX (1956), 287–347.

Fischel, Alfred. *Der Panslawismus bis zum Weltkrieg*. Stuttgart and Berlin, 1919.

Fournier, August. *Wie wir zu Bosnien kamen*. Vienna, 1909.

Franz, Georg. *Kulturkampf: Staat und katholische Kirche in Mitteleuropa*. Munich, 1954.

Funder, Friedrich. *Aufbruch zur christlichen Sozialreform*. Vienna and Munich, 1953.

Goldhammer, Leo. *Die Juden Wiens*. Vienna and Leipzig, 1927.

Graf Taaffe: Eine innerpolitische Studie aus Oesterreich. Leipzig, 1889.

Hantsch, Hugo. *Die Nationalitätenfrage im alten Österreich*. Vienna, 1953.

Heller, Eduard. *Das deutsch-österreichisch-ungarische Bündnis in Bismarcks Aussenpolitik*. Berlin, 1925.

——. "Zum Sturz des Ministeriums Taaffe," in *Historische Studien, A. F. Pribram dargebracht*. Vienna, 1929.

Hertz, F. O. *Die Produktionsgrundlagen der österreichischen Industrie vor und nach dem Kriege*. Vienna, 1917.

Hornung, Otto. *Neu-Österreich*. Zurich, 1890.

K. K. Statistische Zentralkommission. *Statistische Rückblicke aus Österreich*. Vienna, 1913.

Kann, Robert A. "German-speaking Jewry during Austria-Hungary's Constitutional Era (1867–1918)," *Jewish Social Studies,* X (1948), 239–56.

Kiszling, Rudolf. *Die Kroaten*. Graz and Cologne, 1956.

Klopp, Wiard, ed. *Die sozialen Lehren des Freiherrn Karl von Vogelsang*. St. Pölten, 1894.

Knarr, Walter. "Das Ministerium des Grafen Taaffe und die soziale Frage." Unpublished dissertation, Vienna, 1948.

Kramer, Hans. *Die Italiener unter der österreichisch-ungarischen Monarchie*. Vienna and Munich, 1954.

Léger, L. P. M. *La renaissance tchèque au XIXe siècle*. Paris, 1911.

Leichtenmüller, Erich. "Die Wiener Zeitungen und der böhmische Ausgleich." Unpublished dissertation, Vienna, 1952.

Mailáth, Joseph. *Hungaricae Res*. Berlin, 1908.

Manteuffel-Szoege, G. *Geschichte des polnischen Volkes während seiner Unfreiheit, 1772–1914*. Berlin, 1950.

Mayer, Hans, ed. *Hundert Jahre österreichischer Wirtschaftsentwicklung, 1848–1948*. Vienna, 1949.

Mayer, Sigmund. *Die Wiener Juden, 1700–1900.* Vienna and Berlin, 1917.

Medlicott, W. N. *The Congress of Berlin and After.* London, 1938.

Mehring, Moses. "Die deutsch-böhmische Sprachenfrage während des Ministeriums Taaffe (1879–1893)." Unpublished dissertation, Vienna, 1924.

Menger, Max. *Der böhmische Ausgleich.* Stuttgart, 1891.

——. *Die Wahlreformvorlage des Ministeriums Taaffe.* Vienna, 1893.

Molisch, Paul. *Geschichte der deutschnationalen Bewegung in Oesterreich.* Jena, 1926.

——. *Politische Geschichte der deutschen Hochschulen in Österreich von 1848 bis 1918.* 2d ed. Vienna and Leipzig, 1939.

Novotny, Alexander. *Quellen und Studien zur Geschichte des Berliner Kongresses 1878.* Vol. I. Graz, 1957.

Oesterreichisches Statistisches Taschenbuch. Vienna, 1891.

Oppenheimer, Ludwig von. *Austriaca.* Leipzig, 1882.

Petrovich, Michael B. *The Emergence of Russian Panslavism, 1856–1870.* New York, 1956.

Plaschka, Richard Georg. *Von Palacký bis Pekař.* Graz and Cologne, 1955.

Rachenzentner, Alfred. "Die österreichische Agrargesetzgebung vom Beginn der konstitutionellen Ära bis zum Jahre 1889 und die Stellungnahme der Parteien." Unpublished dissertation, Vienna, 1949.

Rádl, Emanuel. *Der Kampf zwischen Tschechen und Deutschen.* Reichenberg, 1928.

Rauchberg, Heinrich. *Die Bevölkerung Österreichs auf Grund der Ergebnisse der Volkszählung vom 31. December 1890.* Vienna, 1895.

Renner, Karl (Rudolf Springer). *Der Kampf der österreichischen Nationen um den Staat.* Vienna, 1902.

Romanczuk, Julian. *Die Ruthenen und ihre Gegner in Galizien.* Vienna, 1902.

Samassa, Paul. *Der Völkerstreit im Habsburgerstaat.* Leipzig, 1910.

Schiff, Walter. *Österreichs Agrarpolitik seit der Grundentlastung.* Tübingen, 1897.

Schmid, Ferdinand. *Bosnien und Herzegowina unter der Verwaltung Österreich-Ungarns.* Leipzig, 1914.

Seton-Watson, Robert W. *Corruption and Reform in Hungary.* London, 1911.

——. *Racial Problems in Hungary.* London, 1908.

——. *The Southern Slav Question and the Habsburg Monarchy.* London, 1911.

Sommeregger, Franz. *Die Wege und Ziele der österreichischen Agrarpolitik seit der Grundentlastung.* Vienna, 1912.

Srbik, Heinrich von. *Aus Österreichs Vergangenheit.* Salzburg, 1949.

Strakosch, S. *Die Grundlagen der Agrarwirtschaft in Österreich.* Vienna, 1916.

Strakosch-Grassmann, Gustav. *Das allgemeine Wahlrecht in Österreich seit 1848.* Leipzig and Vienna, 1906.

Sutter, Berthold. *Die Badenischen Sprachenverordnungen von 1897.* Vol. I. Graz and Cologne, 1960.

Das System Taaffe. Vienna, 1882.

Umlauft, Friedrich. *Die Österreichisch-Ungarische Monarchie.* 2d ed. Vienna, Budapest, and Leipzig, 1883.

——. *Wanderungen durch die Österreichisch-ungarische Monarchie.* Vienna, 1883.

Wendel, Hermann. *Aus dem südslawischen Risorgimento.* Gotha, 1921.

Der Weg Bergab. Leipzig, 1880.

Wertheimer, Eduard von. *Bismarck im politischen Kampf.* Berlin, 1930.

Žolger, Ivan. *Der staatsrechtliche Ausgleich zwischen Oesterreich und Ungarn.* Munich, 1911.

Index

AUSTRIA UNDER THE IRON RING, 1879–1893

was composed, printed, and bound by
Kingsport Press, Inc., Kingsport, Tennessee.
The type is Times Roman.
The paper is Olde Style by the S. D. Warren Company.
The book was designed by
Edward Foss.